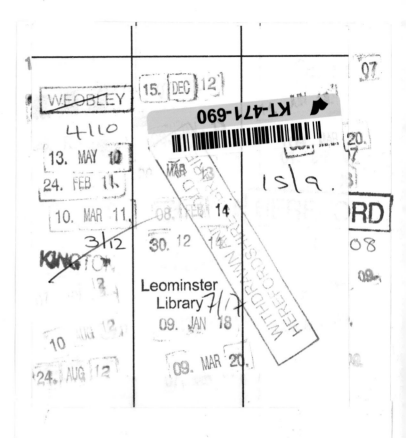

BATTLEFIELD BRITAIN

BATTLEFIELD BRITAIN

From Boudicca to the Battle of Britain

PETER AND DAN SNOW

BBC
BOOKS

This book is published to accompany
Battlefield Britain, first broadcast on BBC2 in 2004
Executive Producer: Jane Aldous
Series Producer: Danielle Peck

First published in 2004

Published by BBC Books, BBC Worldwide Ltd,
Woodlands, 80 Wood Lane, London W12 0TT

ISBN 0 563 48789 5

Commissioning editor: Sally Potter
Project editor: Martin Redfern
Design: Paul Vater and Hon Lam, sugarfreedesign
Art director: Ann Burnham
Picture researcher: Sarah Hopper
Production controller: Christopher Tinker

Printed and bound in Italy by LEGO SpA
Colour separations by Radstock Reproductions Ltd,
Midsomer Norton

2004: INTRODUCTION

Imagine a London where people carry arms as a matter of course. A village suddenly stormed by armed raiders, its men, women and children slaughtered, its houses looted and burned. Rival political groups sorting out their grievances by raising private armies against each other. A country where brother fights brother and father fights son, where force of arms decides who rules and who is ruled. That was Britain for much of its history.

Today, Britain looks like an oasis of calm in a troubled world. With the single exception of the murderous dispute over the future of the people of Ireland, Britain has been a battlefield only once in recent times – when the Royal Air Force fought and won a battle for the nation's survival in British skies in 1940. Otherwise for the last 250 years Britain, though involved in wars abroad, has been a beacon of stability in an embattled Europe. While most of our neighbours have been over-run, we have enjoyed peace at home.

We may have experienced internal tranquillity longer than almost any other country in the world, but this has come only after a number of foreign invasions ravaged and changed British society, after fierce struggles for dominance between warlords from all parts of Britain, and after bitter wars over social and political rights. In the past, Britain has been as bloodily savaged by war and internal strife as any other country in the world.

Battlefield Britain tells the story of eight great milestones in the country's military history, spanning two millennia from Boudicca's battle with the Romans to the Battle of Britain. Each of these conflicts left its mark on the nature and shape of the country we live in today. The annihilation of Boudicca's revolt in AD 61 set the seal on Rome's occupation of Britain. Had Boudicca won, Rome might have abandoned Britain, and the transformation of the country over the next 350 years might never have taken place. The outcome of the Battle of Hastings in 1066 did not just change a dynasty: it transformed

The Battle of Culloden: the view across the lines of the Duke of Cumberland's government redcoats towards the Highlanders.

British culture and language. The fate of Owain Glyndwr's rebellion after 1410 crushed hopes of Welsh independence. The defeat of the Armada in 1588 stopped Catholic Spain adding England to its empire. Naseby in 1645 demolished the idea that a monarch had a divine right to rule alone. The Boyne in 1690 confirmed Britain as a constitutional monarchy, Protestant to this day. Bonnie Prince Charlie's defeat at Culloden in 1746 ended the last civil war in our history. The Battle of Britain in 1940 saved this country from the threat of invasion by Nazi Germany.

We do not claim that *Battlefield Britain* includes all the important struggles in British history. This is the story of only a handful of the hundreds of battles fought within and around the shores of Britain. Alfred the Great, Robert the Bruce and Henry Tudor would no doubt be appalled that we have omitted Ethandun, Bannockburn and Bosworth. Our choices will leave some

disappointed, but we have made our selection to encompass the widest range of periods, terrains and types of warfare.

The most obvious change that has occurred over the course of our story is in the technology of warfare and the tactics that made use of it. Owain Glyndwr's strategy at Pilleth was inspired by the awesome potential of his longbowmen, who could shower arrows downhill on advancing English troops. In 1588 a new generation of English fighting ships faced their sternest test as the Spanish Armada bore down upon the south coast. They were streamlined ships built for speed and manoeuvrability, but they also packed a punch: their well-trained crews could fire devastating broadsides, and the Spanish quickly realized that they were on the receiving end of a revolution in naval technology. Lord Howard and Sir Francis Drake developed a new tactical doctrine to exploit this new generation of military hard-ware. One hundred and fifty years later evolving technology was to be used with equally lethal effect on the clansmen fighting for Bonnie Prince Charlie. As they sprinted across Culloden Moor, swords in hand, the Highlanders sustained horrific casualties from the canister shot and the Brown Bess muskets of one of the world's best-equipped armies. In 1940 British radar, the world's first aerial detection network, was deftly used to guide RAF fighters into battle with the Germans without having to waste time or resources on endless patrols.

But while the science of warfare has changed, there are many constant factors in this very diverse 2,000-year story. Leadership has always been critical to winning or losing a battle. The leadership of Hermann Goering and Sir Hugh Dowding during the Battle of Britain was no less telling than that of Boudicca or the Roman general Suetonius Paulinus 19 centuries earlier. Some led from the front. King Harold and Duke William of Normandy at Hastings, Sir Francis Drake fighting the Armada in the Channel, and Prince Rupert at

Naseby were men who faced the same danger as the soldiers they led. Other leaders, such as Paulinus, the Duke of Cumberland at Culloden and Dowding, distinguished themselves by their strategic direction of battle rather than in conspicuous displays of valour. Whatever his or her contribution, the importance of the leader has often dictated the strategy itself. The death of a commander could mean defeat. 'Decapitation' was not a strategy invented by the Americans during the invasion of Iraq in 2003. At Shrewsbury both sides went all out to kill the enemy's commander. Hastings effectively ended with the death of Harold. The Duke of Medina Sidonia drove his galleon time and again at the ships of the English admirals in a desperate attempt to rob the fleet of its leadership.

Nor is it just the leaders whose inspiration can make a decisive impact. This book is full of occasions when other men, whether born in a castle or a cottage, have performed acts of such courage that they have changed the course of

One of the ring of 100-metre high radar towers built around Britain's south and east coasts during the Battle of Britain. The RAF was the first to exploit this breakthrough in technology by transmitting a radio signal to detect approaching enemy aircraft.

the fighting. At Stamford Bridge in 1066 the entire army of Saxon England was held up by a giant axe-wielding Dane, who held a narrow bridge and traded his life to buy time for the Viking forces on the far bank. At Shrewsbury a knight called Douglas cut an alley through the royal army and might have ended the battle at a stroke if the soldier in royal colours whom he cut down had been King Henry IV instead of his unfortunate standard-bearer wearing royal armour as a decoy. During the Battle of Britain a small number of RAF pilots shot down a much larger force of Luftwaffe planes. It has often been the bravery of the individual soldier, sailor or pilot that has decided the outcome of a battle, as much as the quality of commanders and weaponry.

The weather has been a constant anxiety for military commanders. The wind, arguably more than the Royal Navy's skill, decided the fate of the Spanish Armada. In 1940 the degree of cloud cover determined whether or not German bombers would attempt to break through the RAF's fighter screen and drop their bombs on British airfields and cities. It is true that technology has done much to beat the weather: the modern infantry rifle will fire in the rain when the old matchlock musket would simply have fizzled out. But we have not mastered the elements yet. Even the timing of the 2003 invasion of Iraq was largely dictated by the impending summer heat.

Another constant is the way the fortunes of war can change so rapidly. The brittle psychology of battle means that proud soldiers, sailors or aircrew can be transformed into a terrified mob in seconds. This pivotal moment comes in every hard-fought battle, when a small shift in fortune

Not all battles took place on dry land. During the series we travelled by land, sea and air to experience how they were fought.

Battlefield Britain's graphic displays illustrate the big picture. The photo-real images are reproduced digitally, either on the mapcase (above left) or in a virtual world (above right) to describe each phase of the battle.

can turn victory into defeat. The collapse that followed Hotspur's death at Shrewsbury or Harold's at Hastings, the disarray of the Armada at the sight of the advancing fireships, and the moment when Cromwell reined back his cavalry and wheeled them around to change the course of the Battle of Naseby are classic examples.

In the television series that accompanies this book we set ourselves the challenge of telling the stories of battles in a new way. We decided to separate out the narrative into two broad strands – the overview and the view from the front line. So often in the fog of war the big picture gets obscured and the plight of the ordinary soldier is lost. We looked on the one hand at the grand sweep of each battle – the plans, the geography, the strengths and weaknesses of the commanders. And on the other hand we looked at the front line where the battle was at its fiercest, at the point where the Roman legions clashed with the Celtic warriors, at the young pilot in the cockpit of his Spitfire facing the Messerschmitt.

In telling the story this way we capitalized on a great technical advance – the creation of computer-generated graphics. We have incorporated these groundbreaking images in this book. They allow us to show in meticulous detail the various episodes

of the battles and bring alive the composition of battle lines and their movements. Understanding the ground a battle is fought on is an essential key to following its course.

This book also includes another feature of the TV series – the moments when we experienced for ourselves the weapons and techniques of warfare through the ages. We found out how hard it is to draw a longbow and to fire three rounds from a flintlock musket in under a minute.

History cannot be told by battles alone, but it is notable that most monarchs are primarily remembered for the military achievements or failures of their reigns. And the really great battles – like the eight we have chosen – mark points of ultimate drama when history could have gone either way. You have only to ask what would have happened if the victor of each of our eight battles had been defeated to see how profound their impact was. It is this and the story they tell of skill, leadership and courage that have made the writing of *Battlefield Britain* such a challenging and rewarding enterprise.

Peter and Dan Snow
London, 2004

On a summer's day nearly 2,000 years ago, at the mouth of a valley northwest of London, a British woman – a warrior queen – raced her chariot through tens of thousands of her troops to shout a final word of encouragement. The battle they would fight, the climax of their struggle for freedom from Roman oppression, would cause more bloodshed than perhaps any other battle on British soil. It was a clash between two of the most unevenly matched armies in Britain's history.

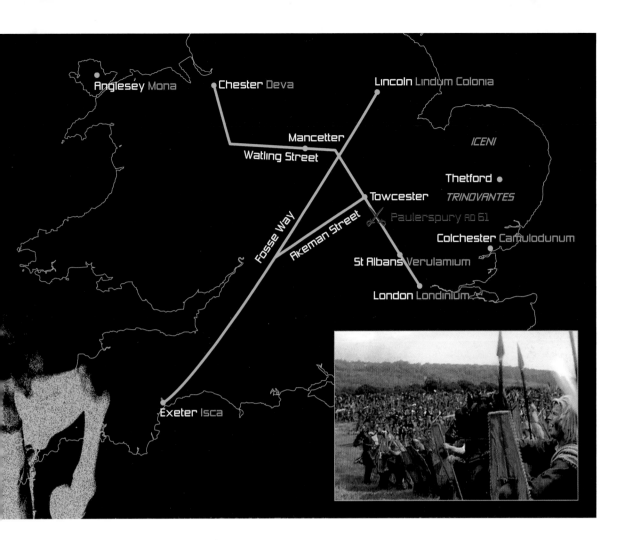

Ten thousand well-drilled professional legionaries were given the signal to adopt their notorious wedge formation. Their task: to cut through and destroy a force of up to a quarter of a million enraged Britons, who were determined to end the occupation of their country.

Britannia – imperial outpost

By AD 60, Rome had spent just 17 years securing its newest conquest, which it called Britannia – the outermost province of the huge Roman Empire, right at the edge of the known world. It had been a tempting prize, rich and fertile; and its restless tribes had constantly undermined

Rome's hold on Gaul. Britain was invaded and later abandoned by Julius Caesar a century earlier, and then permanently occupied by the Emperor Claudius in AD 43. He immediately entrenched Roman rule by ordering the building of a network of roads and forts, and by stationing four legions in Britain: one in Lincoln, one in Exeter and two near the Welsh border. It was an occupation that lasted 400 years – but it came perilously close to a catastrophic end less than a generation after it had begun.

The people who nearly changed the course of history lived in what is now East Anglia. The Iceni, tough people of the soil, were one of a

The temple of Claudius in Colchester was probably still under construction in AD 60. Claudius, who was Roman Emperor from AD 41 to 54, ordered the occupation of Britain, and the temple was intended as a permanent monument to him.

dozen tribes in what is today's England. They lived in farming settlements around their capital, which historians believe may have been Thetford in Norfolk, where first-century Celtic remains have been found. The Iceni and their Essex neighbours, the Trinovantes, were part of the huge Celtic population of western Europe, as were the Gauls in today's France, whom Julius Caesar had brought under Roman rule a hundred years earlier. There was a brisk trade between the Celts and Rome in commodities and in beautiful and highly crafted works of art.

Rome's invasion of Britain in AD 43 led to a different pattern of conquest from region to region. When the Emperor Claudius led his legions triumphantly into Colchester, the main city of the Trinovantes, and declared it the capital of his new British province, the local people lost more than their freedom. Much of their land was confiscated, and they were forced to pay a crippling tax to help finance the occupation and in particular the building of this new Roman capital, which was called Camulodunum. It was to be the crowning glory of the imperial administration, its centrepiece a temple to the

The severed bronze head of the Emperor Claudius. His statue was smashed during the revolt and the head was found in the River Alde in Suffolk in the early 20th century.

Emperor Claudius – who, on his death in AD 54, became a god, like all his predecessors. So confident were the Romans of their hold on their new subjects that they did not even bother to surround Roman Colchester with a protective wall. They were to pay a terrible price for their complacency.

The seeds of revolt

Not all British tribes suffered the fate of the Trinovantes. Some, like their northern neighbours, the Iceni, agreed treaties with Rome that made them client states. It may have been hard for such independent-minded people to swallow their pride and accept this status, but it did give them some measure of freedom. For the Iceni, it meant they were able to keep their own king and queen. The story of King Prasutagus and his queen, Boudicca, would have been lost had not medieval monks rediscovered the work of two ancient historians: Tacitus, who lived 50 years after these events, and Cassius Dio, who wrote a century later. They both spell the queen's

Camulodunum, modern Colchester: prosperous capital of Roman Britain. The temple of Claudius is at the top right.

These are our best guesses as to what the main protagonists may have looked like. We have created the computerized images from the available pictorial evidence and contemporary descriptions. We have also drawn on knowledge of the human physiology of the period.

BOUDICCA

The queen of the Iceni had an overwhelming physical presence: tall, with long hair, steely eyes and a commanding voice. Not only was she a striking woman to look at – she was also, says Dio, 'possessed of greater intelligence than often belongs to women'. So long as she and her husband were allies of Rome, she would have adopted the formal dress and manners of the Romans, but during her rebellion she shed this image and adopted one more appropriate for a warrior queen.

SUETONIUS PAULINUS

The Roman governor who opposed Boudicca was a formidable military commander. We can only guess what he looked like – a stern, battle-hardened Roman soldier, with a distinguished military career behind him in the ancient world's most professional army. He had spent much of it fighting enemies of Rome in the Atlas Mountains of north Africa.

name 'Boudicca'. The spelling 'Boadicea' came later: it may have added a poetic flourish to her name, but it is not what she was called by the people of her time. Dio describes her in colourful language: 'In stature she was very tall, in appearance most terrifying, in the glance of her eye most fierce, and her voice was harsh; a great mass of the tawniest hair fell to her hips; around her neck was a large golden necklace; and she wore a tunic of divers colours over which a thick mantle was fastened with a brooch. This was her invariable attire.'

She may have looked and sounded fierce, but she and her husband made the most of the freedom and privilege they enjoyed as clients of Rome. They did not suffer the indignities and deprivations of their neighbours and many other British tribes. They did not have to pay swingeing taxes, and they were not on the receiving end of what even Tacitus recognizes as the 'rapacity' of the Roman administration. But the good fortune of the Iceni was short-lived. Hoping to secure his people's future, Boudicca's husband, Prasutagus, attempted to buy the Romans off by making a will in which he left only half his wealth to his family; the rest he promised to the Roman emperor. But when Prasutagus died, the Romans reacted with savage disregard for his wishes and with bestial treatment of his family. Soldiers marched into the royal home, confiscated it and all the family wealth, and announced that the Iceni nobles were to be stripped of their estates and enslaved. Boudicca herself was seized and lashed, and – in a piece of horrific depravity – her daughters were gang-raped.

Overnight Boudicca's fury at this treachery and brutality turned her from a supporter of Rome to its bitterest enemy. She found willing allies in the neighbouring Trinovantes. We cannot be sure of the precise timing of these events, but the whole story almost certainly took place between the spring of AD 60 and the summer of 61. The Emperor Claudius had been succeeded by Nero, who had already expressed doubts about the wisdom of retaining an expensive hold on the truculent people of Britain. Rome's grasp of its newest province was now to be tested to breaking point.

Rome's champion

The soldier commissioned by Nero to rule Britain had a reputation as an implacable governor and a formidable general. His name was Suetonius Paulinus. Highly ambitious, and anxious to outdo other jealous rivals in the empire, he believed that the way to enhance his reputation lay less in sensitive governance than in the ruthless suppression of opposition. He was at this time pursuing a merciless campaign in North Wales. His target: the Druids, the Britons' spiritual leaders, who preached a message of resistance to the Romans from their stronghold on the island of Mona, today's Anglesey. He had taken with him two legions, the XIVth and the XXth. They crossed the Menai Strait in flat-bottomed boats, landed on the beaches near the Druids' sacred grove and destroyed them and their supporters in

a massacre that Paulinus no doubt hoped would permanently neutralize British resistance. He was just completing this operation when a messenger arrived with some devastating news. The province he had left behind was in revolt, and at the head of a vast army of enraged Celts was the woman whom his own countrymen had transformed from a docile client queen into the vengeful champion of a repressed people. Worse than that, Paulinus was to hear a catalogue of horror about what she had done to Rome's proud new British capital.

Above: Coin of the Emperor Nero. The excesses of his administration in Britain did much to provoke Boudicca's rebellion.

Left: The Romans crossed the Menai Strait from North Wales (in the background) and confronted the Druids in Anglesey – possibly on this very beach.

Colchester destroyed

In the 17 years since Claudius had triumphantly declared Camulodunum his capital, it had been adorned with all the pomp and splendour of a great imperial city. It was also the site of Britain's first Roman *colonia* – a settlement where veteran legionaries and their families enjoyed a prosperous retirement, farming confiscated British land with the aid of British slaves. That spring they were blissfully unaware of the catastrophe that awaited them.

Suddenly Boudicca and her horde of Britons appeared before the defenceless city. A great host of men, women and children, many armed, were spoiling for revenge and plunder. Colchester's population barely had time to send frantic appeals for help. Paulinus was too far away, and the only legion within reach was the IXth Hispana based at Lindum Colonia, now Lincoln. Its commander, Petilius Cerealis, sent troops racing down the road towards Colchester. But he appears to have been over-hasty, because Tacitus tells us that Boudicca's forces slaughtered his infantry to a man; Cerealis himself and his cavalry were lucky

Above left: The IXth Hispana legion marching in column to rescue Colchester. Its commander's failure to patrol his flanks exposed his men to Boudicca's ambush.

Above right: The men led by Petilius Cerealis pay for his mistake.

Right: The Norman castle in Colchester. It is built on the foundations of the temple of Claudius, which are still visible in the vaults today.

The tombstone of the veteran soldier Longinus, who is seen riding over a cowering Briton. It was shattered by Boudicca's troops in their sack of Colchester.

to escape. Boudicca almost certainly ambushed the legion when it was strung out in a long column on the road without cavalry patrolling the land on either side. It was a great victory for Boudicca, and a humiliating defeat for Rome … a terrifying warning of what was to come.

With all hope of reinforcement cut off, Colchester now lay at Boudicca's mercy. Joining up with her new allies, the Trinovantes, to the northwest of the city, she and her growing army of rebels formed a great raiding party, and their chariots swept through the undefended gates of the capital. The storming of the city was accompanied by slaughter and burning in which

the Britons displayed extraordinary savagery. Som
lucky Romans managed to flee by boat down the
river Colne to the sea, and found safety in Kent o
Sussex; but for most it was death by fire or the
sword. Even veterans' tombs were vandalized: you
can still see the shattered tombstones in
Colchester Museum today. Roman legionaries wh
had settled here for a quiet and comfortable
retirement were massacred with their wives and
children. Some veterans made a hopeless last
stand, barricading themselves into the temple of
Claudius with their families. But Boudicca's force

Colchester under attack

1. The combined armies of the Iceni and the Trinovantes gather outside Colchester.

2. Led by the chariots, they storm into the unfortified Roman capital.

3. The rampaging horde of Britons floods into the town, looting the houses and showing no mercy to the inhabitants.

The temple burns

4. The Britons set fire to the city and surround the temple, where a group of fugitives is holding out.

5. The furious mob sets the temple alight.

6. The temple is burned to the ground and its defenders are killed.

set it on fire, and all who had sought refuge inside this blatant symbol of Roman occupation were consumed in the flames. Any part of Roman Colchester dug up today reveals a continuous red layer of melted and baked clay, bearing witness to the events of AD 61.

Caught unawares

Back in Anglesey, the Roman governor of Britain guessed that the fast-growing commercial capital, Londinium, today's London, would be Boudicca's next target, so he issued rapid orders to his commanders. The two legions in Anglesey were to strike camp at once and march as fast as they could down Watling Street towards London. The commander of the IInd Augusta legion in Exeter was to march post-haste up the Fosse Way to join the other two legions. Paulinus ordered all three to meet him as far down Watling Street as was practicable. Then he himself took an advance guard and rode at top speed to London. Most of its population had already fled south and west; those who were left pleaded with Paulinus to send a rescue force. But he quickly concluded it was

Three of the main arteries of Roman Britain central to the calculations of Suetonius Paulinus in meeting Boudicca's challenge. His legions from Anglesey could travel southeast down Watling Street. He hoped that the legion from Exeter would join him in the Midlands via the Fosse Way or along the short cut – Akeman Street.

too late. In Tacitus's words, 'He determined to save the country as a whole at the cost of one town.' He raced back up Watling Street, determined to make a stand where he could.

His decision not to fight for London may have been a wise one, but it left the commercial centre of the new province at the mercy of a British army that would stop at nothing. Paulinus himself escaped from London with only a day or two to spare. His legions were still a long way to the northwest: there was nothing he could do to save the city. The dreadful fate of the IXth legion, ambushed and annihilated on the road to Colchester, was a sharp warning to him not to face Boudicca without the largest fighting force he could assemble.

On to London and St Albans

What followed in London was one of the most bloodthirsty episodes in British history. The lust for revenge appears to have driven Boudicca's marauding army to extraordinary excesses. Here, and in the next town to fall victim, Verulamium, now St Albans, Tacitus talks of widespread burning and a total of 70,000 being put to death on the gibbet and the cross. Dio gives even gorier details of the bodies of the noblest women being skewered and hung up naked, their breasts cut off and sewn

to their mouths so that the dead women appeared to be eating them. Just as in Colchester, below today's City of London there is a red line of burnt earth, all that remains of the first London.

Boudicca, riding this tide of destruction, made no effort to consolidate or to construct a new alliance; she just pushed on up northwest. That was where Paulinus's military strength lay after his campaign in North Wales. She was determined to get to grips with him and give his legions such a trouncing that the emperor would despair of any further presence in Britain. The Germanic tribes had defeated a Roman army 50 years before and put an end to Rome's occupation

London's Roman wall, still visible today, was not yet in place to protect the city at the time of Boudicca's revolt.

of their lands; perhaps it was this example that spurred the Britons on. Indeed, Boudicca was well on the way to emulating the German feat: she had destroyed one Roman legion and had forced the evacuation of the most prosperous part of Rome's new province. Her forces may have moved slowly, but she was exacting a terrible retribution and building strength all the time. Her strategy was probably the wisest she could have pursued. By all accounts she already had a massive army, too great to sustain without constant movement to new areas for food supplies and opportunities for plunder. And she had the initiative: Paulinus could only guess where she would go next and attempt to plan accordingly.

The big puzzle: where did the two armies meet?

No one knows where the two armies fought the decisive battle for Roman Britain. Paulinus clearly wanted to stop Boudicca as early as he could – before she could seize much more of the richest part of his province. We know from Tacitus how Paulinus agonized before he decided he had to abandon London in order to save his province. Now he had lost St Albans as well. A quick calculation suggests that he did have time to stop Boudicca soon after she left St Albans. He had left London before Boudicca arrived there, and raced off to rendezvous with his legions who were marching down from Wales and, he hoped, up from Exeter. Forced marches must have seen his legionaries push well down Watling Street. Boudicca would have been only lumbering along with her huge mass of fighters and their families, who were travelling with them in wagons. We have another clue to the battlefield's whereabouts from archaeology: no Roman site excavated anywhere northwest of St Albans shows signs of destruction by fire, which suggests the battle may have been fought not far north of the town.

So where do we look for the battlefield? It was Paulinus who chose the place to make his stand

against the marauding Britons. There is only a brief description in Tacitus, who says Paulinus 'chose a place with a narrow entrance backed by woods', with an open plain to its front 'devoid of cover and allowing no suspicion of an ambush'. It is hard to find a site anywhere on Watling Street (now the A5) that precisely matches this picture. The mouth of the valley must have been wide enough to allow Paulinus to stretch his legionaries across it in depth, but not so wide that Boudicca's huge force would have been able to force a way around the Roman flanks. So the *Battlefield Britain* team searched by car and helicopter for a feature such as Tacitus describes somewhere on or near Watling Street as it runs northwest from St Albans.

After exploring all the sites favoured by the experts from St Albans as far as Mancetter, just north of Birmingham – a distance of some 130 kilometres – we agreed with the conclusion of a recent study that the most likely spot was just south of Towcester where the A5 passes close to the village of Paulerspury, 55 kilometres northwest of St Albans. There was a Roman town at Towcester, but no digging there has disclosed any sign of destruction by fire, which suggests that Boudicca may not have got that far. Paulinus's legions certainly could have reached that far south in the time they had.

At Paulerspury a valley opens out from the A5 northeastwards into the large open plain of the river Tove. Paulinus could have taken up a defensive position there – straddling Watling Street in case Boudicca chose to move up the road, but also confronting her across the mouth of the valley if she opted for the more likely tactic of moving her huge army up the river plain rather than risk ambush on the road. The sides of the

The possible site of the final battle at Paulerspury, near Towcester. The Roman front line would have stretched 800 metres across the valley floor.

valley, probably wooded in Roman times, would have offered Paulinus security on the flanks, and his troops would have stretched neatly across the kilometre-wide entrance to the valley. The geography would have done much to make up for his massive inferiority in numbers.

It is only fair to add that Cassius Dio – writing a century after Tacitus, and reckoned to be a lot less reliable – makes no mention of Paulinus using a valley to protect his small force. Instead, he says that the Roman general fought the battle by dividing his force into three separate units to avoid being surrounded.

The prelude to battle

We may not know exactly *where* the battle was fought, but we do have a good idea of *how* it was fought. It was a striking example of a comparatively small, well-drilled force confronting a massed and undisciplined attack.

Paulinus had by now received news that must have driven him into a frenzy of anger and frustration: the legion he had ordered to join him from Exeter, the IInd Augusta, had failed to

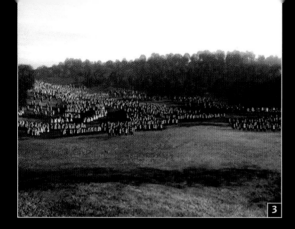

Move and Counter-move

1. Boudicca's army crosses the bridge over the Tove at today's Stony Stratford. She sees the danger of advancing straight on up Watling Street through the forest.

2. Boudicca wheels her army right to follow the river valley northwards towards Paulinus's trap.

3. Paulinus and his legions deploy across a valley, facing out towards the river.

march to meet him. Its commander, Poenius Postumus, had decided that the threat of unrest in the southwest was so great that he would do better to remain where he was. He was expressly disobeying his own commander, who badly needed every man he could muster.

The Romans were outnumbered 10 to one, perhaps as much as 20 to one. Boudicca's army was now enjoying a sense of elation and invincibility that none of Rome's enemies had felt since the German leader Arminius had annihilated three Roman legions half a century earlier. To many of Boudicca's Celtic warriors, who had swept all before them, it must have felt as if nothing could stop them throwing the Romans out of Britain.

Some days after they had set fire to St Albans, Boudicca and her huge force of fighters, together with their families, pack animals and horses, were again on the move northwest, past the site of present-day Milton Keynes. Boudicca was no doubt seeking out allies among the local tribespeople and attempting to keep up the momentum of the advance. When she crossed

the river Tove at the spot where Stony Stratford is today she would have seen Watling Street pass deep into the Whittlewood Forest straight ahead of her, while the open river valley did a great turn to the east and then back north again round the edge of the forest. This is where she would have paused for a moment to decide which way to go. Her scouts would probably have been reporting that the enemy were blocking the road a few kilometres north; they may even have seen the main Roman force taking up station in the valley at Paulerspury, facing northeast towards the river. No doubt Boudicca's heart leapt: battle with Paulinus's main force was now inevitable.

If all this speculation is correct, and if Paulerspury was the site of the battle, our guess is that Boudicca chose not to follow the road into the forest for fear of ambush, but wheeled her huge force off to the right and followed the river valley up to where she found the Roman legions facing her across the mouth of the valley. That way she could move her forces safely over the plain, where there was more likelihood of food and water. Her cavalry and chariots could check

A Roman helmet with neck and cheek guards. The protruding peak (top right) protected the forehead from a downward blow.

the ground ahead and to either side. As her forward units moved up the river valley and turned west towards Towcester, they would have seen the Roman legions commanding the valley entrance ahead of them. This gave Boudicca little tactical choice: she had to fight a battle. To attempt to bypass the Romans would have exposed her army's flank to an attack as it moved past; and once behind them, the enemy would block their road home. Anyway, Boudicca and her army were not trying to avoid battle. On the contrary, it was the moment they had been waiting for. They camped for the night within sight of the Roman lines.

The might of the legion

Anyone watching the early light coming up on the two armies assembling on the day of battle must have been struck by the glaring contrast between them. On one side were no more than 10,000 Roman legionaries moving out of their overnight encampment into their neatly regimented battle lines. Paulinus was deploying

the best part of one and a half legions with around 2,000 cavalry, and perhaps some archers as well. He had the whole of the XIVth Gemina legion and about half of the XXth Valeria Victrix.

The legion was the ancient world's most formidable military machine. Each legion was divided into ten cohorts of around 500 men each, each cohort itself being divided into six units, called 'centuries', of around 80 men each. A century was the basic unit of Roman warfare, commanded by the most feared and respected of the Roman commanders in the field – the centurion. The ordinary legionaries served in the ranks for 25 years before retiring to settle and farm in places such as the new *colonia* at Colchester. But the centurion served for his whole career, and had the sort of reputation for ruthless discipline that the modern sergeant major has in any company or battalion today. The legion's strength was the pride it had in its own record, its powerful sense of cohesion and discipline, and the obedience – or sometimes terror – that led to orders being obeyed without question. Moreover, each legionary was heavily armed. A large, oblong shield with a boss in the middle served to stop missiles and protect the body against sword slashes; it also acted as a battering ram. Everyone wore body armour – the *lorica segmentata* – made of overlapping metal scales, which had replaced coats of mail and provided better protection. And each man carried the short, fat stabbing sword, the *gladius*, which could be used with lethal effect in the close-quarters fighting at which the Romans excelled.

The Roman sword, the *gladius*, was short and broad compared to the far longer slashing swords of most of Rome's enemies.

A Roman legion's front line. The wrap-around shield stretched from chin to knee; the central bronze or iron boss also gave its user an offensive punch.

Century by century the cohorts formed up that morning, the fully armed soldiers clattering along the floor of the valley from the camp, which was probably on the other side of Watling Street. Each legionary carried two javelins, which were to play a vital part in the fighting. When they reached the mouth of the valley the centuries formed up in ranks eight men deep, leaving just enough space between each man to enable them to wield their javelins: the tighter together they stood, the more impregnable the armoured wall they presented to their massed enemy.

Of Paulinus's 15 cohorts, he probably put seven in the front line, with the others behind in reserve: that would be a frontage of over 800 metres – just about the width of the valley floor. His cavalry took up position on the slopes at his flanks to prevent any attempt by the Britons to encircle the legions with their huge superiority in numbers. Behind the neatly arrayed lines was the world's most professional logistical back-up. Surgeons prepared to treat the injured, and spare weapons were stockpiled together with supplies of water for the thirsty troops.

BATTLE EXPERIENCE
Chariots

The most flamboyant of the British weapons was the chariot, perhaps the earliest ancestor of the modern armoured personnel carrier. It was a fast, light, horse-drawn vehicle on two wheels, with a skilled charioteer at the reins and a fearless and agile warrior on the platform behind. The warrior's job was to keep the chariot balanced and to strike terror into the enemy by hurling a salvo of missiles at them as the chariot swept past at close quarters.

We paid a visit to the Tiverton coach-racing circuit to learn the skills that make a good chariot team. After taking turns in the driving seat all morning, Peter was given the reins and despatched on an obstacle course – with Dan on the platform behind, trying to maintain the vehicle's balance by leaning inwards on the curves. As Peter sped around the cross-country circuit, Dan tried to keep the carriage from turning over.

It quickly became obvious that the chariot's warrior must have had a rough ride if the terrain was difficult. It was easy to see why Boudicca would have favoured fighting the Romans on a wide, flat plain, so that early in the battle the charioteers could weave and turn in the no man's land between the two armies. Given the right ground and the right conditions, the Celtic mass of aggressively driven chariots must have done much to raise morale among the Celts as Boudicca's final battle began.

The Celtic war machine

On the other side were the massed ranks of Celtic warriors in Boudicca's army. There may have been as many as 200,000 of them, women as well as men, outnumbering the Romans by as many as 20 to one. Boudicca, an accomplished warrior herself, would not have been that untypical of the ranks behind her. Her warriors' weapons and armour came in an assortment of shapes, sizes and strengths. In the front ranks: the warrior aristocrats with metal helmets, body armour and fine shields, lighter than Roman armour but still effective. Behind them: tens of thousands of other warriors grouped by village and family, and wearing little in the way of protection. Some may have stripped armour from the bodies of dead Romans in previous encounters, but many chose to rely on tattoos and spells to deflect Roman metal. All would have carried either large swords (longer than the Romans' blades and less wieldy) or spears, axes and knives. Unlike the Romans, they would not have been drawn up in carefully drilled ranks. They were used to more open warfare, rushing headlong into battle, slashing around them and looking for chances to exploit gaps in their enemy's ranks.

One of the Celtic Britons' key weapons, which emphasized the contrast between the two sides, was the chariot. This was a potentially terrifying war machine, driven at breakneck speed by a charioteer, with a warrior providing balance on the back, brandishing his or her weapons, seeking out an opponent to confront in single combat and looking for a chance to cast a missile into enemy ranks. Each warrior was poised to leap off and do battle, then jump back on to the chariot and race off to cause terror and dismay elsewhere on the battlefield. Boudicca herself is usually portrayed driving in a chariot; it would have stressed her role as a fearless fighter and champion, and would also have enabled her to command and control her huge force. The Romans recognized that chariots might raise the

BATTLE FACT

Julius Caesar, writing a century before Boudicca, describes the use of chariots by the Britons. 'They drive them all over the field, hurling javelins and inspiring terror. Their horse and wheel noise throw their opponents into disorder.' Contrary to popular belief there is no evidence that they had scythes on the wheels.

other side's morale; they could also deliver key warriors to hotspots around the battlefield where they were most needed. But the Romans' own experience of fighting Celtic charioteers in Gaul had persuaded them that their best defence was not to deploy chariots themselves. They preferred to rely on their own cavalry and their close formations of infantry to deny the charioteers any effective killing ground.

'On this field we must conquer or die'

Both the historians who describe this great battle say that Paulinus and Boudicca made speeches to their troops. The account of a speech is a trick frequently used by historians to provide us with a colourful impression of what motivates and preoccupies commanders before battle. On this occasion it is probably wise to take both Tacitus's and Cassius Dio's accounts cautiously, but they do offer a flavour of what the two leaders may have said. Only a few hundred of their troops, at most, could have been in earshot at any one time, so the likeliest picture is that each leader would have picked a number of spots among their assembled forces to repeat the same words of encouragement several times. Dio certainly refers to the Roman commander moving from one group to another to address them in turn.

Boudicca, we are told by Tacitus, mounted her chariot with her two daughters, rode up to

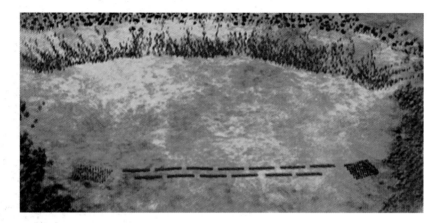

At the bottom of the picture the Romans fill the valley mouth – seven infantry cohorts in the front line, with cavalry on the slopes at either side. Behind Boudicca's massed warriors, women and children watch from an arc of wagons (top).

clan after clan in her huge army and delivered these words:

> It's not unusual to have a woman lead an army in this country. But I am leading you today to avenge not the seizure of my wealth and power, but as a woman who suffered the torture and dishonour of being lashed and having my daughters raped. Roman greed and savagery is now such that nothing is sacred any more ... neither person, age nor virginity. On this field we must conquer or die. That's what this woman is determined to do ... even if men choose to live and become slaves.

Paulinus, Tacitus says, was utterly contemptuous of his enemy:

> Ignore the noise and empty threats of the barbarians. There are more women than men in the enemy ranks. They are unwarlike and unarmed and will break immediately before you, once they recognize the steel will and the bravery of the people who conquered them. Now is your chance – few men that you are – to win glory and gather the laurels of an entire army ... as long as you keep in close order, using your swords and shields to pile up the dead on the other side. Do not think of plunder ... wait till you've won a victory and then all will be yours.

Paulinus's speech is a succinct definition of Roman tactics. Pay no attention, he tells his men, to the posturing of a superficially impressive enemy. Just stay in tight formation, and use the shield and sword in simple mechanical movements to cut through the enemy ranks. He warns them not to act as individuals seeking plunder but to fight as one. Cohesion and disciplined teamwork could beat Boudicca's numbers.

The opening skirmishes

The two battle lines had by now formed up around 400 metres apart – far enough to be out of range of each other's missiles. The first action was probably a display of bravado by the British charioteers racing out in front of Boudicca's line and parading up and down before the Romans, the warriors occasionally throwing a spear into the Roman ranks, both warrior and charioteer howling insults and curses at the enemy. Paulinus may have responded by deploying detachments of cavalry to tackle the chariots, and groups of archers, almost certainly also positioned on the flanks, would have done their best to slay the charioteers. It is a sign of the glaring mismatch between the two armies that the chariots appear to have left the Roman line pretty much unscathed. Their purpose was to intimidate the enemy, but they were useless against well-drilled

Romans. Some legionaries' hearts may have beaten a bit faster, but the real fight was yet to begin.

The opening shots from the Roman side were by the equivalent of today's heavy artillery – long-range catapults, or *scorpios*. These devastating weapons had an effective range of some 300 metres. They shot a lethal wooden bolt, much heavier and broader than an arrow, with a sharp, four-sided iron tip that could cleave a great hole in anything it hit. The wooden arm that pulled back the bowstring was tensioned by coiled springs made of human and animal hair and sinew, giving the weapon a remarkable propellant power. About four bolts a minute could be shot from each *scorpio*, and there were up to 60 in each legion. So when the order was given, around 200 of these deadly missiles could be flying at the enemy in the course of just one minute. They would have taken their toll of the British charioteers prancing up and down between the armies, and – more importantly – they would have caught Boudicca's foot soldiers as they began their advance ... well before they could have brought any of their own weapons to bear on the Romans.

Nevertheless, when Boudicca gave the signal for a general assault by her army it must have been a terrifying moment. You can imagine the great roar that rose from the British ranks as they began their move forward. Massively outnumbering their Roman opponents, they now planned to wreak their revenge on the empire that had caused them so much suffering and treated their leader with such brutal contempt and indignity. It must have taken them all of two minutes to get close enough to the Romans to begin their final charge. At the beginning of their advance they had to endure a further hail of *scorpio* bolts: when they began their final charge, perhaps 50 metres from the enemy line, the Romans brought their second set of weapons into play.

Charge

1. The Roman legionaries hold their ground, in spite of being taunted and showered with missiles by Boudicca's charioteers.

2. As the charging Britons approach, the Romans await the order to hurl their javelins. Their commander had stiffened their resolve by telling them that in the face of overwhelming numbers discipline would save them from extinction.

Javelins

Each Roman soldier carried a light javelin that he could throw around 30 metres, and a heavier one that travelled around 15 metres. As the British began their final charge, the Romans received the order to move forward and throw their javelins one after the other. Keeping in tight formation with his fellow men, holding his shield in front of him, each legionary gave himself just enough room to pull back his arm and cast his javelins. Some of them missed, some of them hit home, and many of them crunched into British shields, making them impossible to hold steady. A shield with a 2-metre shaft impaled in it is useless. There would have been no time to tear the javelin free, and many Britons had no choice but to cast their shields aside as they closed with the enemy. A pile of dead and wounded quickly built up alongside useless shields. Many of the dead were the front-rank troops, the cream of Boudicca's army, their corpses obstructing the mass of attacking Britons behind. But Boudicca still had one major advantage on her side: overwhelming numbers.

The mêlée

Within seconds of the javelins striking home, the Romans found the Britons upon them. Savage close combat ensued. The Britons swung their swords and hacked at the Roman shields and the men holding them. The Romans used their shields to parry the blows, and thrust with their short stabbing swords at the tangle of bodies pressing in on them. The butchery must have been unimaginable, with ghastly

The long iron point of a *pilum*, the Roman javelin. Its thin metal shaft would often bend on impact and deny the enemy the chance to throw it back.

wounds being inflicted by these weapons. Within seconds there would have been bodies, blood and severed limbs everywhere.

As the Romans fought, they also struggled to keep their line of shields straight. Each man probably fought for around five minutes. Then, somehow keeping their wall of shields steady, the men in the front row slipped back through the ranks, allowing the second and then the third ranks to take over the front-line fighting. And so it went on, rank replacing rank, some legionaries filling the places of dead or wounded comrades, others taking over from exhausted soldiers filtering back through the ranks to draw breath and tend to wounds.

We do not know how Boudicca herself fought the battle. It seems likely that she led from the front, probably in her own chariot, shouting encouragement and throwing herself into the thick of the fight. Paulinus, on his side, probably held back so as to maintain an overview of the battle and preserve what he could of his command and control.

The deadly wedge

How long this ferocious mêlée went on we do not know. Both armies remained locked in a largely static struggle for some time, but gradually the ruthless discipline of the Roman line and the sheer solidity of their wall of shields began to take its toll. They used the heavy bosses on their shields to smash forward and they disabled the enemy by stabbing with their short

The Roman *cuneus*, the wedge formation Paulinus used to carve into Boudicca's front line. The size of the wedges in this battle is uncertain: each *cuneus* could be anything from cohort size down to a small handful of men.

swords. Now, with this forward momentum, there was no need to kill an opponent: wounded men on the ground could be dealt with by the ranks behind. The Britons found themselves crushed between the Roman wall of shields and their own troops pressing from the back. They probably found it difficult to wield their long swords.

The Romans must have detected a lessening of the pressure in front of them, and sensed that the time had come to advance. This was the moment for them to put into practice a well-known tactic that they had long rehearsed – their wedge formation. For 400 years, since the time of the Macedonian phalanx of Alexander the Great, the technique of men forming themselves into some kind of arrowhead formation had proved an effective way of smashing through a massed enemy. In the hands of Roman generals it became the *cuneus*, the wedge. A number of soldiers – there is no record of how many – formed one or more pointed wedges at the front of each cohort's battle line. And when the order came to advance, these wedges tore their way into the enemy: the points of the wedges cut holes in the enemy's line and the angled sides of the wedges widened the gaps to allow the legionaries behind to pour through and join the fray.

And so it happened that day. On an order from their centurions, no doubt signalled from a higher level, perhaps by Paulinus himself, the Roman line formed into wedges and the order was given to advance. Slowly, inexorably, the long jagged line of Roman legionaries began to tramp forward, pushing, thrusting, hacking its way into the great mass of disoriented Britons. Everything depended on the Romans maintaining the disciplined symmetry of their formation and the momentum of their advance. They did, and it worked. Once again Rome's great military machine was in motion, and nothing could stop

it. British surprise turned to disarray, retreat and then rout. Mercilessly, the Romans pressed on. They were now out of the mouth of the valley and into the open plain beyond. They did not need to increase their pace; they were moving forward as fast as the tangle of now disorganized Britons could escape. Many of Boudicca's soldiers must have struggled to fight back, turning every now and again to strike a blow at their pursuers. But every time they turned away again they were helplessly vulnerable to lethal blows from those short Roman swords.

Massacre at the wagons

As they ran, walked or stumbled back before this Roman steamroller, the Britons realized with horror that they were trapped by the wall of wagons that they had drawn up in a great crescent behind them at the beginning of the day to allow their families to witness the battle. With her forces corralled in this rapidly shrinking space, Boudicca's rout became a massacre. The Roman ranks now broke open to allow every soldier to enter the fray and butcher the enemy's

men, women and children, and Paulinus ordered his cavalry into the slaughter once they were no longer needed to protect the flanks. Tacitus describes a great pile of bodies – heightened by the corpses of the baggage animals, which were also slaughtered by the Romans. He puts the total British death toll at 80,000, and says the Romans suffered only 400 dead. Even if Tacitus is exaggerating five or ten times over, it was still an overwhelming victory. For Paulinus's troops it was a magnificent triumph, and wind of it must have spread like wildfire around Britain, quickly quelling any ardour for revolt among other tribes. When the news was brought to the unfortunate Poenius Postumus, who had kept his legion, the IInd Augusta, in Exeter and prevented them sharing in the victory, he immediately committed suicide by falling on his sword.

Boudicca's end

The British leader had been so utterly defeated that she despaired of any further resistance and, according to Tacitus, committed suicide by taking poison. Cassius Dio says she fell ill and

The Roman wedge

1-2. The decisive moment in the battle comes when the Romans form wedges and cut their way into Boudicca's forces. The cast-iron discipline of the Roman formation fractures the enemy line and funnels groups of British warriors into V-shaped cul-de-sacs where they are cut to pieces.

3. Those Britons who turn to make their escape are easy prey for the Roman cavalry charging in from the flanks.

The huge mass of Britons retreating before the Roman wedges (in the background) find themselves trapped by the great circle of wagons drawn up to give their families a ringside view.

died, and gives the impression that this happened very soon after the battle. That is all we know. Boudicca may have rejected the opportunity to escape and preferred an honourable death. She may have faced capture and taken poison to avoid being humiliated and executed by the Romans.

She must have wanted at all costs to avoid being taken in triumph by Paulinus to Rome. Whatever the cause of her death, it appears she did not die at the hands of the enemy she had hated so passionately. She was buried with honours by her own people, the Iceni, who spent the next months

BATTLE EXPERIENCE
The wedge formation

What better way to test the impact of the wedge formation, which Tacitus tells us was so effective in defeating Boudicca, than to put it into practice on the rugby field? We spent a day with one of England's top rugby teams, Wasps, at their base in Ealing in west London.

Dan was put at the point of a so-called 'flying wedge', a group of players who form themselves into an arrowhead and charge their opponents. It is easy to see why the 'flying wedge' is no longer permitted under the rules of rugby: it is a fearsome way of carrying an attack deep into the other side's defences. Dan found himself propelled by the momentum of his fellow 'flyers' through the opposition's line, and the next thing he knew he was at the bottom of a pile of bodies on the try line.

The closely packed wedge formation gave the men on the rugby field – as it must have given those on the battlefield – huge driving power. When practised by heavily armed legionaries, it must have pulverized almost any enemy force. Concentrating force on a narrow section of the enemy's line has been a constant feature of military tactics and rugby ever since.

Unimaginable slaughter resulted from the clash between the world's most efficient army and an undisciplined horde. The battle was over. 'Pacification' could now begin. Roman retribution against the rebellious tribes was remorseless.

suffering vicious reprisals at the hands of Paulinus and his forces.

It had been a narrow escape for the Roman occupiers of Britain. If Boudicca had been able to catch Paulinus by surprise, as she had the commander of the IXth legion near Colchester, she might have succeeded in defeating both men. But instead of consolidating her position after she had ravaged London and St Albans, and cautiously waiting for Paulinus to come to her, she pressed on north, probably believing that all would now fall before her. As it was, Paulinus was the one who was able to choose his ground for the battle and decide where and when to fight it. The Britons, so effective at marauding tactics, proved inferior to the legions in pitched battle. But if the Roman line had buckled and collapsed, and Boudicca's revolt had succeeded, the history of Britain might have been very different. We know that the emperor of the day, Nero, had his doubts about the wisdom of

maintaining Rome's grip on Britain. The Britons were known to be an awkward lot, and Britain must have seemed to many Romans to be a province too far. But with the suppression of the revolt the political climate changed, and by the end of the century the totally pacified tribes of Britain settled down, intermarried with the Romans and enjoyed the prosperity that accompanied expanding trade within the empire. Roman rule lasted for three and a half more centuries. It was to leave an indelible stamp on the English language and on the organization and infrastructure of mainland Britain.

As for Boudicca herself, over the centuries her name won a place among Britain's great national heroes and heroines. By a strange irony her fight for the rights of an indigenous people under foreign occupation was trumpeted centuries later by a British people creating their own empire and ruling countless other people across the globe.

1066: THE BATTLE OF HASTINGS

History is often thought to move at a glacial pace, but in the autumn of 1066 it moved at a dramatic speed. The events of that year are seared into the national consciousness to this very day. Harold losing his eye to a Norman arrow and his crown to William the Conqueror are among the most famous events in British history. The Battle of Hastings and its aftermath led to the greatest social and political upheaval to hit this country for the next thousand years.

For the two commanders this would be a clash between two very different strategic approaches. And it would demand an impressive display of fighting leadership from each of them. For the men it would be a harsh test of endurance: the battle was to be one of the longest and closest-fought struggles of the period.

On the morning of 14 October 1066 the army of Anglo-Saxon England stood in a line 800 metres long and up to ten ranks deep on a ridge several kilometres north of Hastings on the southeast coast. Underneath its battle banner, the Dragon of Wessex, stood its last king, Harold Godwinson. This handsome and charismatic warrior was

flanked by his two brothers, and around them stood one of the finest fighting forces in Europe.

On that unusually bright morning they could see the autumn sunlight glinting off the bright spear tips, chain mail and helmets of an equally impressive army in the valley below. This was a foreign army of adventurers and mercenaries from all over western Europe, trespassers on Saxon land. They had spent two weeks in England pillaging, burning and raping, even though they claimed to be doing God's work. Above the vanguard fluttered a white banner with a gold cross, a banner sent by the pope himself. The Saxons must have been particularly struck by the

HAROLD

With a Danish mother, Harold Godwinson had the looks of a Norseman. He was tall and striking, with long flowing hair and a moustache in the Saxon style. In 1066 he was 45 years old and an experienced soldier. His dashing leadership and flair had defeated the Welsh on their own ground. He also won the respect of his men by fighting in the front line. When not fighting, he enjoyed his wealth and had a passion for hunting. He was a charismatic leader, and his coronation, immediately after the death of Edward the Confessor, was highly popular.

WILLIAM

A stocky man of 5 foot 10, with close-cropped red hair and a clean-shaven face, William was in his late 30s at the time of the Battle of Hastings. He had spent his life in the saddle, first ensuring his control of Normandy and then protecting the dukedom from invaders. A canny commander, he was loth to risk all in battles when ambushes and sieges could achieve the same ends. But he was brave and physically strong: he could carry another man's chain mail as well as his own. He was also cruel to the point of brutality, and his men feared him as much as they loved him.

2,000 knights mounted on stallions, a terrifying novelty in these islands, where for centuries men had always fought on foot. Astride a mighty black warhorse, a gift from the king of Spain, rode the commander of the invaders. He too was surrounded by his brothers and closest comrades. A strong, stocky man, he was, like Harold, no stranger to war. His name was William, Duke of Normandy. Both men had come to this sloping field to decide the fate of a kingdom. Only one would leave it alive.

Rivals for a rich prize

The England they fought over was politically united, the soil was fertile, and the churches and monasteries were filled with some of the finest treasures in Europe. Above all, England had the most advanced coinage in western Europe and a system of taxation that had allowed a succession of powerful monarchs to maintain large professional armies and reinforce them in the event of national crisis. But in 1066 England was vulnerable.

In January that year the old king, Edward the Confessor, died. He had no heir, and some of the most powerful men in Europe, such as the mighty Harald Hardrada, king of Norway, cast their eyes on the English throne. But there was also a home-grown claimant to the crown. He was no blood relation to the king but made an ideal candidate in a world where kings were not automatically succeeded by a family member. His name was Harold Godwinson, Earl of Wessex. He and his brothers were almost as rich as the king and possibly even more powerful. Harold was an able and popular commander, and his men had followed him on campaigns in Scotland and Wales. He was the archetypal 11th-century warrior leader – charismatic and brave, but tough and cruel as well.

And there was yet another man who hankered after the English throne. William, Duke of Normandy believed his claim rested on more than cynical, naked ambition. He was convinced that

Above: Coin of William I (1066–87), England's first Norman king.

Right: William on horseback. The statue, outside the great castle at Falaise in the heart of William's duchy, shows him carrying the banner sent him by the pope.

the throne was his by right, and he had such a stubborn, forceful personality that when he pronounced people listened.

William's ancestors were Vikings from Scandinavia. After invading northwest France, they settled and adopted local customs, forcing the king of France to acknowledge them as dukes of the 'Norse', hence 'Normans'. William himself was the illegitimate son of Duke Robert of Normandy and a tanner's daughter. His was a tough and lonely upbringing. Duke Robert died when William was only a boy, and in the power vacuum that followed the young duke had a

Left: The Saxon church at Bosham in Sussex looks just the same today as when Harold worshipped there.

William makes Harold swear an oath to support his claim to the crown of England. In this piece of the Bayeux Tapestry Harold's left hand is held over the sacred relics and an aide to William points to the Latin word *sacramentum* (oath).

turbulent apprenticeship. He witnessed the murder of his beloved steward in his own bedchamber; he saw the disastrous effect of divided nobles; he watched neighbours invade and ravage his dukedom. All this turned William into a ruthless warrior and an aggressive and implacable leader. His fierce reputation deterred raiders from invading Norman land. Amid the violence and unrest of 11th-century Europe Normandy became a haven of security where William's subjects could live out their lives in peace. To his neighbours in Brittany and Anjou he was a brutal warlord, but his fellow Normans were grateful for his protection.

The fateful oath

If there was one thing this warrior duke craved more than anything else, it was a crown. His claim to the English throne derived from the fact that his second cousin, the childless Edward the Confessor, had greatly admired him when he was a young man and may well have promised him his throne. Even Harold, who by 1066 coveted the throne for himself, had earlier sworn that he would support William's claim. It happened during a mysterious visit that Harold had made to France two years earlier. Some say it was a fishing trip that went wrong. Norman propagandists and the Bayeux Tapestry, on the other hand, suggest that

Edward sent Harold, his strong man, to swear allegiance to the duke in order to make the transition from Edward's reign to William's smooth and peaceful.

Whatever the reason, Harold was shipwrecked on the French coast in the summer of 1064. He then had the distinctly mixed blessing of being rescued by William and becoming his 'guest'. He fought for William before the walls of Mont St Michel, and it is tempting to imagine William constantly watching his Saxon rival, looking for strengths and weaknesses as they campaigned together. What is certain is that William decided to use the fact that Harold was in his power – a virtual hostage – to persuade him to swear an oath on the holiest of relics to uphold William's claim to the English throne.

Those events would have dramatic repercussions two years later when, on 5 January 1066, Edward the Confessor died after a long illness. On his deathbed Edward had apparently reached up and taken Harold's hand. This may have been no more than the last act of a delirious old man. But the eager Godwinson clan immediately claimed that by this act Edward had chosen Harold as his successor.

The king is dead! Long live the king!

If Harold's memory of his oath to William troubled him, he did not let it show. He had himself crowned in Edward the Confessor's new abbey at Westminster on the same afternoon that Edward was buried. History was indeed moving at breakneck speed.

We are told that William was out hunting when someone summoned up the courage to give him the news of Edward's death and Harold's corona-tion. William was said by one chronicler to have been 'enraged' and 'spoke to no man, neither dared any man speak to him'. But he did not let his anger cloud his judgement. Within weeks he made it known that he intended to launch a massive invasion of England. Harold, he said, had

broken his oath, flouting the Christian faith and ignoring the will of the dead Edward.

William's ambitions, however, were larger than his resources. His subjects feared his plans would bankrupt Normandy. Ships would have to be borrowed and built, stores gathered and, above all, men persuaded to join him. His ordinary Norman forces were only obliged to protect their homeland and carry out the odd raid into Brittany. William could not command them to join a full-scale invasion overseas – especially not against the warlike Saxons, whose prowess in battle was legendary. He was, therefore, going to need more than his notorious bullying abilities to drum up an invasion force.

William now demonstrated that he was also a highly skilled political operator. He could not commit the duchy to the invasion: the Norman aristocracy was split and arguments raged. So William painted it as his own private war, and he invited his nobles to volunteer privately for a share of the spoils. A group of closely trusted family members and comrades – his brothers, Bishop Odo and John of Mortain, and his most loyal adviser and childhood friend, William FitzOsbern – worked with him to bribe, persuade and threaten nobles and mercenaries from all over Europe to join the expedition. They were told of the rich

BATTLE FACT

The Bayeux Tapestry has a colourful history. Almost as long as a football pitch, it was probably made in England during William's reign, then taken to Bayeux cathedral, where it remained for almost 700 years. During the French Revolution it was removed and used to cover military carts. It was retrieved before the carts left town and narrowly survived subsequent wars and revolutions.

pickings in a conquered England, of land and treasure beyond their dreams. And in a deft propaganda coup William enlisted the support of the pope, who sent a papal banner with his personal blessing. Those who joined the cause would now be doing God's work, and if they enriched themselves along the way, that was their reward for devotion to the Church. It sounded like the opportunity for a good fight, piles of plunder and a guaranteed place in heaven for those who died. Warriors from as far afield as Sicily, at that time a Norman possession, signed up in droves.

The Anglo-Saxon forces: fyrd and housecarls

Back in England, as news filtered through of the gathering threat from Normandy, a flaming star appeared in the sky. To many of the superstitious Anglo-Saxons it warned of disaster; we now know that it was nothing more than a neatly timed pass of Halley's Comet.

Harold, the new king, had lived as a warrior and intended to rule as one. Rather than be cowed by omens or by fear of what lay in wait, he reacted with huge energy. To begin with, he assembled what *The Anglo-Saxon Chronicle* calls 'a naval force and a land force larger than any king had ever assembled before in this country'. He made his headquarters in the natural harbour behind the Isle of Wight. It was a good base for his army and fleet, and one of the most likely targets for any invasion from Normandy.

The army of Saxon England reflected its impressive administrative and social structure. Earldoms were divided into shires, and each shire had a levy of men known as the fyrd, who served in times of war. Every 'hamlet' of farms had to produce one man for military service for a period of two months a year – equipped with armour and weapons, his own food and a horse for transport. If a fyrd man failed to join up he faced big fines and loss of lands, but if he died in battle his heirs could inherit his land without paying any death duties. On top of this, in an acute crisis, every able-bodied man in the shire was called up to protect his home from immediate danger. This 'greater fyrd' fought with knives and small axes; few of them owned swords or armour.

There was also another body of troops in late Anglo-Saxon England: the elite housecarls – full-time professional soldiers who provided bodyguards for the king or for the great earls. There were perhaps 3,000 royal housecarls in 1066, and each earl was accompanied by around 200 of his own. They always fought on foot, and were among the finest infantry in Europe. They used the sword and spear, but some were also axemen. The Saxon axe was a terrifying weapon: the axeman had to use both hands to swing it, and so had to rely on others to shield him. Housecarls were bound by more than payment from their commander. Their loyalty was absolute, and it was a disgrace to leave the field of battle alive if their lord had fallen.

Meanwhile, on the other side of the Channel William assembled his forces at the port of Dives, just west of the mouth of the Seine. This huge camp was home to 10,000 men and 2,000 horses, which needed 13 tonnes of grain and 13 tonnes of hay each day. To feed such a force and restrain it from plundering the local farmland was an astonishing achievement.

Above: A Viking longboat: a design used from Norway to Normandy.
Opposite: An 11th-century Viking sword. This type of sword was also used by the best warriors in Saxon and Norman armies.

William's disciplinary measures were so effective that one chronicler tells us that a weak or unarmed man could ride 'singing on his horse wherever he wished without trembling at the sight of a squadron of knights'.

Harold's huge army in southern England waited all through the long summer. The beacons that had been erected on the headlands to warn of the enemy landing remained unlit, and the fyrd's enthusiasm began to wane. The men wanted to bring in the harvest and were impatient to go home. *The Anglo-Saxon Chronicle* said simply, 'The men's provisions were finished and no one could keep them there any longer.' No doubt cursing himself for mobilizing too early and casting a glance south to where he knew William was waiting for a fair wind, Harold disbanded his army. He returned to London hoping that the brutal autumnal gales would keep William's expedition in Normandy until the spring.

'Thunderbolt of the North'

Harold had hardly reached London in September 1066 when he received shocking news. England had been invaded, but not in the south and not by William. It was another ambitious foreigner with

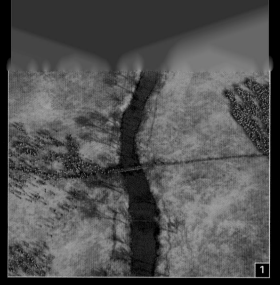

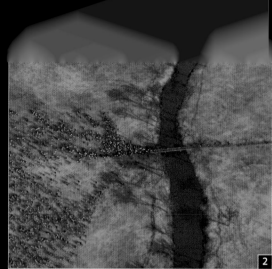

an eye for plunder, Harald Hardrada, the giant king of Norway, known as the 'Thunderbolt of the North'. One of his chroniclers called him 'the strongest man living under the sun'. Together with Harold's treacherous younger brother Tostig, Hardrada had sailed his 300 Viking longboats up the river Humber. On landing, he had unfurled his banner, known as the 'Land Waster', depicting a raven to warn his enemies of the fate that awaited their corpses. This was no simple Viking raid: Hardrada had brought many thousands of men. It was an invasion.

While Hardrada was brushing aside local opposition, Harold reacted with astonishing speed. He summoned his housecarls and ordered the fyrd to join him on the way north. In one of the most famous lightning marches in British history, Harold's forces covered over 300 kilometres in about five days. Modern research suggests that between battles the Saxons travelled on horseback, but even so this was an extraordinary feat. Gathering the Midland fyrd along the way, Harold reached Tadcaster on the night of 24 September.

There he learned that the Viking leader had no idea the Saxon army was in the area. Indeed, the next day Hardrada was expecting the official submission of the city of York. He was planning to receive hostages at a river crossing to the east of the city, called Stamford Bridge.

Caught napping

Harold resolved to launch his Saxons against the Vikings next day. It was sunny, and the Viking chronicler tells us that the unsuspecting invaders 'were all very cheerful' as they marched to Stamford Bridge from the spot where they had left their ships 20 kilometres away. Given the warm weather and their recent victory, they were not expecting a fight and had left their cumbersome chain mail behind. Each suit weighed about 30 kilograms and was made from tiny interconnected iron rings hammered or riveted together; it would stop all but the most powerful blows from a sword or spear.

As the Vikings ambled towards Stamford Bridge, Harold led his Saxons straight through the deserted centre of York. They were fully armed and motivated for battle against an age-old foe. Here was a chance to drive the hated Vikings, who had been raiding the country for 300 years, from English shores once and for all.

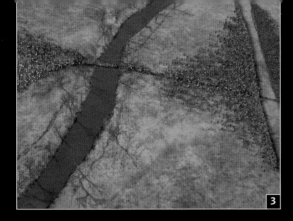

1. The Vikings are lounging about on both sides of a bridge across the river Derwent. Suddenly, the Saxons appear (bottom left) and catch them by surprise.

2. While some Vikings flee across the bridge, others desperately try to hold the Saxons back.

3. The Saxons sweep away Viking resistance and pour over the bridge. There they find the Vikings formed up facing them behind a wall of shields (far right). The Saxons assemble their own shield wall opposite, leaving only a narrow gap between the two sides.

The Saxons stream across the narrow bridge. For some time they were held up here by a Viking axeman, who bought his countrymen vital time to form a defensive line on the east bank.

At Stamford Bridge the Vikings waited for their gifts, hostages and tribute, and amused themselves with a little cattle stealing. Suddenly those with the keenest eyes spotted a cloud of dust on the road from York. At the base of the cloud, the Viking chronicler tells us, they saw what looked like the 'glint of sunlight on broken ice'. It was the armour and weapons of the approaching Saxons, with King Harold at their head.

The Battle of Stamford Bridge

The Vikings were spread out on both sides of the river Derwent connected only by a small bridge. The English, approaching from the west, trapped those on the west bank in a bottleneck. Some scrambled to get back across the bridge, while others stood and fought against overwhelming odds.

Hardrada and Tostig argued. Should they retreat to the ships, or stand and fight? Tostig, the Saxon renegade, knew that his own people, led by his brother Harold, would be invincible in a fight with the disorganized, outnumbered and armourless Vikings. He begged Hardrada to return to the boats and organize resistance there. But Hardrada had never run from a battlefield. He ordered his banner to be unfurled and commented grimly that, although he would doubtless be killed, he would give the English one hell of a battle.

One Viking, whom *The Anglo-Saxon Chronicle* describes as 'worthy of eternal fame', had brought his chain mail armour with him. After the Anglo-Saxons had scythed through his panic-stricken comrades on the west side of the river this giant stood astride the bridge and held up the entire army. With a massive axe he hewed down 40 Saxons as they tried to rush the bridge. Other Saxons shouted that if he surrendered he would be treated with the highest respect and rewarded handsomely

for his valour, but he sneered at their promises and refused to move. He was only brought down when one enterprising Saxon floated beneath the bridge in a barrel and stabbed upwards with a spear through the wooden slats of the bridge right into the Viking's unprotected groin.

As the Saxons burst across the bridge, the Vikings on the east side hurriedly locked their shields together in a wall; the Anglo-Saxons did the same. Viking chroniclers claim that, as the two lines looked at each other, the Saxons shouted that if Tostig surrendered he would get his earldom back and a third of the kingdom. 'What about Hardrada's share?' Tostig shouted back. The reply came that all Hardrada would get was 'seven feet of English soil' to be buried in. Tostig refused to abandon his ally, and the Saxons advanced up the hill towards the Viking shield wall.

As the two sides clashed, Saxon steel caused carnage among the Viking ranks. Hardrada seems to have left the protection of the shield wall and ferociously charged the English with a sword in each hand. The Saxons gave way until Hardrada was killed by an arrow in the throat. His body was carried back to his own Viking lines during a lull, and the Saxons offered terms, but the Vikings shouted back that they would rather fall in battle than accept mercy from an Englishman. The battle was hard fought, but the Vikings were outnumbered and their lines began to fragment. Tostig was felled in the shadow of the 'Land Waster'. Reinforcements had run the 20 kilometres from the ships, but had had to shed their armour to move fast enough. They were too late: by the time they arrived all they could do was sacrifice themselves for a cause already lost. The Viking army was slaughtered, their leadership destroyed.

After his victory at Stamford Bridge Harold showed mercy and allowed Hardrada's son to take his father's body home. Just 24 of the 300 Viking ships were enough to carry the survivors back.

A 10th-century Viking helmet. No Viking headgear has ever been found to support the popular myth that they had horns.

William's huge invasion fleet, which had waited two weeks at the mouth of the Somme for a favourable wind, sets off on its 100-kilometre voyage to Pevensey.

The road to Hastings

But as the exhausted Anglo-Saxons celebrated, they were soon given news of a more menacing invasion 400 kilometres to the south. On 28 September Duke William of Normandy had landed in Pevensey Bay, totally unopposed.

William had left Dives on 11 September heading east to get closer to Britain, but his fleet was hit by storms and driven into the bay of the Somme. For two grey, rainy weeks it sheltered at St Valery-sur-Somme as the westerly wind kept the ships in harbour. The relics of St Valery were paraded to enlist the saint's help for a favourable wind and to buoy up sagging morale.

That wind finally came on the 28th, and William prepared to set out to sea on his flagship *Mora*, a present from his wife. Terrified horses were manhandled into the boats, last-minute supplies of fresh food were stowed away, and at dusk more than 700 vessels sailed out of the mouth of the Somme with a southerly breeze filling their sails.

The night crossing would make it difficult to keep the fleet together. William hung a lantern from his masthead so that the other boats could follow. With no compasses, the sailors must have used the wind direction and stars to guide them across the Channel. At dawn William's ship was all alone, bobbing about in sight of the English coast. Always mindful of morale, he ordered a large breakfast and ate it with conspicuous ease, telling the ship's anxious company that the other ships would join them. He was right: within a few hours the fleet had formed up again.

BATTLE FACT

A typical Norman vessel, which was 15 metres long, required the wood of some 74 trees to build. If William had constructed all the ships in his fleet, he would have had to denude Normandy of much of its forest. To avoid this, most of his fleet was almost certainly borrowed or requisitioned.

D-Day at Pevensey

The Norman fleet entered Pevensey Bay, a large, shallow natural harbour that has since silted up. William first sent ashore his archers, who reported that the old Roman fort guarding the bay was empty and that there were no hostile troops in the vicinity. William probably could not believe his luck. The horses and supplies were landed, and engineers immediately set about using wood to shore up the old fort as a base.

As William himself landed, he tripped over in the surf and cut his hands on the shingle. A cry of consternation went up from the superstitious soldiers around him. But a quick-witted nobleman called out that William had seized England with both hands and was going to guarantee it to his successors with his blood. Talk of a bad omen evaporated.

When William heard that Harold and his army were up in Yorkshire, he rejoiced but did not change his plans: he decided to stay close to his ships and his supply route to Normandy. Then, in order to lure Harold south, William started to ravage the area surrounding his bridgehead. The sources tell us of burning houses, and of children crying for their slaughtered fathers: according to the Domesday Book, two decades later these areas were still wastelands. William gambled that Harold would rush south with his exhausted army; meanwhile, the Normans could rest and prepare for the battle ahead.

William had judged Harold perfectly. On 1 October, when he was brought the news that William was ravaging his beloved Wessex, Harold immediately rode south from York with his house-carls and ordered the southern levies of the fyrd to be assembled. Speed had won him victory at Stamford Bridge; perhaps it would work again.

Harold paused a few days in London. His family urged him not to dash down to the coast: he should send his brother to contain William while he himself remained in London to build up a bigger army. They reminded Harold of the oath he had sworn not to fight William. But a furious Harold claimed the oath counted for nothing since it had been sworn under duress; he would lead the army himself. He decided that speed and surprise were worth more than the advantage of waiting for reinforcements.

He left London on 11 October at the head of an estimated 7,000 men. His veterans were exhausted, their numbers thinned by the fighting in the north. But two days later Harold was within reach of Hastings and some of his southern levies were beginning to join him. He had nothing like the numbers he could have had if he had waited a few days longer, but his mind was set on bringing William to battle as soon as possible.

Preparations for battle

In those days there were huge inlets either side of Hastings, which meant that there was only one practicable route to London. About 12 kilometres north of the coast it crossed a prominent ridge where the modern village of Battle stands. By Friday, 13 October Harold's army had arrived on the top of the ridge. He and his forces were now effectively blocking William's road north. A decisive battle for the crown of England was inevitable.

That night, the Norman chroniclers tell us, the English ate and drank till all hours, 'carousing, gambolling and dancing and singing', while the pious Normans and their French allies confessed their sins and prayed. At 9 a.m. on the 14th the Normans moved forward to face the Saxon army who were camped on its dominating ridge. The valley below was marshy, with a stream running along the bottom. In the vanguard the papal banner gave reassurance to the Normans; it may also have caused creeping doubts among pious Englishmen as to the righteousness of their cause. The French troops sang 'The Song of Roland': his heroism in the time of the great Charlemagne two centuries earlier would inspire them on a long and bloody day.

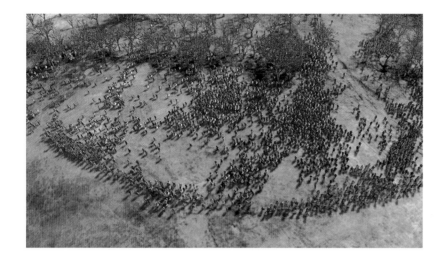

Harold's Saxon forces emerge from the woods behind the Senlac ridge and form a shield wall facing south to block the road from Hastings to London.

William had risen before dawn, taken the sacrament and addressed senior officers and troops. He told them that the battle could end only in victory or death; they could expect no mercy from the Saxons. He then donned his chain mail, and initially put it on back to front: it was another bad omen, but his quick wit came to the rescue. He said that just as he was today swapping round his hauberk, so he would swap his dukedom for a kingdom. To top it all he placed around his neck the very relics on which Harold had sworn his oath two years earlier. He wanted his men to know that God was with them.

The braying of dogs

Standing at the bottom of that hill, looking up at the thick, tightly packed line of long-haired Saxons screaming their war cries, many of William's men must have regretted their decision to follow their ambitious duke to this alien land. They did not understand the Saxons, whose language sounded to the Normans like the 'braying of dogs'. Most had probably never faced men who wielded the mighty broad axe. Its giant hardened steel blade – nearly 30 centimetres long – mounted on a metre-long shaft made it a fearsome weapon. And the more so in the hands of the Saxon housecarls, who now stood at the front of Harold's ranks swinging their axes in huge arcs, daring the Normans to attack them. The Saxon army was not just an awe-inspiring sight; its sound alone was enough to strike terror into an enemy. Their war cry, 'Ut! Ut! Ut!', had been used for generations; centuries earlier, in the mouths of their Saxon forebears, it had terrified the Romans in the dark German forests. A Norman chronicler said the Saxons 'count it as the highest honour to die in arms that their native soil may not pass under another yoke'.

The Normans deployed into three divisions, as ordered. The forces from Brittany were on the left, the Normans in the centre, and other French and Flemish allies on the right. In each block archers formed the front ranks; behind them were the

BATTLE FACT

The ridge at Hastings is now known as Senlac. Some believe this comes from the Norman French name given to it in the years after the battle: 'Sanguelac' means 'blood lake'.

Early on the morning of 14 October the approaching Normans found the Saxons drawn up in a formidable defensive position on the hill where Battle Abbey stands today.

heavier armed infantry, with the cavalry in reserve. William himself was in the centre with his inner circle. One of them, his brother, Bishop Odo, resplendent on a white charger, and mindful that a man of the cloth should not take up the sword, brandished his mace: it was ideal for the crushing of skulls, and not outlawed in the Bible.

'Dex aie!'

The Saxons were standing shoulder to shoulder, their shields interlocked in a 'wall'. William's battle plan was to soften them up with sustained archery, then send in the infantry to tear holes in their tight ranks. These gaps could then be exploited by the cavalry, who would burst through and finish the job. The cavalry stallions, trained to bite, kick and head butt the enemy, were warriors in their own right. If they could get in among the Anglo-Saxon infantry behind the wall of shields, they would be unstoppable.

Harold ordered that the shield wall should remain intact: no one was to break formation and charge down the hill. He knew that if he could fight a purely defensive battle on the crest of this ridge, he could hold William off and fight another day.

Fresh troops were arriving all the time: the northern earls Edwin and Morcar were on their way south, and the Bayeux Tapestry shows that troops were turning up even as the battle started. Harold knew that if he could fend off the Norman attack with a jagged wall of shields, the spears and swords of his infantry poking through it, he would be victorious. Even a bloody stalemate would mean an English victory: William was in a foreign land and could not replenish his ranks. But if a chink could be opened in the Saxon wall and William's formidable horsemen could get through, Harold's army would be routed.

As men fidgeted with their helmets and checked their saddles and stirrups, the Normans shouted their war cry, 'Dex aie!', meaning 'God's help'. They would need it.

An uphill struggle

William's minstrel, Taillefer, sensed his chance for immortality. He rode up to the duke and begged him, in payment for all his years of service, to let him strike the first blow. A Norman chronicler tells us that William acquiesced and Taillefer rode forward, singing 'The Song of Roland' and

BATTLE EXPERIENCE
Shield walls

The Anglo-Saxon *schildburh*, literally 'shield fort', was the most important formation for infantry forces of this period. The wall of shields protected a dense mass of troops behind it, who were free to throw missiles and add their weight to push the front rank forward. The shield wall would have bristled with spears over 2 metres long and swords to deter attacks from cavalry. No horse would impale itself, and as long as the troops held their nerve, the formation should have been impregnable.

We went to see a modern descendant of the shield wall in the Metropolitan Police Public Order Training Unit. They gave us a display of the skills they use to maintain public order, and we compared their shields and equipment with those of the Saxons. The similarities were fascinating. The police told us they never use long, densely packed shield walls precisely because they are considered too intimidating, but they formed one just for us with Dan in the middle of it.

Dan's first impression was of the strength and unity of the tightly bound group. Police officers behind helped bind the front rank by bracing them with their shoulders in the small of the back. Shield walls need constant management, with advice and orders flying to and fro. The key is to know and trust the man or woman next to you. As other policemen imitating rioters charged into the wall, all the individuals in it were bonded together to form a solid, unbreakable mass. Teamwork is as vital now as it was to the Saxons a millennium ago. No wonder the Saxons fought with their friends and relations close beside them.

performing tricks with his sword. He then fell upon the English ranks and killed two men before he was dragged off his horse and hacked down. William then ordered his archers forward to await his signal.

Harold and his brothers stood, dismounted, in the centre of the Saxon line at the top of the hill. The men of the London levy had the hereditary duty of guarding the king and his banners, just as it was the honour of the men of Kent to bear the brunt of the first attack. One of the banners was Harold's own, the jewel-encrusted image of a fighting man; the other was the Dragon of Wessex, the same dragon that had fluttered above the great Alfred when he had dealt so decisively with Danish invaders of England two centuries earlier.

At around ten o'clock, the battle began. The Normans began by loosing off their arrows straight up the hill, where many either struck the Saxon shields or sailed overhead. One of the mysteries of Hastings is the lack of English archers; perhaps this was another effect of Harold's hasty and incomplete mobilization. But it meant that no arrows were being shot at the Normans for them to recycle; they risked running out. William did not wait for his ineffective barrage to thin the Saxon ranks: he ordered his infantry forward.

With a blast of trumpets the Normans set off up the 200 or so metres of steadily sloping ground. Simply keeping in ranks in heavy armour was hard enough. As they neared the English they met a swarm of missiles: small throwing-axes, stones tied to sticks, spears and rocks. Nevertheless they persisted through the hail, with officers keeping their men in formation by kicking, prodding and hitting them with the flats of their swords. Waiting for them was an unbroken line of the finest foot soldiers in Europe, the Saxon housecarls.

What fighting there was at this point cannot have lasted long. However valiantly the Norman forces threw themselves at the shield wall, it didn't budge. Men could see their opponents over the top of their shields, but were unable to strike at them because their arms were pinned to their sides by the press of other warriors. The chroniclers tell us that the two sides were so tightly packed that the dead could not fall, 'for each corpse though lifeless stood as if unharmed and held its post'. The wounded could not escape, and were crushed or trampled. Between the Saxon shields their holders' knives and swords jabbed and cut, often aiming for the ankles and shins of their enemies. The Normans now had to clamber over their own dead as they struggled up the hill, only to be met by huge Saxon axes that could cut through chain mail and shatter wooden shields.

The Norman infantry wavered and William committed his horsemen, even though the Saxon shield wall had not yet been penetrated. They powered up the hill, forcing their way through the mass of Norman infantry until they too were pounding the shield wall. But the Saxons were not as intimidated by seeing horses in battle as

William had hoped. The wall held. The galloping stallions stopped short of impaling themselves on the spears and swords that jutted through it, and wheeled away. If any Normans came close, the Saxon shield bearers would open a small chink in the wall to allow the axemen to take a huge swing that could cut a horse's head off.

A scene from the Bayeux Tapestry showing the tightly packed Saxon shield wall inflicting early casualties on the Normans.

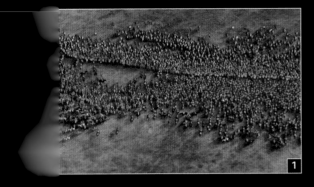

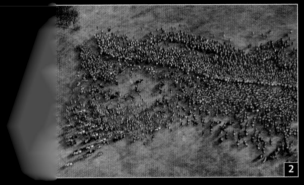

Panic

Against an enemy so resolute, the Norman attack stalled and then became a retreat. The Norman chroniclers claim that the Bretons on the left were the first to break off their attack and run headlong back down the hill. Their panic infected the rest of the army, and it seemed that the critical moment of the battle had been reached. The terrified troops shouted that William was dead and all was lost.

The sight of the Bretons streaming away was too much for some of the Saxons. Caught up in the emotion of battle, with the prospect of a broken enemy running before them, several hundred jubilant Saxons forgot their king's strict orders to hold their shield wall intact and broke ranks to pursue them. The Bretons were chased into a wooded, boggy area where their horses got stuck, and it quickly became a killing ground.

At this moment of extreme danger, William acted with great resolution. He threw back his helmet so that he could be seen and bellowed, 'Look at me – I am alive and with God's help will

Bretons flee

1. The Normans (bottom) are pressing hard on the Saxon shield wall (top), when the Bretons on the Norman left suddenly panic and flee back down the hill.

2. The panic spreads. More of William's forces turn and run.

Unable to resist the temptation, part of the Saxon line breaks ranks and chases the Bretons down the hill.

The penalty of indiscipline. Hundreds of Saxons who have disobeyed Harold's orders to stay defending the top of the ridge pay the price – slaughter at the hands of William's cavalry.

be the victor!' He roared that there was no safety in flight because the pursuing Saxons would massacre them; they had to stand firm together if they were to survive the day. He and his brother Bishop Odo led a strong unit of horsemen across to the left side of the field where, wielding their maces, they attacked those Saxons who had gone after the fleeing Bretons. Conditions were now perfect for the Norman knights. The Saxons were caught on open ground outside their protective shield wall; some of them tried to head for a little hillock, still there today, and huddle together in a forlorn shield wall of their own. It was to no avail. The Bayeux Tapestry suggests that some of the bloodiest fighting that day took place at this point: the exposed Saxons were surrounded and slaughtered, watched by the rest of their army only 300 metres away.

It was a pivotal moment in the battle. By annihilating those Saxons who had left their shield wall, William had turned a moment of great crisis into a success for his side. The massacre had taken place in full view of the main force of the English army, but they were ordered to stay put and not go to their comrades' aid. If Harold had seized this opportunity to launch a full-scale attack down the hill, William would still have had at least 2,000 horsemen to destroy any Saxon infantry caught in the open. Harold knew that his one chance of victory was to remain rooted to the spot in tight formation and let William's attacking force break themselves on his shield wall. Harold must have cursed when he saw his Saxons charging off to chase the Bretons, but he had been powerless to restrain them. Because he was fighting on foot and probably in a forward line of his housecarls, he had effectively lost the overall tactical control that William, on horseback, had maintained throughout.

Drawing breath

There was now a lull in the battle. Saxons darted out of the wall to retrieve their missiles and strip the valuable chain mail off corpses. On both sides water was passed through the ranks, supplied by the women and boys who accompanied the army.

William used this time to re-evaluate. He had scored a major success, but he did not allow this to blind him to a more critical problem: he had made scarcely a dent in the shield wall at the top of the hill. But his slaughter of the Saxons who had broken ranks gave him an idea. What if, instead of smashing the shield wall at a stroke, he could grind it down? If enough Saxons could be drawn out and killed by his cavalry, the wall would lose its strength and gaps would appear. So William decided to use guile. By staging a series of attacks and mock retreats, encouraging the eager Saxons to follow him down the hill where his cavalry could set upon them, he would wear down the enemy numbers in a battle of attrition.

Grinding down the Saxons

At least, this is what the Norman chroniclers would have us believe. It may be that William did indeed repeat a tactic the Normans had used before – feigning retreats to draw the enemy out of their defences. Equally, that account may be the invention of Norman spin doctors, when in reality the Normans simply attacked and were bloodily repulsed.

Either way, over the next few hours the Normans made several surges up the hill and retreats down it. Each time a few Saxons, carried away by enthusiasm and lacking the Normans'

After the failure of his first attack, William (centre) raises his helmet to show he is still alive. In a dramatic gesture, his standard-bearer points this out to the Norman army.

discipline, followed their enemy down the hill only to be picked off by William's cavalry or just overwhelmed by the greater numbers of the Normans. These constant cavalry charges inflicted a steady trickle of casualties in the shield wall, giving the exhausted Saxons no respite. The battle became a relentless ebb and flow. But while the best Saxon troops were kept permanently fighting, the Normans were able to rotate their men, enabling themselves and their horses to rest.

We are told that William was always where the action was thickest, and that two or three horses were killed under him. One chronicler tells us dramatically that the duke's horse was killed by one of Harold's brothers, whom William then 'hewed limb from limb'. But he was still without a horse and in serious danger. Suddenly he spotted one of his knights riding past. The knight was terrified by the slaughter around him and ignored

William's cry for help. But William seized him by the nosepiece of his helmet and flung him to the ground, then helped himself to his horse and rode off to fight again. What happened to the knight is not recorded.

The crisis

As the light began to fade in mid-afternoon, William knew his window for victory was narrowing sharply. If Harold could hold out for the rest of the day, he would gain reinforcements, whereas William, whose ranks were also thinning, had no such hope. So he gathered every man who could still walk or ride and placed them in one solid block rather than the three divisions he had started with. He then ordered his archers to stand behind these troops and shoot in high arcs over their heads so that the arrows would fall on the unprotected rear ranks of the Saxon army. He may have hoped that the combination of archers and advancing infantry would prove too much for the Saxons, who would now have one threat to their front and another whistling down on them from above.

For the Saxons this was the climax of another long day in a month of long days. The housecarls and elite troops who had stood in the first couple of lines had taken significant casualties and their places were increasingly filled with less experienced, less well-armed men. The soldiers were now too exhausted to roar their defiance or even to lift their sword arms. The hail of arrows and a renewed Norman attack proved a breaking point for many men of the fyrd, who used the dusk to sneak off into the trees behind their position.

The details of this final attack and of the heroic last stand of the Saxon army are hard to decipher. We can guess that the depleted shield wall contracted just enough to allow William's men to gain a foothold on the ridge, where the savage fighting continued. But one event in particular has become a defining moment in British history: a Norman arrow struck Harold in the eye. The general consensus seems to be that the arrow did not kill him and that he lived his last few minutes in agony surrounded by his loyal housecarls. The Normans saw their chance. A group of knights made a concerted and bloody effort to hack their way through to the stricken king. Given the personal nature of command at that time, a prime aim in battle was to destroy the enemy's morale by killing their leader and trampling his banner. This is exactly what happened at Hastings. The housecarls fought desperately to save their king, but the Norman knights were too strong for them. They reached the wounded Harold and cut him down with a blow to the thigh. His body was virtually dismembered, and the banners of Wessex and of Harold himself were hurled to the ground.

The famous scene from the tapestry showing the death of Harold. Some believe the king is shown twice – first, on the left, pulling the arrow from his eye, and then, right, being cut down by a sword blow to the thigh.

Battle Abbey today. The abbey stands at the top of the hill that Harold defended. It faces south down a long grassy slope to the lake (just visible on the left) where the Normans assembled for their attack.

'Few in number but brave in the extreme'

When, in the gathering gloom of that October evening, the Saxon rank and file saw their banners fall they knew that England had lost a king and, more importantly, the army had lost its leader. The English force disintegrated. Some ran. Others were cut down in small groups. But the housecarls remained true to their word and refused to leave the field. One chronicler says in admiration, 'The English were few in number but brave in the extreme.' Some are said to have organized a desperate rearguard action behind the battlefield in a ravine called Malfosse, where they unhorsed some Norman knights. But the Saxons were brushed aside by the tireless William, who rode to the rescue.

When he returned to the battlefield it was said that he 'could not look without pity upon the carnage'. Perhaps as many as 4,000 corpses littered the field. Heaps of bodies indicated where the fiercest fighting had been. That night and the next day Normans stripped the armour off the dead and collected armfuls of valuable swords. No doubt they were also busy chasing off scavenging bounty hunters seeking to enrich themselves by robbing the bodies. The Normans buried their own dead, and allowed family and friends of the English to take their bodies away if they wished. But many did not, and 70 years later a traveller saw heaps of whitened bones.

Somewhere among the dead was the last Anglo-Saxon king of England. Harold's body was apparently identified by his mistress, Edith Swan-neck. She walked through the carnage, searching bodies for intimate birthmarks or tattoos, and eventually found her dead lover. But when

King William I on his throne. His coronation was a fiasco: the shouts of acclamation were misinterpreted by his Norman soldiers, who thought it was a riot and set fire to several nearby houses.

Harold's mother appealed for her son's body, the Conqueror would not surrender it – even in exchange for its weight in gold. Instead, so the story goes, he dumped it in a shallow grave on the seashore as a taunt to his defeated enemy. Harold's final resting place would be on the coast that he had so signally failed to guard against William's invasion.

The commanders

Harold and William were two of the most impressive commanders in British history. Without William's talent for organization and discipline the invaders would probably never have left France. His role in the battle was equally decisive. He was always in the thickest of the action – a brave and inspirational leader. He skilfully switched tactics with the flow of battle. He turned an early reverse into a successful counter-attack. He relentlessly whittled down the Saxon numbers and then had his archers create havoc among the enemy troops while he led an all-out attack with his cavalry and infantry.

Harold was extremely unlucky. He had to fight two major battles at different ends of the kingdom within three weeks of each other, in itself a remarkable feat. But there was more to his defeat than bad luck. His battle plan at Hastings was a model of defensive tactics and he held his enemy off for most of the day. But his plan was inflexible, and he himself fought on foot. This meant that, unlike William, he was ill equipped to adapt to the changing battle situation. Harold may for a moment have been within sight of victory, but in the end it was William who made the most of his opportunities while Harold did not.

Aftermath

The Anglo-Saxon state collapsed. William had himself crowned on Christmas Day 1066 in Westminster Abbey but it still took him several years of hard campaigning to secure his new kingdom. After fighting in Devon, Wales, Yorkshire and Scotland, he finally established himself as the supreme ruler in Britain. Over the next five years the land of the Saxons was distributed among William's followers, who installed themselves in impregnable castles. By 1070 the Saxon earldoms had ceased to exist, and by 1086, the date of William's great census, the Domesday Book, some 200 barons and 100 major abbeys and churches controlled 75 per cent of the country's wealth. After 1070, no Anglo-Saxon was appointed to high political or religious office for the next 200 years.

The Norman Conquest instigated one of the biggest transformations in English history. A small and exclusive warrior aristocracy took control of a huge native population. French language and culture replaced Saxon. England moved away from its Scandinavian roots towards the Latin ways of the Mediterranean. The mingling of the two traditions did much to shape the English language and the political and cultural fabric of the country that lasts to this day.

BATTLE FACT

Battle Abbey was built as an act of penance by King William I for all the blood he had shed during the conquest of England and to honour the dead in the Battle of Hastings.

1400-c.1410: THE BATTLE FOR WALES

All parts of the British Isles have been racked by conflict at some point during the past 2,000 years – Wales no less than anywhere else. In the early years of the 15th century, when war was a way of life all over Britain, Wales was caught up in the struggle to be free of English rule. The torch of rebellion was lit by a Welshman whose name has become a legend, and whose lightly armed troops ran rings around English armies in a ceaseless war of attrition. He was to take his land to the threshold of independence and lead his forces deep into England itself. His name was Owain Glyndwr, and his Battle for Wales was not fought in a day, but lasted over a decade.

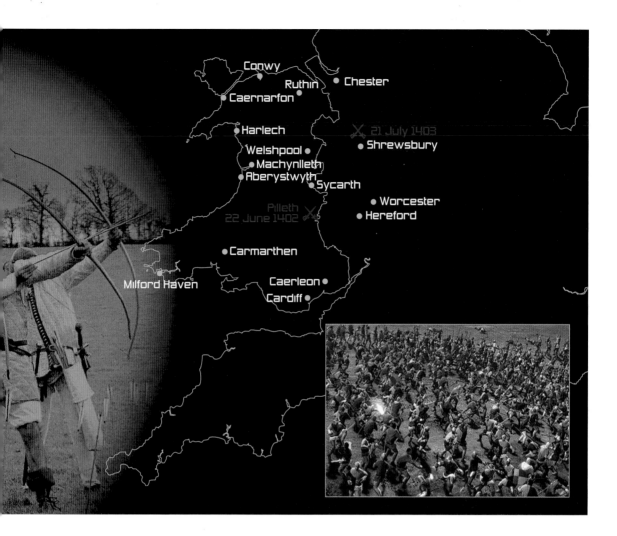

Wales conquered

For 200 years after the Battle of Hastings the Norman kings of England and their successors the Plantagenets were too busy elsewhere to deal with the troublesome Welsh. They settled for vague oaths of allegiance from native Welsh princes and planted English 'Marcher' Lords in huge castles on the Welsh border or marches. But this was not enough for Edward I, who in 1280 marched into Wales at the head of the biggest army seen in Britain since his ancestor William the Conqueror landed at Pevensey in 1066. One of his lieutenants captured the last Welsh prince, Llewellyn, and sent his head to Edward. The king then took over Llewellyn's final

bastion in Snowdonia and started a programme of castle-building to place a ring of steel around Wales. Castles such as Conwy, Caernarfon and Harlech became formidable symbols of English control that survive to this day.

Under English rule Wales was treated like a colony run for profit. Around the castles new towns or 'boroughs' sprang up, in which only the English could trade. The settlers set up new monopoly businesses and their privileges were ruthlessly enforced. In 1375 nine Welshmen were arrested at Clynnog, 16 kilometres from Caernarfon, for brewing ale to sell. English moneylenders lent the native Welsh money to pay their taxes and charged them

HENRY IV

Henry Bolingbroke reigned as King Henry IV from 1399 to 1413. He had a reputation for chivalry which made him famous throughout Europe when he was a young man. He won tournaments; he was the first crusader to reach the battlements during the famous siege of Vilnius in Lithuania; and he made a pilgrimage to Jerusalem. He became king by deposing his cousin Richard II and secretly having him put to death. His short reign was spent largely in the saddle, reeling from one crisis to the next but he left England stable enough for his son to launch a series of spectacular campaigns in France after he died.

Harlech Castle. Today's landscape is still dominated by this English stronghold, one of a ring of castles built by Edward I to control Wales.

crippling rates of interest. Any Welsh nobles who had managed to hold on to their lands were still denied top jobs and patronage. Welsh clergymen were excluded from high positions in the Church.

In 1399 any loyalty that Welsh nobles still felt towards the English crown was further undermined when the weak and unpopular Richard II was deposed by his cousin, Henry Bolingbroke, the wealthiest noble in Britain. Succession was believed to be ordained by God, and the removal of a king was therefore heresy. It was a severe shock to many in England and Wales when Bolingbroke became the new king, Henry IV. He had a struggle to persuade nobles in both England and Wales that he was the rightful heir, as other relatives of Richard's had better claims to the throne.

Henry did not make a good start. He installed his friend Reginald de Grey as a Marcher Lord, even though he was deeply unpopular in Wales. Grey promptly picked a quarrel with a local Welsh nobleman – unfortunately for him, the man whom the Welsh saw as the legitimate ruler of Wales, Owain Glyndwr. Glyndwr was from royal Welsh stock but his family had cooperated with the English and thrived under their rule. He himself had had the upbringing of a young English noble. He spoke four languages, had served in royal armies and even studied in London. Grey had made a terrible blunder.

It is unclear exactly what the row was about. One suggestion is that Grey and Glyndwr argued over a piece of land. The Welshman appealed to Parliament in London to settle the dispute. Chroniclers tell us that the Bishop of St Asaph warned Parliament not to ignore Glyndwr because the Welsh might revolt. But Parliament threw out the appeal, contemptuously dismissing Glyndwr and his countrymen by saying that it cared 'nothing for these bare footed clowns'. Parliament would regret its arrogance.

Revolt!

Spurned by London, on 16 September 1400 the Welsh leader met with his close family, senior

The site of Owain Glyndwr's fortress home on a round hilltop at Sycarth, south of Welshpool.

Welsh clergymen and a soothsayer at Glyndyfrdwy in the Dee valley of North Wales, and together they decided to raise the banner of revolt. They proclaimed Glyndwr Prince of Wales, a blatant challenge to the crown. Since Edward I's time this title had been reserved for the eldest son of the English king. This act of defiance showed that from the outset Owain Glyndwr had decided to turn his private quarrel into a national struggle against English rule.

Glyndwr's first target was the castle and borough particularly associated with the hated Lord Grey: Ruthin in North Wales. The attack took the town completely by surprise. The English garrison sought refuge in the castle, and from the safety of its stone keep watched Glyndwr's men ravage Ruthin. This raid set the pattern for the early stages of the revolt, in which lightning guerrilla attacks were carried out: symbols of English rule were burnt or destroyed, and boroughs ransacked. The castles may have provided sanctuary to some, but with garrisons of no more than 10 or 20 men, there was little

GLYNDWR

Only romanticized images exist of Owain Glyndwr (pronounced 'Glindoor'). They depict him with long, flowing grey hair and a noble bearing. It is true that he was born into a princely Welsh family, but he was given an education befitting a young English noble. The mound on which his fine timber-beamed house stood in Sycarth in Powys can be seen to this day. Glyndwr was famed for his hospitality and for serving that medieval delicacy, white bread. When it came to war, he was a man of great courage and determination. The speed of his manoeuvres, his use of guerrilla tactics and exploitation of the Welsh terrain made him a gifted commander. But he was not just a soldier; he also possessed the abilities and vision of a statesman.

The inhospitable terrain of Snowdonia, where Glyndwr's forces were secure from English attack.

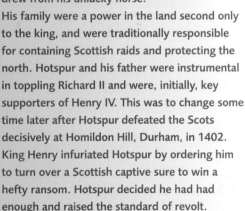

HOTSPUR

Henry Percy earned his nickname, Hotspur, at a young age because in his eagerness to get to battle his spurs became hot from the blood they drew from his unlucky horse.

His family were a power in the land second only to the king, and were traditionally responsible for containing Scottish raids and protecting the north. Hotspur and his father were instrumental in toppling Richard II and were, initially, key supporters of Henry IV. This was to change some time later after Hotspur defeated the Scots decisively at Homildon Hill, Durham, in 1402. King Henry infuriated Hotspur by ordering him to turn over a Scottish captive sure to win a hefty ransom. Hotspur decided he had had enough and raised the standard of revolt.

their occupants could do to stop the rampaging Welsh rebels. Glyndwr's ranks swelled with new recruits. Chroniclers tell us that even Welsh scholars from Oxford and Cambridge rushed home to join the revolt, as did landless labourers who had been working in England.

'The hour of freedom has struck'

Henry IV was quick to respond. He had been the finest warrior in England in his youth, and now he acted with great determination. His hold on the throne was precarious. He had to demonstrate that rebellions against him would not be tolerated, especially as Glyndwr was calling for a full-scale national uprising against English rule.

Henry marched an army into Wales, but could not find Glyndwr. The rebel leader had slipped off into the mountains of Snowdonia where he knew Henry's lumbering army would never find him. But wherever Henry marched in the rest of Wales he persuaded Welsh nobles to swear allegiance to him. They knew they could not defeat him in open battle.

Henry returned to England, no doubt congratulating himself on a job well done. Wales appeared pacified, Glyndwr was a fugitive in the mountains, and his own son, Henry, was installed as Prince of Wales. The king appointed yet another Henry, Henry Percy (known as 'Hotspur'), to crush what remained of the revolt. He seemed the right man for the job: he was England's foremost warrior.

In 1401 Glyndwr unleashed a new wave of violence, renewing his attacks on English garrison towns such as Harlech and Caernarfon. His cousins Rhys and Gwilym captured Conwy Castle while its garrison was attending church on Good Friday. To the king's great embarrassment, the Welsh held the castle for two months before agreeing to withdraw. Meanwhile, Glyndwr marched south and achieved the first major military success of his rebellion when he and 400 followers found themselves surrounded by 1,500 of Henry's troops at Hyddgen in Montgomeryshire. The Welsh fought their way out of the trap and slaughtered their enemy. Sources tell us that at least 200 Englishmen died.

Through the summer of 1401 Glyndwr conducted a lightning campaign around Wales. But support for the revolt was not universal. It depended largely on local magnates, who traditionally commanded the obedience of their tenants. Although there were individuals who joined the rebellion spontaneously, it was the nobles who held the key to recruiting in any real numbers. As his campaign wore on, Glyndwr threatened, bribed and cajoled noblemen who were still undecided, appealing to their patriotism. In a letter written to a fellow noble in 1401 he said that 'the hour of freedom has struck' and he was going to 'free the Welsh from English oppression'. Glyndwr's forces waved the dragon banner of King Arthur and the ancient Britons, staking their claim to be the last of the Britons fighting the Saxon and Norman invaders.

Glyndwr took Radnor Castle and ordered its entire garrison to be beheaded. He carried off vast booty from Welshpool, where his forces plundered the Prince of Wales's personal baggage train. Northwest Wales was rapidly coming under his

Henry IV's army on the march in Wales. With its lumbering supply wagons, it was exposed to hit-and-run attacks from Glyndwr's guerrilla forces.

sway. A furious assault on Caernarfon Castle was beaten off so narrowly that the king's council considered suing for peace. But Henry was not a man to negotiate with his enemies. Again he set out at the head of an army to bring Wales under control. Again Glyndwr melted into the countryside, refusing to let himself be drawn into a pitched battle with the king's superior forces.

Henry used every stratagem to crush the revolt. He seized the property of those who had joined Glyndwr, and had his sympathizers hunted down and killed. He took the children of prominent Welshmen hostage to ensure the loyalty of their parents. But still the rebellion grew.

Effigy of Sir Edmund Mortimer. For generations his family had the task of pacifying the Welsh borders.

The English chroniclers were impressed by the number of people who were willing to die for Glyndwr. Bad autumn weather in 1401 forced Henry to end that year's campaigning early. But he was growing increasingly impatient and demanded more action from Hotspur, his commander in Wales. Hotspur may have favoured compromising with the rebels but the king was surrounded by men, such as Lord Grey, who insisted that the revolt must be crushed at all costs.

The following year began with raids across North Wales. Using sturdy ponies and travelling along mountainous routes, Glyndwr could move his forces with considerable speed to achieve surprise. The beleaguered Hotspur had to organize a fleet to relieve the castles along the coast, which were being besieged by rebel forces. Glyndwr even captured his enemy Lord Grey in an ambush, and the king was forced to pay an exorbitant ransom for his supporter's safe return. This windfall was invaluable to Glyndwr, who desperately needed funds to pay his warriors and to buy weapons and stores.

But Glyndwr's greatest success came in June when, whether by accident or design, he came face to face with an English army. The confrontation was to be a breathtaking story of tactical trickery, treachery and – in the end – savagery.

Out of the mountains

Glyndwr surprised the English by bursting out of the mountains of Maelienydd – in today's Powys – into the lands of one of the most powerful Marcher Lords, Sir Edmund Mortimer. The Mortimer family had long been the scourge of the Welsh. The chronicler Thomas Walsingham tells us that when Mortimer's land was raided and ravaged he summoned 'almost all the militia of Herefordshire' and set out to crush Glyndwr.

Mortimer's army numbered up to 2,000 men. It was based on a core of knights and men at arms from his private retinue, full-time 'retained' soldiers wearing a surcoat of the Mortimer livery over their armour. Each of these men had a contract under

BATTLE FACT

Owning state-of-the-art plate armour in 1400 would have been as costly as owning a top sports car today. To make sure it fitted perfectly a life-size cast of the buyer was sent to an armourer.

which they agreed to supply Mortimer with more troops from their lands in time of war. These troops included soldiers with a wide range of weapons, such as billhooks or spears, but the great majority were archers. It is likely that three-quarters of Mortimer's force were longbowmen, all recruited from the estates of his retainers. Archers with the longbow had been used by the Plantagenet kings to win stunning victories over the Scots and French. Lethal at 300 metres, and capable of delivering 20 arrows a minute, the longbow was a devastating weapon. Many of Mortimer's longbowmen were Welsh because his lands spanned the border between England and Wales.

These troops were reinforced by local knights, men such as Sir Walter Devereux and Sir Robert Whitney, who brought their retinues with them. The infantry ranged from heavily armoured knights to foot soldiers carrying spears, bills, halberds, axes or clubs. Many would have worn chain mail over a leather jerkin. For the wealthier soldiers, 'plate' armour was now increasingly common: overlapping plates of iron made for better protection.

Although most of the forces on the Welsh side probably belonged to Glyndwr's lieutenant Rhys Gethin 'the Fierce', Glyndwr was almost certainly there too. His and Gethin's forces were not as numerous as those of Mortimer, nor as well equipped, but having no armour, they were faster and more agile. The Welsh were largely guerrilla fighters, who often sacrificed armour for speed and agility. Their real strength was their skill with the longbow, for which they were renowned.

The hill of Bryn Glas today, towering over the village of Pilleth. This is the view Mortimer's army would have had on its approach from the east. The valley where Glyndwr hid part of his force is on the right. The clump of Wellingtonia trees on the hill was planted a century ago to mark the bloodiest point of the battle.

Pilleth

To suit his troops and tactics Glyndwr chose to fight from the top of Bryn Glas hill, just west of the village of Pilleth. This gave the Welsh a commanding position looking down a steep slope, and to their left was a hidden valley where it seems Glyndwr concealed a sizeable part of his force. On 22 June 1402 Mortimer's army approached along the Lugg river valley. The armour of the commanders, knights and retainers would have been carried in slow-moving carts, with pieces of plate armour stored in hay-filled barrels. Also in the carts were ale and food casks and a huge number of sheaves of arrows for the archers, each one containing 24 shafts.

There are no detailed accounts of the Battle of Pilleth, but we can piece together what probably happened from the available evidence. Advancing up the valley, the English would have spotted the comparatively small number of men Glyndwr had placed prominently on top of the hill. It must have seemed to Mortimer that he had the Welsh outnumbered, so he ordered his men to attack up the slope.

Squires helped the knights into their armour. This was a laborious process, but it could take as little as ten minutes if it was well practised. The plate armour would have weighed 30–40 kilograms, so it was put on only at the last minute before battle. Less well-off men at arms had to make do with chain mail coats made up of thousands of interlocked iron rings.

When they were ready, the English troops formed themselves up into lines of infantry with V-shaped wedges of archers at intervals. This was a powerful defensive formation, and if the Welsh had charged wildly downhill, they would have been cut down by longbow volleys. Anyone lucky enough to escape the arrows and reach the English infantry would have been met by a tight-packed line of swords and spears. Glyndwr knew this, and waited on top of the hill hoping to tempt the English to climb up to him: for Mortimer's formation, impregnable in defence, would be unwieldy and vulnerable in attack.

Mortimer accepted the challenge. And as the English began the long, steep climb, Glyndwr's longbows must have launched a steady barrage. With a lifetime of practice behind them, the Welsh archers used their yew bows, taller than a man, to send their ash-wood shafts skimming down on the English. The bodkin-headed arrows, tipped with about 10 centimetres of narrow-shafted steel, could pierce chain mail as if it were linen. Thanks to the slope, Glyndwr's archers hit Mortimer's troops long before they were able to shoot back, and the attackers must have taken terrible punishment as they laboured up the 1 in 4 gradient. Even those with plate armour suffered: if an arrow hit at 90 degrees, it could punch straight through. There must have been a steady toll of casualties as arrows whistled through gaps between the shields and pierced exposed feet and limbs with such force that the victims were thrown backwards down the hill. Mortimer's tight-knit formation began to fragment as soldiers paused to catch breath or lost their footing. And still Glyndwr's men at the top of the hill refused to come down and fight. They kept up the shower of arrows on Mortimer's men, who were clamber-ing uphill, desperate to get to close quarters with their enemy. In spite of their terrible casualties, Mortimer's attacking force still thought they out-numbered the opponents that they could see ahead of them. But the battle was now to take an extraordinary turn.

Duel of the longbows

1. The Welsh, high on the hill (right), have a huge advantage over the English (left) in the longbow exchange.
2. With casualties mounting, the English struggle up the steep slope.

Plucking arrows from where they've stored them in the ground at their feet, longbowmen loose off their opening barrage.

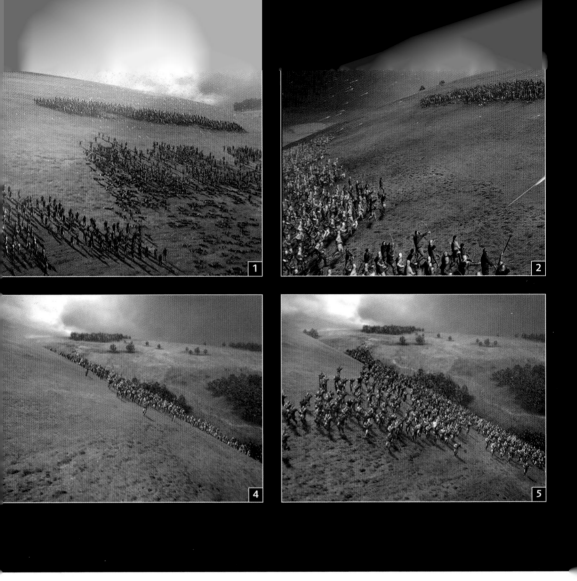

Ambush!

Suddenly the Welsh archers in Mortimer's army unleashed a volley at point-blank range into the mass of their own infantry. Nobody knows why they did it. It could have been prearranged. Or perhaps Mortimer's Welsh archers, realizing that things were looking bad, saw changing sides as their only chance of self-preservation. It may also have been the lure of Glyndwr's reputation: by now his achievements were an inspiration to people all over Wales, and his very presence on the battlefield may have been enough to make Mortimer's bowmen turn on their own army.

This act of treachery in Mortimer's ranks must have shattered his army, but Glyndwr still had a final blow to deliver. With a roar, his troops from the hidden valley streamed over the brow of the hill and fell upon the flank of Mortimer's bewildered survivors. At the same time the troops on top of Bryn Glas at last swept down the hill to join the slaughter. Ambushed, exhausted and betrayed, Mortimer's army was annihilated.

The leading English knights were killed and Mortimer himself captured. Medieval chroniclers suggest that 800 English corpses littered the field of battle. Welsh women apparently mutilated the

Treachery

1. Without warning, Mortimer's archers (left) turn their arrows on the rest of his army (centre).

2. The Welsh (top right) seize their chance and begin to charge down the hill.

3. Betrayed by their archers, Mortimer's army (left), in desperation, close with their enemy.

Ambush

4. Suddenly the rest of Glyndwr's army, which had been concealed in the valley to the right, appears over the brow of the hill.

5. As they charge, they present a new threat to the English from yet another direction.

6. They attack the right flank of Mortimer's battered force.

bodies, stuffing severed genitals into dead men's mouths. The comprehensive defeat of a superior force of well-armed English troops by Glyndwr's guerrillas was a huge embarrassment to Henry. His enemies gloated. Just days after the battle the news was all around Europe.

Glyndwr's understanding of the strengths and weaknesses of both his army and that of his enemy had won him a striking victory. He had adapted his successful guerrilla tactics to the ground at Pilleth and shown he was a match for a regular army, not just in a hit-and-run campaign, but in a pitched battle.

BATTLE FACT

Archery was so important in this period that Edward III, who reigned from 1327 to 1377, banned football to make time for it.

Conspiracy

Glyndwr was now a serious threat. His forces, which numbered many thousands, controlled North and Central Wales by keeping the small English garrisons bottled up in their castles. Franciscan monks raised money for him and supported his cause throughout Britain. That summer he attacked Southeast Wales, burning Cardiff, Abergavenny, Newport and Usk. Yet again he avoided Henry's massive army by careful use of the terrain. The elements were on his side, too: Henry's army spent only three weeks in Wales, in September, and during that time there were floods, snow and such strong winds that on one occasion the king was almost crushed when his tent collapsed on him.

Foiled militarily by Glyndwr, Henry tried to mobilize the law to strangle the revolt. In October Parliament enacted punitive legislation. Welshmen were barred from public office. No Welshman was to bear arms unless he was loyal to the king. No victuals or warlike equipment were to be imported into Wales unless for use in royal castles. Bards were banned from making a living out of singing to the common people: their epic accounts of Glyndwr's deeds were helping to transform him from a disgruntled rebel into a national icon.

These draconian laws alienated the Welsh even further. Glyndwr's power was growing by the month. If he was to force Henry to recognize him as Prince of Wales, he needed external help. Guerrilla campaigns alone do not win wars. He needed to capture castles, and that required considerable money and expertise. So he started to correspond with Irish, Scottish and even French leaders, encouraging them to support his revolt.

In November he gained one notable ally who was not a foreigner – none other than his defeated enemy and prisoner, Sir Edmund Mortimer. King Henry had arranged for his close friend Lord Grey to be ransomed at great expense, but was content to let Mortimer languish in Glyndwr's mountain stronghold. Mortimer suspected that the king was happy to have him out of the way because Mortimer's

family had a better claim to the throne than Henry's. Glyndwr saw his opportunity and promised to uphold Mortimer's claim to the throne if he, Mortimer, would support Glyndwr's fight for an autonomous Wales. At the end of November Mortimer married Glyndwr's daughter and sealed the alliance.

Henry had made a big mistake in failing to ransom Mortimer. Glyndwr had cunningly exploited a dynastic quarrel and won himself a useful English ally. He could now go further to exploit English opposition to Henry IV. Glyndwr's timing was perfect, for a massive rebellion was brewing in England. At the heart of it were Hotspur and his father, the Earl of Northumberland – the Percy family who up to now had been Henry's closest comrades in arms, but had grown disaffected. The king was not only critical of the way Hotspur was conducting the campaign in Wales, but was also failing to reimburse its costs. All Glyndwr needed to do was to tap into this bad feeling and form an alliance to topple Henry and establish his own rule in Wales. Now he had the perfect middleman, for Mortimer was Hotspur's brother-in-law.

And so, in early 1403, the leader of the Welsh rebellion allied himself with two powerful English families, the Mortimers and the Percys. If they could now act as one, they would be more than a match for Henry.

Prince Hal

On 10 July Hotspur raised his standard of rebellion in Chester. Cheshire men were stalwart fighters: strengthened by their support, Hotspur set off south to try to capture the king's son, Prince Henry, known as Hal, who he heard was in Shrewsbury with a small force. Historical details are sketchy, but it is probable that Hotspur also saw Shrewsbury as a base where he could meet up with Glyndwr and await his father, the Earl of Northumberland, who was marching south with another force. They could then confront King Henry with their three united armies.

King Henry V succeeded his father in 1413. As the young Prince Hal, he had fought tough battles against Glyndwr's rebels.

We will never know the precise rebel plans because Henry IV acted with speed and decisiveness. He was in Nottingham, and when he heard about the new rebellion he summoned the militias of 16 counties and, after an exhausting march, arrived at Shrewsbury the night before Hotspur. It was not just the safety of his son that Henry was worried about; it was also the strategic importance of Shrewsbury. He knew he had to get between Glyndwr and Hotspur and prevent them from joining up. Divided, he could defeat them; united, he knew they could win.

In spectacular fashion, Henry turned the tables on his enemies. Hotspur expected to find only Hal and his men in Shrewsbury; now he was faced by the king's and his son's forces combined. Glyndwr and Northumberland were still a week away. Hotspur could stand and fight – with the odds against him – or retreat. He had little choice: his rebel army was only a few days old and hardly committed to his cause, since he had used a mixture of threats and promises to get it to march to Shrewsbury. If he tried to retreat, pursued by royal forces, his army would disintegrate: it would be a pathetic end to his rebellion. There was nothing for it but to pick the most favourable ground and trust to the superior quality of his men to offset his enemies' numerical advantage. This was not so far-fetched. Hotspur was a veteran of many battles. With him was one of Scotland's best fighters, Earl Douglas, and many fine knights and their followers. The Cheshire men alone, according to a 14th-century chronicler, were 'better trained in arms and more difficult to control than any other people in the kingdom'.

The Battle of Shrewsbury

On the night of 20 July Hotspur identified a ridge north of Shrewsbury that would make a good defensive position. The ground was open in those days, covered with low, scrubby vegetation. While waiting for the royal army, Hotspur's men plaited wild pea plants into tangled barriers to impede the enemy advance.

Hotspur had 10,000 men. He placed his bowmen on either flank and his infantry in the centre. Except for a small reserve, everybody fought on foot. Horses were vulnerable to longbow arrows, and cavalry had for now disappeared from British battlefields. The two royal armies appeared from the direction of Shrewsbury. Prince Hal advanced from the southwest, keeping his forces slightly separate from his father's, who approached from the southeast. Together they numbered approximately 14,000 men. It was the biggest concentration of troops on a British battlefield since Hastings.

Henry was desperate to avoid bloodshed. His short reign was going badly enough without the cream of England's warrior class cutting each other to pieces. Envoys were sent into the no man's land between the two armies to seek a peaceful solution. The Bishop of Shrewsbury begged the rebels to lay down their arms and accept a royal pardon. One rebel knight deserted Hotspur with his followers and rode over to the king, who promptly knighted some of his companions.

But neither side would back down. It seems that the king and his advisers thought the rebels were stalling in the hope of reinforcements arriving. So, with only a few hours left until sunset, the king ordered the attack to begin. Hotspur called for his favourite sword, only to find that it had been left behind. In a superstitious age, this was not a good omen.

'Like a thick cloud'

Both sides sent forward their archers to soften up the enemy. On the king's signal the Earl of Stafford, who commanded the royal archers, ordered his men to let fly. Hotspur's archers did the same, and the first battle in history with massed longbowmen on both sides had begun. It would lead to bloodshed on a prodigious scale.

The archers drew back their great bowstrings to the ear, which meant they could not aim by eye. Instead they let years of experience direct them. Their muscles must have been strained to the utmost – each heave of the bow was equivalent to lifting a grown man. The arrows were described as coming 'so thick and fast that it seemed to the beholders like a thick cloud'. Only the full-time 'retained' archers would have had chain mail; the rest would have been defenceless against the hail of arrows. A chronicler described men dropping dead like 'apples falling in autumn when stirred by the west wind' as thousands of archers each shot over a dozen arrows a minute.

The exchange cannot have gone on long. The royalist archers walking uphill through matted pea plants took terrible punishment, wavered and then fled – straight back into the ranks of their own infantry who were following them. The archers, desperate to escape, caused havoc among the royal foot soldiers. Tangled up in the undergrowth, with arrows falling around them and their front ranks in disarray, the royalist army was soon in chaos. Hotspur decided to seize his chance. At his signal there would have been a clicking sound across the battlefield as hundreds of helmet visors were lowered. Then Hotspur led his entire force off the ridge and plunged headlong into Henry's army.

The press of battle

The critical phase of the battle had arrived. The royal shield wall had been disrupted by its own archers retreating through it. Now the troops struggled to regroup so that their shields touched rim to rim again. The men behind reached over the heads of the front rank to strike at the enemy with maces and swords. But under the impetus of Hotspur's charge, the ranks broke and savage hand-to-hand fighting ensued.

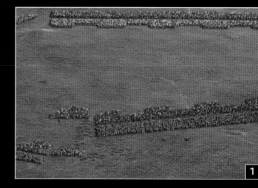

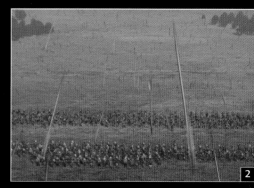

The battle lines at Shrewsbury

1. The armies of King Henry (bottom right) and Prince Hal (bottom left) take up position on low ground, looking up at the ridge on which Hotspur's rebels are deployed in two lines.

2. A bird's-eye view looking down the hill as the arrows shot by the rebels on the ridge rain down on the royal army below.

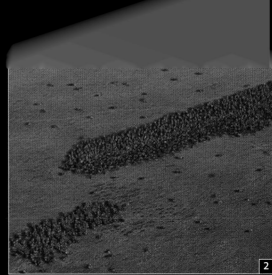

A medieval mêlée is hard to imagine. With men weighed down by plate armour and chain mail hacking, slashing and thrusting, the noise of metal hitting metal must have been deafening. There was an array of weapons on either side that defied categorization: in addition to swords, daggers, axes, war hammers, maces and spears, there were some that were no more than improvised farm tools. Others, such as the pole axe, were designed for use in abattoirs. Hammers, swords and maces crushed limbs and forced men to the ground, where lighter-armed troops such as archers could finish them off with long slender daggers, stabbing through chinks in their armour in the groin, eyes or armpits.

Telling friend from foe in this sea of violence must have been a daunting task. There were no uniforms, although some men could be identified by their lord's banner, a large flag bearing his coat of arms. The retained men of the lord wore his colours in a surcoat worn over their breast plates and would have stuck close to his banner. Their first duty was to watch their lord's back and protect him from the enemy.

When a man's visor was down his vision was impaired and he could not see his own feet without bending forward. Even so, armour was not as unwieldy as is often supposed: men could turn cartwheels in it or vault into saddles. It did have one great drawback, however: lack of ventilation. Body heat could not escape, and many would die from suffocation and heat exhaustion in the press of battle.

The nature of this gruesome fighting was far from the chivalric ideals of the age. There was no room for fancy sword play. The cross-guard on the hilt of the sword was used to poke people's eyes out, the pommel to smash into an opponent's head. Killing your enemy outright was time-consuming and unnecessary. It was enough to break a bone, cause temporary blindness or spike his foot. Once on the ground, a man was out of the battle.

The result of Hotspur's charge was devastating. His knights had smashed their way into the king's army, and his light troops were despatching the wounded, who littered the ground behind them. Hotspur now gathered his close companions and told them to target the king. His experience told him that the quickest way to end a battle was to

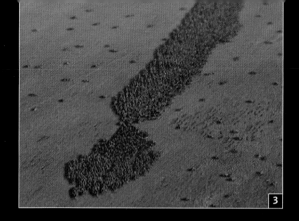

Prince Hal to the rescue

1. The forces of Hotspur and the king are locked in a ferocious hand-to-hand struggle (centre).

2. Prince Hal's smaller force (left) manoeuvres to outflank Hotspur.

3. Hal begins to attack the rebels' right flank and rear.

The bloody slaughter of a medieval mêlée.

destroy its leadership. His surest way of snatching victory was to kill Henry. With the fearsome Earl Douglas at his side, he 'made an alley in the midst of the army' and headed for the royal standard. Douglas felled many men and twice thought he had killed the king, only to find that Henry had employed knights to dress like him both to confuse his enemy and to show his own army that he could be everywhere at once. This cunning trick no doubt enraged Douglas when he cut down one of these 'doubles', only to find it was the unfortunate royal standard bearer Sir Walter Blount.

But with the royal centre being pushed steadily back, King Henry's position was precarious. The next move could decide the battle. Luckily for Henry, that move came from his son.

BATTLE EXPERIENCE
The longbow

The longbow is still used in a sporting context by archers in many parts of Britain. We spent a day with the Margam archers in South Wales, who demonstrated the skill required to shoot such a powerful bow. It has the longest range of any manually drawn bow, and its arrows can travel up to four times the effective range of a musket. But – unlike the musket – this was not a weapon you could learn to use in days, weeks or even years. It took half a lifetime. Henry VIII offered a prize for the best shot over 400 yards – just under 400 metres. But he was making the offer to longbowmen who had trained their muscles to pull these massive bows since they were young boys.

We managed – by the end of the day – to draw back the bowstring of an 18-kilogram bow and shoot an arrow over 100 metres. But the draw-weight of the longbows that were used at the battles of Pilleth and Shrewsbury was over 70 kilograms. We could hardly shift the bowstring on a 36-kilogram bow.

The most striking thing about these weapons is the rate of shooting they can sustain. The Margam archers could each shoot around 20 arrows a minute, which would mean that in a battle situation 2,000 archers shooting for two minutes could loose off a staggering 80,000 arrows.

Prince Hal's forces had been drawn up slightly south and west of his father's and now faced the exposed right flank of Hotspur's troops, who were flooding down the hill to attack Henry. Ironically, the more the royal centre buckled, the stronger Prince Hal's position on the left became. His forces were now in a position to wrap around Hotspur's flank and rear. Hal, already a battle-hardened veteran at 16, would, as Henry V, become perhaps the greatest warrior king in English history. Not a man to let slip an opportunity, he now led his men in a disciplined charge and crashed into the rebel army's flank.

'Wounded, bruised and bleeding men'

Hotspur's army was inflicting massive casualties on the king's forces, but they refused to break, and now the pressure on them was relieved by Hal's attack. In the end Hotspur was proved right: one of the armies did collapse when it lost its leader. But it was not the royal army, it was his own. The story goes that Hotspur lifted his visor to gulp some fresh air and was killed instantly by an arrow slamming into his mouth. Henry bellowed to the rebels that Hotspur was dead. Those rebels who were not trapped by Prince Hal's flanking movement fled; thousands more were cut down. Hotspur's men were pursued a great distance from the battlefield. 'In all directions,' a chronicler tells us, there was 'a chance medley of weary, wounded, bruised and bleeding men'.

All the chroniclers were struck by the brutality of the battle and the sheer numbers of dead. One, Adam of Usk, tells of the loss of the 'flower and the glory of chivalry of Christendom'. They all agree that no one had ever witnessed a battle with so many casualties. Prince Hal had been shot in the face by an arrow but surgeons saved his life. Many other nobles and soldiers lay dead and dying through the night. To local people and many of the survivors the carnage was a great opportunity. Looting the dead was endemic: indeed, it was one of the few perks of being a soldier.

When Hotspur's body was brought to Henry, he wept and ordered it buried. But then he had a change of heart: he wanted to prove the rebellion was over. So the corpse was exhumed and displayed in Shrewsbury. Henry then ordered it to be cut in quarters and sent in sacks to London, Bristol, Newcastle and Chester for display. Hotspur's head adorned the gates of York, a brutal warning to the rest of his powerful northern family.

Back to Wales

A dazzling opportunity for Glyndwr had been lost. His chances of taking the battle to Henry had disappeared with his failure to link up with Hotspur's army. Now Glyndwr was back on the defensive and Henry could turn his whole attention to Wales. By early September the king was back at the head of an army, putting down opposition, receiving local submissions and issuing pardons; Glyndwr melted away into the hills. Castles were relieved and resupplied, but again Henry found the Welsh countryside very inhospitable, particularly for his horses. Feeding such a large force was virtually impossible. After a few weeks Henry took his army home and, like a returning tide, Glyndwr's men flooded back, besieging castles and ravaging the land. At the end of 1403 there was stalemate. The king could not defeat Glyndwr's elusive forces, and they could not defeat the king.

The destruction of Hotspur's army meant that the Welsh needed to look elsewhere for military backing. A statesman as well as a soldier, Glyndwr knew that there was one country that wanted Henry defeated as much as he did: England's oldest enemy, France.

He found the French compliant, and through the winter of 1403–4 they supplied his forces and blockaded enemy castles, operating with impunity because Henry lacked the money to build a fleet. With the help of French ships, Glyndwr captured the sturdy castles of Harlech and Aberystwyth. Now he had the powerbase to hold parliaments, receive

Glyndwr summoned a Welsh parliament to this house in Machynlleth, emphasizing the true extent of his power by 1404.

foreign envoys and consolidate control of West Wales. He was the de facto Prince of Wales, ruling unchallenged all the land between Caernarfon and Ceredigion. The people of neighbouring Shropshire even had to make a treaty with the 'land of Wales' to stop Glyndwr's armies ravaging their lands.

But if Glyndwr was to consolidate his hold on Wales and establish his country's independence, he needed more help from abroad. In May 1404 he sent an envoy to the king of France, Charles VI, with a request for an army and supplies. He wrote that 'my nation has been trodden underfoot by the fury of the barbarous Saxons'; with French help he could defeat them for good. The king sent him a ceremonial sword and promised troops would follow. A small force did leave France in July, but never arrived in Wales. Glyndwr had to wait another year for the opportunity to force Henry to bow to his power.

Wales invades England

The year 1405 offered Glyndwr his greatest opportunity. In August 3,000 French troops landed at Milford Haven. He met them with probably his biggest ever concentration of troops, 10,000 men, and together they marched east towards the border to take on the English king.

The French had not had an easy voyage and most of their warhorses had perished. About 800 of the soldiers were heavily armed knights who had paid a considerable sum to equip themselves for the expedition and would be invaluable to Glyndwr. There were 600 crossbowmen and the rest were lightly armed troops, probably the escorts of the knights. The crossbow was actually more accurate and powerful than the longbow, but its loading time was far longer. Crossbowmen spent so much time reloading that they were very vulnerable and needed a companion with a shield to protect them.

Glyndwr's Franco–Welsh army burnt English towns in South Wales and captured the castle of Carmarthen; he gave its garrison special passes to guarantee them safe passage out of Wales. Glyndwr then crossed the border into England, confident that this was the most powerful military force he had ever led. Welsh hopes were raised high. Henry, who was at Leicester, realized this was not a mere raid and set off for Worcester. For the first time in the rebellion it looked as if a major pitched battle between the two was inevitable.

Worcester

From the little we know it seems that the Franco–Welsh army camped on Woodbury Hill, 12 kilometres northwest of the city of Worcester. A formidable vantage point, used by Iron Age tribes for a hill fort and subsequently by the Romans, it was known locally for generations as 'Glyndwr's Camp'. The king led out of Worcester an army approximately the same size as his opponent's and probably camped on the slopes of Abberley Hill, a couple of kilometres away from Woodbury Hill across a wide valley.

What followed was a stand-off. Both armies had perfect defensive positions and were reluctant to attack because to do so would put the attacking force at a serious disadvantage. A stalemate suited Henry. He knew that Glyndwr's army was deep in enemy territory, where food and supplies would be as difficult for them to find as they had been for Henry during his futile expeditions through Wales. In addition, there was no sign of the popular uprising Glyndwr had been hoping for. For once time was on Henry's side. Why risk all in a costly battle when he was confident that the enemy army would starve and have to crawl back to Wales?

On the Franco–Welsh side there must have been arguments and divisions. Perhaps Mortimer, remembering the massacre of his army at Pilleth on slopes not much steeper then these, dissuaded the Welsh leader from risking battle. Glyndwr would

Glyndwr's coat of arms on part of a horse's harness.

The battlefield that never was. The view west from Abberley Hill, where King Henry's camp was in the summer of 1405, towards Glyndwyr's position on Woodbury Hill.

also have been aware that, although the French knights were well armed, the majority of his army consisted of light guerrilla troops. They would prove no match in open battle for the English army, unless the English could be persuaded to attack up the steep hill.

The French for their part had come to Britain looking for glory and riches. It is easy to imagine their impatience as, according to the chronicler de Monstrelet, the armies 'drew up and each evening

they went back to camp'. They were not alone in their frustration. On the other side, hot-headed English nobles became furious as the days dragged on and no battle took place. In order to satisfy their thirst for glory Henry is said to have allowed jousting tournaments in the valley between the two armies. Henry was no stranger to tournaments. When he was a young earl his chivalric prowess had been renowned throughout Europe. Now young French and English nobles vied for honour while the rest of their armies stared sullenly at each other across the valley.

The jousting was probably conducted with real weapons, and there must have been casualties. There was other skirmishing, too. Scouts clashed, and Welsh troops scouring the area for food were ambushed by detachments from Henry's army. A chronicler tells us that overall 'upwards of two hundred of either side were slain and more wounded'. Meanwhile, Henry's plan to starve the enemy army was working. 'The French and Welsh', we are told, 'were also much oppressed by famine and other inconveniences for only with great difficulty could they obtain any provision as the English had strongly guarded all the passes.'

After a week it was clear that Glyndwr had over-extended himself, and his only option was an orderly but depressing withdrawal. His forces made their way back towards South Wales with the English army snapping at their heels until they were across the border. King Henry IV had achieved an important victory at almost no cost. The confrontation on Woodbury Hill was as decisive as any battle. Never again would Glyndwr be in a position to impose terms on his enemies. The French, who had promised so much, saw that there was little popular support for Glyndwr's cause in England and went home, never to return.

The final years

Glyndwr scored notable successes in the next two years but he was increasingly on the defensive. Prince Hal, now recovered from the wound he

received at Shrewsbury, was appointed commander of the royal forces in Wales and took a firm grip on the English reconquest. Bit by bit Glyndwr was pushed out of Anglesey, South and East Wales. By 1407 he controlled only the mountainous north. In an age of shifting loyalties, many of his supporters accepted offers of pardon from Prince Hal. The castle of Aberystwyth fell to the English in 1408, and Harlech the following year after a long and expensive siege. These operations were among the first examples in Britain of the sustained use of cannon.

The loss of Harlech was the most powerful

Henry preferred to bide his time at his camp at Abberley Hill, waiting for his enemy opposite to run out of supplies.

expression of Glyndwr's waning power. Along with the castle, he lost his wife, daughters and granddaughters, who were taken to the Tower of London. Distinguished allies, such as Mortimer, were killed or captured. Glyndwr had lost the base that gave his rule legitimacy. He could no longer claim to be the Prince of Wales. He was now once more a guerrilla leader, living in the mountains with a dwindling number of supporters.

Each year the number of raids and ambushes decreased, and by 1413 Glyndwr had disappeared from view, still refusing to accept the personal pardons offered by the new king, Henry V, the former Prince Hal. Some said that he never died, but, like King Arthur, was simply waiting until Wales needed him again. Others claimed that he found peace in the Golden Valley in Herefordshire, living with his daughter and dying in his bed in 1415. For many of the men who fought for Glyndwr a future beckoned in the ranks of their former enemy. Led by Henry V, an army containing many of Glyndwr's veterans crossed to France in 1415 and won the greatest victory of the Hundred Years' War: the Battle of Agincourt.

Monnington Court in Herefordshire. This house is on the site of the residence of Glyndwr's daughter, who may have sheltered him in his last years.

A seal showing Glyndwr enthroned as Prince of Wales.

Contrasting commanders

Glyndwr showed great courage and determination throughout the rebellion. With the startling exception of Pilleth, his forces were often beaten in open battles, so he avoided them when possible, and relied on surprise, sudden ambushes and over-whelming numbers. He used the terrain and climate of Wales to exploit his advantages over heavily armed columns of English troops. He attacked English supply routes and targeted convoys carrying pay to the soldiers in order to paralyse the armies marching against him. Through raids and ransoms he got the money he so badly needed to keep his armies together. Glyndwr was an inspired military commander. But ultimately it was the king and his son who won the Battle for Wales.

The Shrewsbury and Worcester campaigns showed Henry to be a decisive commander with a good strategic grasp and a willingness to avoid battle if diplomacy and the threat of force would achieve the same goals. Therefore it is all the more bizarre that he showed none of these qualities in most of his attempts to put down the revolt. His four campaigns in Wales were inadequately prepared and lacked overall strategy and momentum. His was a world of castles, armies and pitched battles – not mountainous passes, guerrillas and ambushes. His inability to defeat Glyndwr was matched by his unwillingness to negotiate or reach a compromise. Only the advent of Henry's son Hal as commander in Wales saw the development of a strategy for defeating Glyndwr and the first successes of English forces in Wales.

The collapse of Glyndwr's rebellion ended all hope of creating an autonomous, native Wales. Wales was now indissolubly annexed to the kingdom of England. No one else has ever attempted to seize back Welsh independence by force. The Welsh people would henceforth have to find other ways to express their strongly held sense of national identity.

King Henry IV. In later life, the once striking young warrior turned into a fat old man with a leprous disease.

1588: THE SPANISH ARMADA

It must have been an unforgettable sight. At 3 p.m. on 29 July 1588, a little way off Lizard Point in Cornwall, one of the greatest invasion fleets in history stretched from one horizon to another. As it came within sight of land the lead ship slowed, neatly spilling the wind out of her sails. In a conspicuous display of seamanship, the rest of the fleet followed her example: 120 ships, each with the red cross of religious crusade on their sails, slowed to a standstill and the 29,000 men on board had their first glimpse of the Cornish coast.

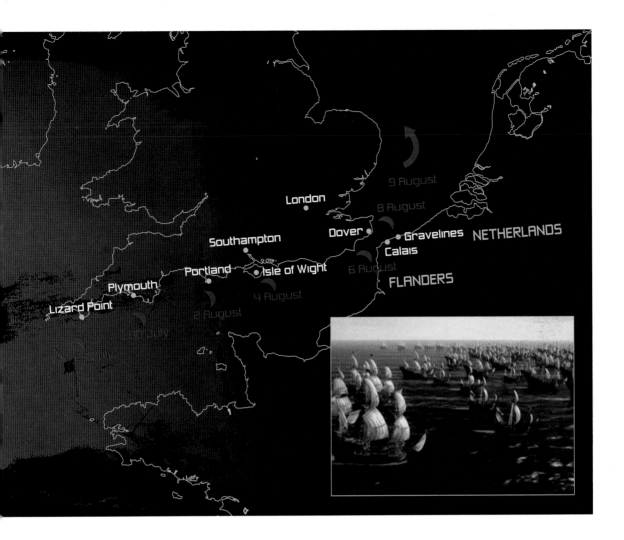

Then the leader, a massive galleon of 1,000 tonnes, more like a castle than a ship, hoisted a mighty banner that stretched from topmast to waterline. On it was an image of the crucifixion, with the Virgin Mary and Mary Magdalene kneeling before the cross. It was a banner blessed by the pope himself. The Spanish king, ruler of half the world, had come to settle a score with England and its defiant queen.

Europe divided

In 1588 Europe was divided on religious lines as never before. Several states had rejected the Catholic Church and embraced Protestantism. But the pope had a champion, the most powerful man on earth, a Catholic sovereign who believed he had been chosen by God to restore unity to the Christian world. He was Philip II, king of Spain.

Philip ruled over a massive empire comprising Spain, the Low Countries, southern Italy, Sicily, Portugal, Mexico, Brazil, Peru and the Caribbean islands. His first cousin was emperor of Germany and Austria. Fervently anti-Protestant, Philip let it be known that if his son grew up a 'heretic', he would gladly carry the wood to burn the young man at the stake. He had smashed Turkish naval power as it advanced on Christendom from the east. Now he was bent on crushing those in Europe whom he saw as worse than the infidel Turks, those who had been

Philip II, king of Spain from 1556 to 1598. The rosary reminds us that Catholicism was his driving force.

Rogue state

Philip had once thought England and its queen would be easy prey. As a young man, he had been married to Elizabeth's Catholic half-sister, Mary. On Mary's death in 1558, he confidently proposed to her successor, his young Protestant sister-in-law. He was surprised when Elizabeth rejected him, and enraged when she adopted policies clearly designed to damage him, his empire and his religion.

Elizabeth was ruling over a country of increasing prosperity and ambition. In the midst of a Europe torn by civil war and religious hatred, England remained at peace. Business was good and Protestantism, the religion of trade and commerce, was popular. Instead of imposing taxes to pay for wars, Elizabeth left the money in her subjects' pockets – her entire annual revenue was no more than Philip received from just one of his Italian cities.

Elizabeth's England was looking beyond the horizon of Europe to where the wealth of the New World beckoned. But this was part of Philip's empire, reserved for Spanish merchants, so the buccaneering spirit of English sea captains brought England into direct confrontation with Spain. In 1563 John Hawkins, an English seafarer, sailed across the Atlantic with Elizabeth's backing. He took his young cousin Francis Drake, son of a farmer and Protestant lay preacher. The small fleet was guaranteed safe conduct by the Spanish, but was then attacked and destroyed in San Juan de Ulua, Mexico. English seamen were burnt as heretics. Drake's ship escaped and limped back to Plymouth. He never forgot this Spanish treachery, and from then on waged a personal war of revenge.

Elizabeth's sea captains now terrorized the Caribbean, carrying off the wealth of the New World. It was only a matter of time before these activities brought England to the brink of war with Spain. But the spark that was to ignite it came from the Netherlands. And it was Elizabeth who moved first.

shown the true faith and had consciously rejected it: the Protestants.

One hotbed of Protestantism was his own territory in the Netherlands, now in full-scale revolt against Spanish rule. Philip had sent an army there 20 years earlier and it was still fighting to put down the rebellion. He neutralized France by bankrolling the powerful Catholics who controlled the French government. The only other gap in the imperial jigsaw was the troublesome nation off the northwest corner of Europe – England, with its heretical views and its scheming queen.

BATTLE FACT

Philip had a religious obsession with saintly relics. By the end of his reign there were 7,422 in the Escorial Palace in Madrid.

Alexander Farnese, the Duke of Parma. The nephew of Philip II, he was one of the foremost military commanders of his age.

War

The immediate cause of nearly every major war in the last 500 years of British history has been the fear of a strong hostile power controlling the Low Countries. The presence of a threatening enemy in Flanders and the Dutch provinces made Britain feel vulnerable to invasion. In 1585 Philip of Spain's talented nephew the Duke of Parma was poised to crush the Protestant rebellion and recapture the whole of the Netherlands. His 25,000 veteran troops would then be ideally placed to hop across the Channel and topple Elizabeth and her Protestant pirates. Elizabeth saw the danger, and in September 1585 sent 6,000 men to the Netherlands to aid the rebels.

Philip was furious. Freebooting attacks by England's seamen were mere pinpricks; supporting open rebellion in one of his empire's wealthiest provinces was a stab at his jugular. Elizabeth would have to go. And Philip conceived an ambitious plan to conquer England and its queen. He would send an invasion fleet – an armada.

The Spanish fleet that approached the Lizard that July afternoon in 1588 represented a compromise between two invasion plans. One was to send a massive expeditionary force from Spain and land it on the south coast: a very expensive undertaking. The other was to send Parma's army, the best troops in Europe, from the Low Countries. But the English navy was strong enough to stop any sudden dash across the Channel, and in any case Parma did not have enough ships to carry his men. So Philip decided to combine the two plans. A fleet would sail from Spain to accompany Parma's army across the Channel. English resistance would be brushed aside and London occupied.

In Spain it was a genuinely popular cause: the Protestants were widely hated, and the depredations of the English pirates had to be stopped. The ports of Naples, Genoa, Lisbon, Cadiz and Barcelona bustled with activity. Foreign ships were chartered or impounded.

DRAKE

The son of a fervent Protestant farmer from Devon, Francis Drake received only rudimentary education but was an expert sailor. He rose quickly to become a renowned privateer, the terror of Spanish possessions in the New World. Between 1577 and 1580 he completed the first English circumnavigation of the globe, acquiring enormous wealth and claiming California for Queen Elizabeth. At the age of 48 he accepted the position of vice-admiral for the Armada campaign – the only time in his career that he was not in overall charge.

Sir Francis Drake sailed around the globe in the *Golden Hinde*.

Supplies came in from every corner of Europe. Some unscrupulous English armourers even exported cannon to Spain.

'Prepare in England strongly'

Elizabeth's strategy was threefold. She would look to the Royal Navy for defence, and she would raise an army to defend the coast. But she would also go on the attack.

At four o'clock on the afternoon of 29 April 1587 an English fleet appeared off Cadiz in southern Spain. The rumour immediately flew around that this was the fearsome admiral known as 'El Draque', and panic ensued. A hundred ships lay in the port in various states of readiness for the invasion. As the English squadron boldly glided into the harbour, some ships cut their lines and tried to escape. Many collided or ran aground in the chaos. Terrified civilians stampeded through the town, desperate to find refuge; 25 women and children were crushed to death. Drake made quick work of the weak galleys that tried to defend the harbour, while other vessels in his squadron burnt or captured every ship in the port.

From Cadiz he laid waste the coast and, most damaging of all, destroyed a convoy carrying seasoned wooden staves. The Armada would now have a serious shortage of watertight barrels for storing biscuit, meat, water and gunpowder. Drake had succeeded in delaying the invasion by a year and severely weakening the fleet that eventually sailed. Even so, he wrote to the queen's adviser, 'I dare not almost write of the great forces we hear the king of Spain hath. Prepare in England strongly and most by sea.'

MEDINA SIDONIA

Although he was the richest and most powerful feudal lord in Spain and the best administrator in the kingdom, Medina Sidonia had never fought at sea. He did not want to serve. He wrote to the king's secretary: 'I am sea sick and always catch cold. I have had no experience of the sea or of war ... I feel I should give but a bad account of myself, commanding thus blindly and being obliged to rely on the advice of others without knowing good from bad.' Even his mother did not think he was up to the job.

Alonso Perez de Guzman, Duke of Medina Sidonia.

Medina Sidonia

Even without Drake's raids, assembling the Armada was an administrative nightmare. By the autumn of 1587 the cost was running at £200,000 a month, and not even the wealthy Spanish crown could sustain such spending. Preparations were in chaos: crews were not ready, clothing had not been issued, some ships had too many guns and others had no guns at all. To make matters worse, on 9 February 1588 Santa Cruz, Spain's greatest admiral, died, followed days later by his vice-admiral.

Undeterred from his divine duty, Philip found another man to command the Armada. His name was Don Alonso Perez de Guzman, Duke of Medina Sidonia. He had begged not to be appointed, but the king would not take no for an answer. Medina Sidonia was sent to Lisbon, where the Armada was assembling, and for four months he worked tirelessly, settling jealousies amongst his proud subordinates, stockpiling food and weapons, and assembling more ships.

At last everything was ready. The admiral went to the cathedral in Lisbon and took the expedition's sacred banner from the altar. Every man made his confession. The ships were checked for hidden women. The brothel ship that usually accompanied military expeditions was left behind as inappropriate for a crusade. Blasphemy, gambling, feuding and swearing were forbidden. At daybreak and dusk the ships' boys were ordered to sing 'Ave Maria' and 'Salve'. On 28 May this so-called Holy Enterprise glided out of Lisbon, each ship with the red cross of crusade on its sails. Medina Sidonia had triumphed, and perhaps, as he lay seasick in his bunk on that first night in the Atlantic, he could take comfort from the knowledge that without him the Armada would never have left harbour. With that achievement under his belt, his invasion of England should be a walkover.

England expects

In the spring of 1588 England's navy was in reasonably good shape. Elizabeth had wisely not let her

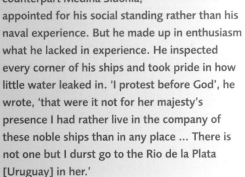

HOWARD

Charles Howard, 2nd Baron Effingham, was 52 years old in 1588. A cousin of Queen Elizabeth, he was, like his counterpart Medina Sidonia, appointed for his social standing rather than his naval experience. But he made up in enthusiasm what he lacked in experience. He inspected every corner of his ships and took pride in how little water leaked in. 'I protest before God', he wrote, 'that were it not for her majesty's presence I had rather live in the company of these noble ships than in any place ... There is not one but I durst go to the Rio de la Plata [Uruguay] in her.'

Lord Howard, the commander of the English fleet at the time of the Armada, depicted here in later life.

impatient captains, such as Drake and Hawkins, take her precious ships into the Atlantic winter gales to attack the Spanish. The vessels were in good repair, with scraped and tallowed hulls. Short of cash, the queen spent less in the whole of 1587 than Philip spent on the Armada in a month. Powder, shot and victuals had been carefully stockpiled.

The fleet was to be commanded by the 52-year-old Lord Howard, a staunch Protestant. Like his opponent, Medina Sidonia, he had the breeding to ensure the respect and obedience of other officers – he was a cousin of the queen. Howard was no great seaman but he was ably assisted. His vice-admiral was Drake, who, for the only time in his career accepted the role of second-in-command.

Alongside him were other men who are now maritime legends: John Hawkins, whose ship designs had revolutionized fighting at sea, and Martin Frobisher, pirate and slave trader, whose 1,100-tonne *Triumph* was the largest ship in the English fleet. Howard and his commanders knew that the Armada had left Lisbon and was making its way slowly up the coast of Portugal, beating into contrary winds. The English fleet was mobilized. Howard and Drake went to Plymouth with the majority of the ships, leaving Lord Henry Seymour in the narrowest, eastern part of the Channel to keep an eye on the Duke of Parma lurking in Flanders.

Howard heard that the Spanish had been scattered in the Bay of Biscay by gales and had returned to Corunna to regroup. The English fleet sailed off to try to attack the Spanish before they could recover, but bad weather forced them to return to Plymouth. On 21 July the English dropped their anchors back home in Devon, and on the same day the Armada left Corunna. On the 29th they sighted the Lizard. An English scout ship caught sight of them and dashed back to tell Drake and Howard. The phoney war had ended. England now had to fight for her survival against the world's greatest superpower.

'Time to finish the game'

The story has it that the messenger with the news of the Armada's arrival found Drake and Howard playing bowls on Plymouth Hoe. Drake had his response ready before Howard could even open his mouth: 'We have enough time to finish the game and beat the Spanish too.' Drake's quick tongue and cool head have become legendary, but they disguised what was a desperate situation for the English fleet. The Armada had achieved tactical surprise. The English ships were riding at anchor in harbour and therefore extremely vulnerable to the kind of attack Drake had made at Cadiz the year before. Many ships were still taking on supplies.

The tide and wind were against them, so they were bottled up in Plymouth for the next few hours. Drake was right: there was no point interrupting the game of bowls because there was nothing they could do.

While the English fleet was trapped in Plymouth, the Armada was just 12 hours' sailing away. Medina Sidonia called a council of war. Two of his most experienced commanders, Juan Martinez de Recalde, Spain's greatest sailor, and the young warrior aristocrat Don Alonso de Leiva, urged the admiral to sail the Armada into Plymouth and catch the English in harbour. But Philip had given Medina Sidonia strict orders to ignore the English fleet and concentrate on the rendezvous with Parma. So when the council broke up the Armada's captains took in sail in order to slow down for the night.

The English spent the dark hours desperately clawing their way out of Plymouth. Rowing boats had to tow the great galleons out into the open waters of the Channel. By the morning of 30 July the English fleet, only around 55 strong at this point, was out at sea. The Armada, more than twice the size, had missed a golden opportunity to crush the enemy in harbour. As the sun came up, the Spanish resumed their stately procession up the Channel. The English were nowhere in sight.

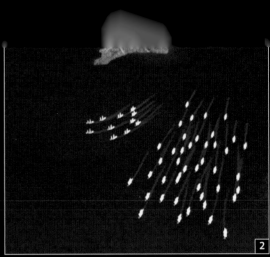

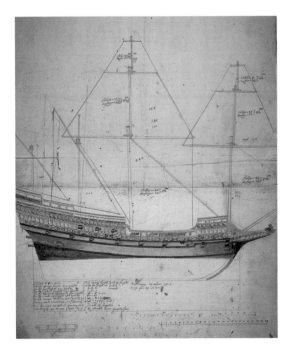
An English Elizabethan galleon. Designed for speed and manoeuvrability, it was greatly superior to its Spanish rivals.

The weather gauge

Drake and Howard now took a bold decision to place themselves between the Armada and the wind. They were out to grab what seamen call the 'weather gauge'. With the westerly wind behind them, blowing them on to their enemy, they would be able to control the timing, nature and range of the battle. Drake took his small squadron along the shore, struggling into the wind, tacking frequently. Howard took his ships out to sea, aiming to pass south of the Spanish fleet and then come round behind it. It was a difficult and daring manoeuvre, but it was an unqualified success.

At dawn the following morning, the 31st, the Spanish were shocked to catch their first sight of the English fleet not in front of them, as expected, but behind them to the west. The English were bearing down on their rear, favoured by the westerly wind. Experienced sailors, such as old Recalde, knew that the deft English manoeuvre proclaimed the arrival of a new generation of warships. The English galleons were longer in relation to their breadth than the Spanish ships. They had deeper keels. They lay low and snug in the water with much smaller fore and stern

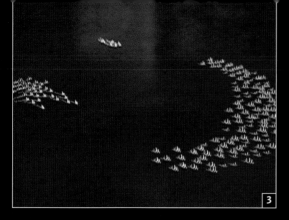

1. 30 July. As the Armada glides eastwards, the English fleet (top) sails out of Plymouth .

2. Determined to claw their way to windward of the Armada, Drake (left) tacks off west, while Howard and the main body of the English fleet head south.

3. Dawn, 31 July. The British gain the weather gauge. Drake (top) and Howard (left) now have the wind blowing them towards the Armada, which now forms into a crescent.

Howard's squadron approaches the Armada from behind.

> **BATTLE FACT**
>
> The Armada had 5 million kilograms in weight of ship's biscuit, over 180,000 litres of olive oil, 14,000 barrels of wine, 2,431 guns and 123,790 cannon balls of all weights.

superstructures. They were better at sailing into the wind, and more agile than any warship built before.

'The sea seemed to groan'

But if the Spanish were awed by the speed and nimbleness of their enemy, the English too saw a sight that day which they would never forget. The Armada impressively manoeuvred itself into its chosen battle formation: a giant crescent with the most powerful ships guarding the 'horns' on either side. One English observer was astonished not just by the discipline of the Armada but by its sheer scale: 'Beneath the weight of it the sea seemed to groan.'

Its size and weight were colossal by the standards of the day. There were over 120 ships with 29,000 men on board. In total, the vessels displaced 58,000 tonnes – a weight that made it the largest fleet that had ever sailed. Everything an invading army would need – a siege train, tents, ammunition, ready-made defensive barricades – was carried in store ships. These vessels nestled in the centre of the crescent, protected on either wing by giant galleons with raised 'castles' on the bows and sterns. These towering superstructures were designed to strike fear into the enemy, and they bristled with soldiers, muskets loaded, swords sharpened ready to storm the decks of any ship foolish enough to come alongside. The Spanish were relying on the age-old tactic of grappling an opponent's ship and pouring armed men over the side to seize it.

For an unreal moment both sides watched each other with numb uncertainty. They were on the threshold of a new era of warfare. No two fleets armed with such lethal firepower had ever fought before. Howard took the initiative first. He sent an 80-tonne barque, the *Disdain*, to perform an act of etiquette. A medieval gesture was to start the first modern naval battle. The *Disdain* sailed to within hailing distance of the Spanish fleet. Then it fired a cannon into its midst. England was now at war with Spain. Hostilities could commence.

The Battle of Plymouth

The English were quick to make the next move. Drake and Howard led their squadrons into battle. Howard's flagship, the *Ark Royal*, and Drake's *Revenge* surged respectively towards the southern, seaward tip and the northern, inshore tip of the crescent. These exposed 'horns' of the Armada's

formation were protected by the strongest, best-gunned galleons. They were troubleshooters, which could be deployed to meet a threat, allowing the rest of the fleet to keep in neat formation.

The English ploy was to keep their distance and rely on the agility of their ships and the firepower of their cannon. These revolutionary tactics were born of necessity. The fact was that the Armada could not be defeated in the traditional way. Its ships carried nearly 20,000 soldiers among its crews, ten times as many as its opponents, and the English knew they would be overwhelmed if the Spanish could grapple their ships and board them.

Howard's attack was the first of its kind in history. Previous naval encounters had been head-on collisions, where both sides made for each other, fired their guns once and then tried to board the enemy and settle the issue by hand-to-hand fighting. Now the English sailed in file one behind the other, firing one broadside and then swinging round to fire the other broadside before sailing off to reload, letting other ships take their place. The result was that the Spanish ships found themselves under constant bombardment.

The *Ark Royal*, Howard's flagship: the first of a long line of warships with the most distinguished name in the Royal Navy.

Left: The Battle off Plymouth. Recalde's *San Juan* (centre right) with ungainly 'castles' on its bow and stern takes punishment from the more agile English ships.

Below: English sailors in action. The great numbers of soldiers aboard Spanish ships knew nothing of seamanship, unlike all English crewmen, who were trained to fight and to work the ship.

Recalde, the veteran seaman who had predicted glumly that the English would employ these tactics, now tried to tempt the enemy closer. Trying to force a ship-to-ship mêlée, he allowed his vessel and one other to fall behind, offering a tempting prize that he hoped English greed would find irresistible.

Infuriatingly for the old Spanish commander, the two arch buccaneers Drake and Frobisher did not take the bait. They kept their ships 400 metres off, blasting away at Recalde's ships and damaging the foremast and rigging of his *San Juan*, and did not allow him close enough to grapple and send his 600 troops over the side. Eventually Medina Sidonia, with his powerful squadron, tacked back to help Recalde. Drake saw the threat, pulled back and allowed the damaged *San Juan* to rejoin the rest of the fleet.

Stand-off

For the next few hours the English foiled every attempt by Medina Sidonia to close with them. The official Spanish log states, 'The Duke collected the fleet but found he could do nothing more. For they [the English] still kept the weather gauge and their

ships are so fast and nimble they can do anything they like with them.' But while the speedier English ships may have been able to jab annoyingly at the Spanish fleet, they were not able to sink, capture or disable any of it: it was difficult to inflict major damage on wooden vessels with long-range cannon fire. Howard called off the attack. He had tested the Armada's strength, but needed reinforcements before renewing the action. Meanwhile, the Armada,

Portland Bill. The tidal rip off this prominent headland in Dorset is as notorious as any in the world.

only slightly bruised by the English, proceeded east towards its rendezvous with Parma.

The most serious damage to the Armada that day was self-inflicted. With the ships only 50 metres apart, it was perhaps unsurprising that the massive flagship of the Andalucian squadron, the *Rosario*, collided with two other ships and lost its bowsprit and, soon afterwards, its foremast. Medina Sidonia tried to take her in tow; in the end, however, he was persuaded not to risk the whole enterprise, but to leave her to fend for herself. At the same time an explosion tore apart the *San Salvador*.

What caused it is unknown, but myths abound: one suggests a cuckolded gunnery officer plunged a lighted match into a barrel of gunpowder. The 950-tonne ship was a floating wreck and half of its 400-man crew were killed. After a day of towing, it too was abandoned.

The English watched with trepidation as the Armada sailed on. Its formation seemed to be impregnable, and the only thing Howard could do was keep as close as possible. Drake was asked to lead the pursuit, with a lantern hanging from his stern to guide the rest of the English fleet through the dark.

But that night Drake did something that would be unthinkable today: he acted like the true pirate he was and ignored his orders. Dousing his lantern, he slipped back to raid the wounded *Rosario*. No sooner did her Spanish commander hear that 'El Draque' was alongside than he surrendered his sword without a fight and handed Drake his ship and the 55,000 gold ducats aboard. Mysteriously, only half of this money found its way into the queen's treasury. During the 16th century war and enrichment went hand in hand.

Many of the ships in the English fleet were owned by private businesses motivated by financial gain as much as by patriotic fervour.

Drake's outrageous action meant that the English fleet scattered in the dark and had to spend much of 1 August frantically regrouping as a light breeze pushed the Spanish fleet across Lyme Bay. It was taking them ever nearer to that Spanish army in the Netherlands.

The Battle of Portland Bill

At 5 a.m. on 2 August the Armada was just east of Portland Bill when a light breeze blew up from the northeast. Suddenly the Spanish had the advantage: with the wind behind them, they had the English at their mercy. Recalde was still repairing his damaged ship, so de Leiva commanded the powerful rearguard. They bore down on Howard and engaged in the fiercest naval gun battle the world had yet seen. But even this did not produce a result. Time and again the unwieldy Spanish ships tried to get to grips with their enemy, but each time the swifter and more agile English managed to escape.

Martin Frobisher was under the most pressure. He found himself trapped east of Portland Bill and attacked by the giant Spanish galleasses, oar-powered galleons with sails and heavy guns. He replied by firing shot after shot into the ranks of the slaves manning the oars. This caused panic, especially as the galleasses also got caught in the Portland Bill tidal race. They left Frobisher alone and turned on Howard, attempting to board the English flagship. But Howard kept his distance, firing three shots for every one from Spanish cannons.

As the day went on the battle petered out, mainly because the English began to run very low on powder and shot. Many Spanish ships, however, had been severely damaged. Medina Sidonia's own flagship, *San Martin*, had been hit by 500 rounds. The Spanish were learning bitter lessons: the English were not just outsailing them, their gunners were better trained too.

BATTLE FACT

The best rations were reserved for the slaves who manned the oars of the galleasses – not from any sense of humanity, but because they needed to be strong for rowing.

The Isle of Wight

The next day, 3 August, the wind hardly blew as the two fleets approached the Isle of Wight. Medina Sidonia seems to have decided that, until he heard that the Duke of Parma and the land forces in Flanders were ready, he would find somewhere his fleet could wait. Between the Isle of Wight and the Strait of Dover there were no natural harbours capable of sheltering a force like the Armada. The only place to stop and anchor was in the calm water of the Solent. The problem was compounded by the fact that Parma himself did not control a port deep enough to accommodate the Armada. It could not just arrive and wait for the troops to embark: the timing of the rendezvous had to be perfect, and with no word from Flanders, Medina Sidonia was not even sure that Parma knew he had left Spain.

Drake nearly found himself another prize that morning. He caught up with a Spanish straggler, a transport ship called the *Gran Grifon*, and approached her in the light wind. Her decks were thronged with soldiers desperate to get to grips with their elusive enemy. But Drake glided to within close range and gave her first one broadside and then another. He crossed her stern to 'rake' her, hurling cannon balls down the whole length of the ship. The *Gran Grifon* suffered over 100 casualties but was towed to safety by other Spanish ships.

Howard now organized the English fleet into four squadrons to pursue a wider strategic aim: to keep the Spanish out of the Solent at all costs. The obvious men to command the squadrons were Howard himself, Hawkins, Frobisher and Drake.

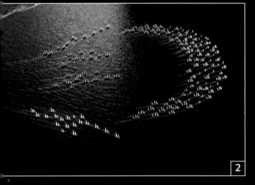

The Battle of the Isle of Wight

1. 4 August. Just south of the tip of the island Howard forms four squadrons and heads for the Spanish fleet.

2. Frobisher (top) heads northeast, while Drake (bottom) heads southeast to attack the Spanish fleet.

Frobisher's predicament

At dawn on 4 August the two fleets lay in a dead calm less than 2 kilometres apart off the Isle of Wight. When a light wind began to blow, Frobisher, in the *Triumph*, seized the initiative and led his squadron close inshore up the east side of the Isle of Wight to try to block the entrance to the Solent. But he was soon in trouble. He saw Medina Sidonia heading for him with a powerful group of galleons, possibly aiming to force their way into the Solent. In the light wind the Spanish galleons were overhauling him. He put 11 rowing boats into the water to give his warships a tow until a breeze filled the *Triumph*'s sails and she picked up speed. Recalde chased after her and claimed he was making ground when the Spanish admiral's signal gun ordered the recall. Recalde was furious. He could not believe he was being ordered away just when he reckoned he had Frobisher in his grasp and could secure access to the sheltered water of the Solent.

But Medina Sidonia had other priorities. A vicious attack had been launched on the southern end of the Armada: Drake had taken the initiative again. He led his squadron against the Armada's

With Frobisher (top) under pressure, Drake (bottom) sees the danger of the Armada heading north into the shelter of the Solent and decides to distract it.

less well-protected southern flank while many of the big galleons were being drawn away to the north. The *San Mateo* took the brunt of Drake's attack and fled for shelter into the centre of the Armada. The ships around her were driven back too. Medina Sidonia saw the danger and rushed to shore up his crumbling formation. A Spanish officer wrote, 'We who were there were cornered so that if the Duke had not gone about with his flagship … we should have come out vanquished that day.'

But Medina Sidonia's diversion to the south meant he was drifting past the eastern entry to the Solent and on towards a major navigational hazard. Suddenly a keen-eyed Spanish lookout saw a dark patch in the water ahead. It was the Owers, one of the most infamous sandbanks in southern England. The Armada rapidly changed course to the southeast – and headed clear out into the English Channel. Medina Sidonia had saved his fleet from the enemy and the shallows but was now on an unstoppable course towards the army in Flanders; and he had absolutely no idea whether it was ready for him.

The English celebrated their success, and Howard knighted Frobisher and Hawkins. A light breeze now nudged both fleets towards the Strait of Dover. Howard wanted to conserve his powder and shot, while the Spanish used the benign weather to patch holes and repair rigging. They had been bruised but not seriously damaged, and the threat of a Spanish invasion was still very real.

Calais

In the Low Countries the Duke of Parma was getting worried. He had heard nothing from the Armada since a message arrived from Corunna signalling its intention to leave. His army was spread across Flanders: it would take him several days to consolidate his forces and embark them on the ships. He had another problem, too. He was bottled up in port by a Dutch fleet that could sail in the shallow coastal waters the deep-draught Armada ships dared not approach. Neither he nor the

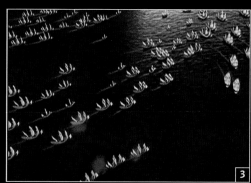

Drake's diversionary attack

1. Drake's squadron in line ahead makes for the southern tip of the Armada.

2. Drake moves into the attack.

3. Medina Sidonia (right) swings his main strength south to tackle Drake.

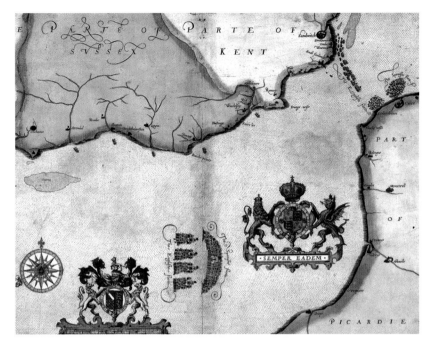

One of Robert Adams's contemporary charts of the Armada's progress. Here he shows the Spanish crescent, pursued by the four English squadrons in mid-Channel. Later, the Spanish fleet is seen anchored off Calais with the English to its west and Seymour's reinforcements heading south from Dover.

Armada had enough shallow-draught warships that could protect his barges from Dutch attack when he tried to rendezvous with the Armada. Here was the fatal flaw in the strategic plan. No decision had been made as to where and how Parma and Medina Sidonia were to join forces. Philip had suggested that Parma should sail out to join the Armada in the Channel, but that would be virtually impossible. The grand plan was unravelling.

On 6 August, while Parma was fretting, the Armada dropped anchor off Calais. But the anchorage was open to the prevailing winds and swift tidal currents: it was untenable for any length of time. Days before, Medina Sidonia had written a final letter to Parma in which he had said, 'Unless we can find a harbour we will perish without doubt.' A lack of proper barrels meant that the Armada's water supply was dangerously low. The men on board had fought a running battle up the Channel and were hungry and exhausted. Repairs and resupply required a safe haven away from the open sea and the English fleet.

That English fleet now anchored off Calais, just a couple of kilometres away from the Spanish. Reinforced by Seymour's squadron from Dover, Howard was no longer outnumbered. France's neutrality meant that the Armada was not allowed to enter the port of Calais, but small boats plied to and fro with supplies, and one of them brought the first word from Parma. It was not good news: none of Medina Sidonia's messages had reached Parma until the day the Armada anchored off Calais. The Spanish admiral was shocked to hear that Parma had not embarked a single man for the invasion of England. It was only now that he had confirmation of the Armada's arrival that Parma could begin to load into barges his army of 27,000 men with their horses and provisions. But it would take him six days: all this time the Armada would be at anchor without shelter, with the English to windward and the threatening Dutch sandbanks to leeward. The Armada could only wait, but Medina Sidonia knew the English would not let him wait in peace.

The attack of the fireships. It was actually after dark when the blazing ships spread panic in the Armada. The fighting in the foreground, as a sleek English ship fights its way between a huge galleon and a red-oared galleass, in fact took place the next day.

Fire

Howard and his commanders were as uneasy as the Spanish. The Armada was a mere 40 kilometres from Parma's HQ in Dunkirk. For all the English knew, Parma could link up with the Spanish fleet that very day. To make matters worse, the constant flow of traffic between the Armada and Calais made many in the English fleet worry that the French were not observing the strictest neutrality. At a council of war on the flagship *Ark Royal* the assembled captains decided that the situation called for radical action. The very survival of Tudor England was at stake.

At midnight Spanish sailors noticed eight great lights blazing in the English fleet. The lights drew closer, and as they grew larger, the Spanish realized with horror that the English had deployed the most dreaded weapon of all. That evening eight armed merchant vessels had been commandeered and their owners compensated. They became sacrificial ships to be soaked in oil, loaded with combustibles and then sent floating in flames among the Spanish warships.

Sailors in wooden ships were terrified of fire. Sails, rigging, decks and masts could all ignite within minutes. Few sailors or soldiers could swim. Medina Sidonia had anticipated the English use of fireships, and a team of small boats headed out to try to grapple them and tow them to shore. They valiantly towed the first two burning ships away from the fleet, but as they approached the third ship the fire ignited its cannon, each loaded with two balls. The crews of the Armada's anchored ships panicked. Many cut their cables and abandoned their anchors as they scrambled to escape the packed anchorage. Ships collided in the chaos.

Medina Sidonia behaved impeccably. He took the *San Martin* out to sea, waited for the danger to pass, and then anchored close inshore a couple of kilometres north of his original spot. He had ordered his other ships to do the same, but it was

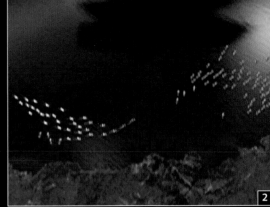

to no avail. Some ships fled great distances. The southwest wind blew many far beyond Calais, towards the port of Gravelines. The Armada was spread along the French coast, its impregnable formation shattered. At dawn the English gleefully attacked: the Battle of Gravelines had begun.

Medina Sidonia's handful of ships is bombarded by the English fleet that surrounds it.

Gravelines

With trumpets blaring, the English fleet of royal galleons, heavily armed merchant ships and private men-of-war closed with the Spanish. Only five ships had stayed behind with Medina Sidonia, and Recalde commanded one of them. He may have had his disagreements with his admiral, but he was not about to abandon him to the English. Medina Sidonia fired a cannon to order the Armada to regroup while he held off the English onslaught. The Spanish admiral and his little band of ships made ready to resist.

Once again, the greed of the English was almost their undoing. This time it was Howard's turn. A massive Spanish galleass had broken its rudder in a collision the night before and was now limping into Calais. Howard spotted this juicy prize and led his entire squadron in a disorganized chase. They forced it aground and had almost stripped it bare when the neutral French, upset by these Englishmen rampaging on their beach, opened fire and forced Howard to withdraw. One of the Armada's greatest ships had been destroyed, but it had kept many of the best English vessels out of the battle for three hours.

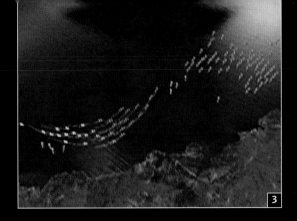

The Battle of Gravelines

1. 8 August. Medina Sidonia (bottom left) with just five ships is attacked by the English (left). The rest of the Armada (right) is in disarray.

2. The Spanish admiral's rearguard action has given the rest of the Armada time to reorganize.

3. The English (centre) attack in line ahead as the Armada re-forms its crescent.

While Howard had been conducting his bit of piracy, Drake led the remaining ships straight at the Spanish. The English knew this was their best chance of decisively defeating the Armada, and pounded the enemy ships from close range. As Drake's *Revenge* passed Medina Sidonia's *San Martin*, the two admirals must have been close enough to shout to each other, but with the roar of the guns nobody would have heard a word. The *Revenge*'s stern cabin was shot through by the *San Martin*'s cannon balls. The *San Martin* herself fought bravely, but was on the receiving end of a devastating attack. One by one Drake's squadron passed her by, firing their broadsides and then moving on to find other targets. Behind Drake, Frobisher brought his guns to bear on the stalwart Spanish flagship.

Medina Sidonia's plucky rearguard action allowed the rest of the Armada to regain some semblance of order. But for the flagship the price was high. Rigging crashed down on the heads of sailors and the *San Martin* was holed above and below the waterline. She was hit over 200 times and her decks were awash with blood. Imagine the rage of Spanish soldiers crowding the decks, waiting for a grapple

and the hand-to-hand battle that traditionally followed it, impotently watching the English ships pounding them with heavy guns. The Spanish thought it cowardice. Time and again they dared the English to come alongside and duel man-to-man.

By 10 a.m. many of the other Spanish ships were rejoining the fray with their crescent formation restored, and for the rest of the day there was a running battle. Both fleets drifted northeast. The Spanish tried to maintain their defensive huddle and avoid the sandbanks near the shore. The English, with the wind behind them, used their skilled seamanship to fire into the Armada at close range and then wheeled away to avoid the grappling hooks and to reload their guns.

Victims

Unlike in the earlier battles, the fight was at such close quarters that ships were now being fatally damaged. The *San Mateo* and her sister ship the *San Felipe* both suffered heavily. At one stage the *San Felipe* was totally surrounded by English ships. While she could return only musket fire, English cannon tore holes in her hull, broke her rudder,

The Battle of Gravelines. The English in line ahead (left) pound the Spanish from the closest range yet.

felled her foremast and killed 200 men on her decks. Her captain roared at the 'Lutheran hens' on the English ships to come closer. The *San Mateo* came to her rescue and was badly mauled. Her only recompense was a boost to morale when one foolhardy Englishman leapt on to the *San Mateo's* deck as the two ships passed very close. He was immediately cut down. The *San Mateo* fought until, an eyewitness said, 'she was a thing of pity to see riddled with shot like a sieve'. Casualties were mounting. The cannon balls smashed through the thick hulls sending showers of splinters, some over 30 centimetres long, into the crowded gun decks. The upper decks, packed with enthusiastic but helpless soldiers, were built for defence only against small arms fire. They had no protection against the English cannon.

The Spanish inflicted relatively little damage in return. On one ship the Earl of Northumberland's lunch was ruined by a cannon ball that smashed into his cabin, grazing his feet and knocking down two men. In general, however,

Spanish gunnery was so ineffective that many eyewitnesses assumed they had run out of powder. But discoveries from wrecks disprove this theory. Most of the Armada's cannon came from different parts of Europe and had different calibres. Picture the frantic confusion on the dark gun decks as men tried to find the right shot for the right cannon. The Spanish had not expected to fight an artillery duel and the men had not been trained for it. The soldiers had been told to fire once and then assemble on deck, ready to board the enemy ships.

To make matters worse, the Spanish gun carriages had only two wheels and were harder to manoeuvre than the English four-wheeled carriages. The unwieldy weapons were so hard to load that soldiers were seen climbing down the outside of the hull to put the ball and charge into the muzzle. During the time it took even an experienced Spanish crew to fire their cannon once, the English were probably firing their guns two or perhaps three times.

Outclassed

The English used this advantage to rake the Spanish time and again. They did not try to storm the battered hulks, but moved on to smash more ships. Two naked divers braved the North Sea and enemy fire to make heroic efforts to patch up the *San Martin*, which was leaking like a sieve. The *San Juan de Sicilia* was reported 'completely shattered' and half her crew dead, the *Santa Maria de la Rosa* was damaged 'whereof they thought she would have sunk'. The leading Armada ships bore the brunt of the damage in order to save the lighter-armed transport ships from annihilation. The *Reganzona* was typically brave, refusing to abandon her place in the rearguard, even though her guns were dismounted, she was listing danger-ously and 'running with blood'. By mid-afternoon the *San Felipe* and the *San Mateo* were floating wrecks. Their commanders refused to abandon ship, and the vessels drifted helplessly on to the Flemish sandbanks, where the crews were set upon by jubilant Dutch rebels who had followed the course of the battle from the shore. The *Maria Juan* sank outright: she was surrounded by English ships and sank so suddenly that just a single boatload of crewmen escaped.

Only the weather saved the Armada from further destruction that afternoon. At four o'clock a squall blew up from the northwest. The English headed for the open sea with virtually no gunpowder left, while the brisk northwest wind blew the Armada further towards the dreaded Flemish shoals. The Spanish had lost the capacity to fight.

The English navy had defeated the Armada. In just 24 hours the tightly knit Spanish fleet, anchored a mere 40 kilometres away from its army in Flanders, was reduced to an ill-organized collec-tion of battered ships moving further and further away from the army. A thousand men had been killed and 800 wounded. Many of the ships were now unseaworthy. The *Gran Grifon* and the *Trinidad Valencera* had sustained hull damage so

Constant firing of cannon was exhausting English supplies of ammunition. On the Spanish side many of the casualties were caused by flying splinters.

BATTLE FACT

On both sides, conditions for the men firing and reloading the cannon on the cramped gun decks were terrible. Sailors were killed by their own recoiling cannons, they choked in the thick cloud of powder smoke, and the noise of the cannon was so loud that the men's ears bled.

BATTLE EXPERIENCE
Cannon firing

The battles against the Armada were the first naval encounters in history in which firepower played a decisive role. We went to an army test range on Salisbury Plain to try out a replica Tudor cannon. We found the loading process complicated enough, and we were on dry land – not, like the sailors in 1588, on a pitching ship in the darkness of a confined gun deck. They had to ram home a powder charge, and then insert a cannon ball and wadding, making sure the ball did not roll out of the end of the gun as the ship lurched over a wave. The cumbersome weapon was then aimed and fired by applying burning matchcord to the touch-hole, which ignited the charge and hurled the ball out of the muzzle. Before loading again, the barrel had to be sponged out and 'wormed' to get rid of any embers or powder residue that might hinder reloading.

With our replica cannon we managed to hit a wooden target at a distance of 100 metres, which made us wonder why the 16th-century English gunners had failed to sink more than a couple of Armada ships. But after a look at the target and a few seconds of thought, we soon saw why. The damage caused by our ball was unimpressive. A fairly neat hole several centimetres across is not going to sink a buoyant wooden ship. Besides, with the ship bouncing around, you would have had to be spectacularly lucky to hit an enemy below the waterline, and any holes were easily blocked with wooden plugs. Even so, the relentless and constant pounding of the English cannon did enough damage to the Spanish ships to make many of them unable to withstand the storms they suffered on the way home.

severe that their crews were forced to run them ashore. The captain of the *San Marcos* passed cables around his ship to tie her up like a bundle in case she split open.

The remaining ships were on an unfriendly lee shore, one of the most treacherous in Europe. Their route to the army was blocked by the English, and the strong prevailing wind was against them. They did not know that the English had run out of powder. Even if they had known, the wind would have made it extremely difficult to sail the fleet back to Calais. The Holy Enterprise was over. But would the crippled ships ever get home?

The banks of Flanders

The wind that had forced the English to break off the fighting now pushed the Armada inexorably northeast up the coast of Flanders. They knew the treacherous sandbanks were somewhere ahead, but had no pilots or charts to guide them. The fleet spread out again, ignoring its formation and with its morale in shreds. Only old Recalde and de Leiva stood by Medina Sidonia as he proudly offered battle to the hovering English. The *San Martin* fired a cannon to re-form the Armada, but the order was largely ignored. Later, Medina Sidonia arrested all captains who had not obeyed. One commander was hanged from the yardarm and his body paraded around the fleet to restore discipline.

Meanwhile, the Flemish sandbanks came ever closer. The colour of the water changed and soundings showed the water getting shallower. A man in the bows threw a weighted line over the side and measured the depth as the rope ran through his fingers. Eight fathoms, seven fathoms: the biggest ships needed five fathoms of water.

Disaster was only minutes away. Once aground, the ships would slowly break up as the sea pounded them further on to the shoals. The English were to seaward, while Dutch crowds on shore waited to pounce on anyone who managed to get to land. Various officers came to Medina Sidonia and

begged him to take the papal banner in a small boat and make for a safe haven in Flanders. He refused; instead he made his confession and prepared to die like a Christian soldier. He shouted to one of his squadron commanders: 'We are lost. What shall we do?' The commander shouted back: 'As for me, I am going to die like a man. Send me a supply of shot.'

The wind to the rescue

Then, quite suddenly, just when defeat seemed final, the wind backed to the southwest and the Spanish ships struggled out into the open water of the North Sea. The Armada had avoided total destruction by a matter of minutes. Medina Sidonia wrote, 'We were saved by God's mercy.'

That night councils of war were held on board the *Ark Royal* and the *San Martin*. The English fleet was to continue to shadow the Armada. A protesting Seymour was sent back to the Strait of Dover to keep an eye on Parma in case he attempted a cross-Channel dash. Drake wrote that he doubted whether the Spanish would now try to

A siege gun recovered from the wreckage of a Spanish galleass, the *Girona*, near the Giant's Causeway in Northern Ireland.

rendezvous with Parma. He added that many of the enemy were injured and 'without doubt many killed', also 'by report of such as are taken their ships, masts, ropes and sails are much decayed by shot'. Drake guessed right. While the English council of war opted to wait and see, their Spanish counterpart decided to go home. The invasion of England had been abandoned. The Armada was defeated but not yet destroyed.

There was only one practicable route home for the Armada's ships, which were being driven by the wind far up the North Sea. They would have to sweep around the north of Scotland and Ireland and then turn south. It would be a hazardous voyage for the battered ships with their weakened crews and inadequate supplies. And they were to run into tempestuous weather.

The English fleet followed the Spanish as far as the Firth of Forth. There it broke off the chase and returned home to replenish its exhausted supplies.

Ireland

The main body of the Armada passed between Scotland and Orkney and into the Atlantic. Here it was hit by a massive gale, the first of many. Ruined vessels, running low on water and with irreparable leaks, ran for safety towards the jagged coast of Ireland. They had little knowledge of it and no detailed charts. Ship after ship was smashed on exposed beaches from the Giant's Causeway in the north to the Dingle peninsula in the south. Thousands drowned, among them Philip's favourite, de Leiva, with his glittering crew of aristocrats.

And even for those who managed to scramble ashore there was no refuge. The English lord deputy in Ireland was taking no chances, for a Spanish landing could provoke an Irish uprising. He had fewer than 750 soldiers at his disposal to ensure that no Spanish came ashore and stayed, so the chilling order went out to 'apprehend and execute all Spaniards found'. Hundreds of Spanish soldiers and sailors struggled ashore, only to be brutally murdered by detachments of English troops.

Medina Sidonia and a group of ships led by his *San Martin* avoided the Irish coast and on 21 September limped into Santander in northern Spain, 44 days after their defeat at Gravelines. Over the next few weeks other ships struggled back. The crews were enfeebled by scurvy, influenza, typhus and malnutrition. Medina Sidonia almost died of dysentery. Recalde, his second-in-command, made it home but died days later, too ashamed to face his family or friends.

The ships were in an even worse state than their crews. The state-of-the-art galleon *San Marcos* was broken up for her timber and guns. One ship sank the moment she put down her anchor. Another ran aground in Laredo harbour because her remaining crew were not strong enough to drop the anchor. At least 45 of the original 120 ships, and nearly 11,000 men, had been lost. Even Philip's unquestioning faith was shaken as the full extent of the disaster became known.

Left: Elizabeth I, queen of England from 1558 to 1603. This 'Armada' portrait is filled with images of the great sea battle with Spain.

Opposite: A gold ring recovered from the wreck of the *Girona*. An inscription on it reads: 'No tengo más que dar te', meaning 'I have nothing more to give thee'.

The fate of the English

Back in England, things were not much better for the victors. The sailors who had driven off the Armada were left to die as the country celebrated its victory. Typhus tore through the fleet, killing thousands. The water men drew from harbours for cooking and cleaning was contaminated with excrement and corpses. There were no supplies of food.

England, which had exerted itself to the limit to beat the Armada, failed to find the resources to feed its victorious sailors. They starved as they obeyed orders to stay cooped up on their ships in case the Spanish returned. The rumour went round that they were being retained so that the Treasury would not have to pay them. Those who were demobilized were given no money or food. The streets of Dover, Rochester and Harwich were lined with emaciated sailors too weak to go home. Howard, devastated, pawned his family silver in an attempt to give his men food and shelter.

The English had lost fewer than 100 men to the Spanish guns. Yet a year later as many as half of the 16,000 men who had fought the Armada were dead. It was a shameful end to a great English victory.

The Armada had been destroyed by a combination of Philip's bad planning, English fireships, gunnery and seamanship, and finally by the weather. This great maritime enterprise marked the zenith of Spain's military and political power, and although the loss of the Armada's ships did not greatly affect the military balance, it bequeathed to the English victors a deeper and more abiding legacy.

England had defended its land and religion. Most importantly, it had created a myth that was to last three and a half centuries: an almost religious belief in the invincibility of England and her navy. Generations of supremely confident seafarers were to extend English and then British influence around the globe and create the biggest maritime power the world had ever seen. The defeat of the Armada was to become the foundation myth of the British Empire.

1645: THE BATTLE OF NASEBY

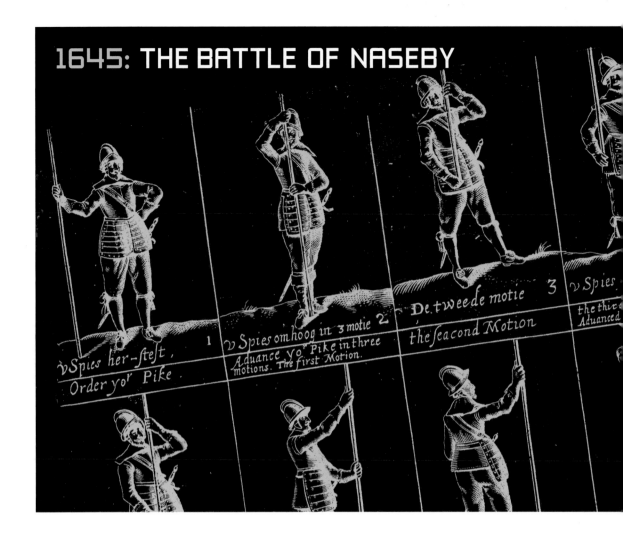

The elite cavalry of the king's Lifeguard left Market Harborough at two o'clock on the morning of 14 June 1645. Even though it was almost midsummer, it was pitch dark as they heaved themselves into their saddles and headed south to meet an enemy who had appeared seemingly out of thin air. By six the infantry were marching. After three years of warfare the veterans among them had grown used to lugging their huge pikes, over 5 metres long, their cumbersome muskets and jangling bandoliers. Last of all came the wagons and carriages of the supply train. A squadron of cavalry guarded this baggage and the army's women and children who travelled with it.

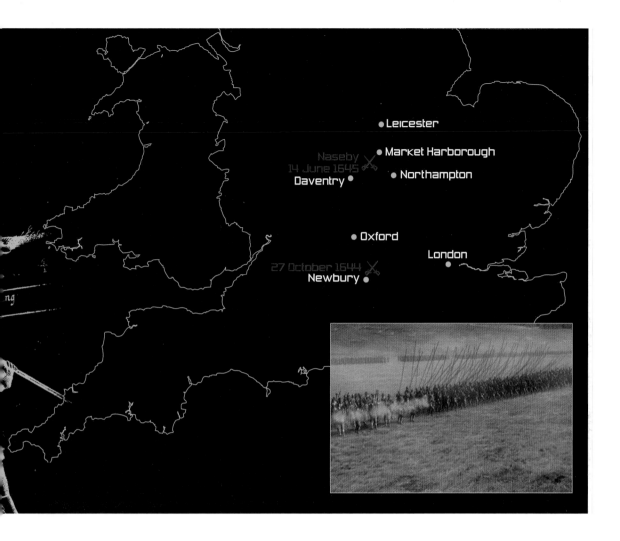

The king's army was not marching to war with the nation's enemies in France or the Low Countries, but with its fellow countrymen in the rolling hills of Northamptonshire. Britain was at war with itself. For the first time in a century and a half there was vicious fighting in every part of the country, from Cornwall to Scotland. It was a war in which, according to a recent study, more British people would die per head of population than in any other war in our history. By the time the vanguard of the royal army reached Clipston village later that morning, they knew a major encounter was inevitable. As they halted on high ground, they saw the forward elements of their enemy, the forces of

England's Parliament. Within hours the greatest battle of the Civil War would take place on the open ground to the northwest of the village of Naseby, and it would have a decisive impact on the struggle between King and Parliament.

King Charles

It is hard to imagine this Civil War occurring without the personality and policies of King Charles I. There were other factors, such as long-term economic, social and religious pressures, that aggravated the situation, but without Charles, full-scale war would almost certainly have been avoided. When he inherited the throne from

CHARLES

Having been an extremely shy and sickly young man, Charles had grown into an elegant and dignified figure by the time he ascended to the throne in 1625 at the age of 24. But he was doomed never to be a successful monarch. He lacked the self-assurance to negotiate, and his obstinacy led to his downfall. Above all, he was steeped in the ideology of divine kingship. Charles believed that he had a religious duty to wield total power, not to share it with the people he ruled.

papist'. He reformed the Church's prayer book, and his new liturgy prompted many to believe he was intent on restoring Britain to the Catholic fold. It seemed that Charles was going out of his way to antagonize his subjects. By the late 1630s a huge reservoir of opposition was building up against him and his coterie of bishops and Catholic advisers.

When Charles was forced to call Parliament because of his desperate need for money, his uncompromising arrogance led inexorably to armed struggle. In 1642 his high-handed storming of the parliamentary chamber provoked such outrage among his subjects that he had to flee London. Parliament raised an army to resist his return: Charles in turn declared war on Parliament. The Civil War had begun.

'I fight for your halfe crowne'

Soon nowhere in England was free of conflict. Both the king and Parliament ordered the counties

James I in 1625 he ruled in a radically different way from his father. He made savings that allowed him to live without parliamentary subsidies. He scrapped the political bargaining of his father's court and adopted the more ritualized, autocratic style of European despots.

Charles boosted revenue by finding loopholes in ancient tax laws to enable him to make ends meet without having to call Parliament. This was unpopular: people felt they were paying semi-legal taxes to the king without their representatives having any say in how it was spent. There were other grievances, too. The king's wife, Henrietta Maria, was French and Catholic, the two *bêtes noires* of 17th-century Englishmen. Her influence was seen as deeply malignant. The king had failed to intervene to help fellow Protestants in the religious conflict now known as the Thirty Years' War, which had been ravaging Europe since 1618. He even let hated Spanish troops march across the south of England in 1639 on their way to fight Protestants on the Continent. Charles gained a reputation as a 'closet

Charles I on horseback by Anthony van Dyck (c.1637).

to supply them with troops. This made neutrality hard to maintain, and most people reluctantly had to choose sides.

Parliament portrayed itself as standing for decent, English values. Parliamentarians believed the king was tainted by foreign influences and Catholic beliefs. Radical Protestants, called Puritans, were among Parliament's most fervent supporters. Parliamentarians gave Royalist troops the nickname 'Cavaliers', from the Spanish word *caballeros*, meaning 'armed horsemen'. It suggested that Royalists were dissolute gentlemen with Catholic, foreign airs and a propensity for violence and pillaging.

Charles certainly did use foreign troops, and this played into the hands of Parliament, especially when he recruited hated Catholic Irishmen. But most peers and gentry favoured the king. No doubt they felt personal ties of loyalty, but, more importantly, the one thing they feared more than Charles's despotic rule was anarchy and the collapse of the social order. The Royalists saw the Parliamentarians as low-born townspeople out to cause social upheaval. They gave them the nickname 'Roundheads', a reference to the shaved heads of the London apprentices who had been so vocal in the mob that had driven Charles from his capital.

Social class or religion were not the only reasons to support one side or the other. Ideological arguments divided families and ruined long friendships. Sir William Waller commanded an army in the southwest against a force led by his close friend Sir Ralph Hopton. Both had opposed the king throughout the period of political turmoil, but when war was declared Hopton reluctantly joined the king's side. Hopton believed that sovereignty should reside in the monarch. Waller did not.

Others had no ideological basis for fighting at all. Foreign mercenaries flocked to England. One, called Carlo Fantom, said, 'I care not for your cause, I … fight for your halfe crowne and your handsome woemen.' Others were forced to fight by their landlords, or were press-ganged by soldiers at gun-point.

For two years the course of the fighting that was to lead to Naseby dragged on inconclusively. Both sides were strong enough to threaten each other, but not to deliver the knockout blow. The Royalists secured the West Country and the north, while the Parliamentarians controlled London, southern and eastern England and the Midlands. In the east, Parliament's supremacy had been established with the help of a military novice: Oliver Cromwell, a Huntingdonshire squire and MP who found he had a gift for commanding cavalry.

From its base in London, Parliament controlled valuable resources. But one thing held Parliamentarians back from all-out war. Most of them could not imagine a country without a king at its head. This left the parliamentary leadership confused about its war aims. Its campaigns had no forthright purpose. So the war dragged on.

CROMWELL

Oliver Cromwell had a broad, ruddy face, shorter hair than was the fashion and, famously, warts. When he sat for a portrait years after Naseby he insisted that he was painted, as he put it, 'warts and all'. A hard-working member of the gentry, before the war he had ploughed his own fields. He had a conviction that he 'acted in the Lord's business' and possessed extraordinary energy: while others vacillated, he acted. Realizing that the clash between King and Parliament was bound to lead to war, he raised a regiment of horsemen and seized Cambridge Castle before it could be used for the Royalist cause. By 1645 his 'Ironsides' were the best troops in the country.

Above: Oliver Cromwell, the 'warts and all' portrait.
Right: The head of a typical civil war pike, with protective metal 'cheeks' running down the shaft.

Newbury

In October 1644 the war was two years old, but although Parliament won a major victory at Marston Moor, near York, the king was still far from defeated. So when, later that month, three separate Parliamentarian armies with a total of 19,000 men surrounded a force of 9,000 Royalists at Newbury, it was Parliament's best chance yet.

The Roundhead high command was notoriously divided. All strategic decisions were taken by a committee in London, although there was provision for a council of senior officers in the field to take urgent measures. The system rarely produced decisive leadership. However, on this occasion the council resolved on a risky but potentially brilliant plan of action. They would make the most of their numbers and divide their forces. Two-thirds of the army, commanded by

Sir William Waller, would march around in a huge flanking movement and attack the Royalists from the west, while the other third, under the Earl of Manchester, would attack from the east. This great encircling move might just defeat the Royalists so comprehensively that it would end the war. And so, just before midnight on 26 October, thousands of Parliamentarian soldiers shouldered their pikes and moved off into the night. With them on the 20-kilometre march were the horsemen of Oliver Cromwell.

Cromwell had found religious zeal as a Puritan while studying at Cambridge, and this was reflected in his sober dress and character. His sincerity, fervour and commanding voice made him an impressive figure in Parliament. These attributes served him equally well on the battlefield where, despite having no military experience, he excelled. His horsemen became known as 'Ironsides' after their bravery at Marston Moor. Cromwell insisted that his Ironsides were to be 'godly and honest men ... who [are] upon a matter of conscience engaged in this quarrel'. Unusually, he promoted men on merit rather than birth or class: 'I had rather have a plain russet-coated captain that knows what he fights for, and loves what he knows, than that which you would call a gentleman and is nothing else.' His men wore a cuirass – an all-in-one breast plate and back plate – over a stout leather buff coat, and a helmet. They were armed with long, straight swords and a pair of pistols, and some had carbines or short muskets strung on their backs.

These horsemen were joined on the encircling march by foot soldiers. The only infantry Parliament could count on were Londoners; the rest of the local militias had been disbanded when they had proved unwilling to get involved. But even the Londoners had to be cajoled to leave the

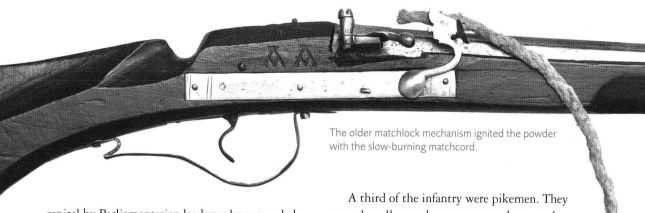

The older matchlock mechanism ignited the powder with the slow-burning matchcord.

capital by Parliamentarian leaders who persuaded them that the best means of defending their homes was to attack the king.

About two-thirds of the marching infantry carried muskets. Some had the latest kind, with barrels only a metre long, which meant they could be used without the forked rests that older, heavier muskets required. Nearly all the muskets were of the matchlock type: they had a crude mechanism that dropped a lighted matchcord into the priming pan to ignite the powder charge in the barrel. These matchlock muskets were inefficient in wet weather, and vast supplies of matchcord had to accompany the army. New firing mechanisms, known as firelocks or flintlocks, were being introduced: flint instead of a match created the spark that ignited the powder in the priming pan. But these weapons were more expensive and so far less common.

Around his neck each musketeer carried a bandolier, a leather belt on which 12 or more wooden containers were strung, each containing enough coarse gunpowder to fire a single round. At its base was a pouch in which musket balls and cleaning equipment were kept. Suspended below the bandolier was a flask containing fine powder to prime the musket. Soldiers also carried swords. Most had no uniform jackets and wore civilian clothes unless they were lucky enough to get their hands on buff coats for added protection. Helmets were still compulsory headgear, but most musketeers couldn't be bothered to carry them around and left them behind.

A third of the infantry were pikemen. They were the tallest and strongest men because the pike, at 5–6 metres long and with a 20-centimetre steel tip or head, was a daunting weapon to handle. Officers had to keep an eye open because 'many base soldiers' would cut the long staff down to make the pike easier to carry. Its length was vital, because it was deployed to keep cavalry far enough away to allow the musketeers to fire unhindered; without the protection of pikemen, musketeers would be charged down and dispersed.

On this night march the pikemen would have been in full armour. This consisted of back and breast plates with extensions called 'tassets' to protect the upper leg. At the waist of the back plate was a small hook on which the men hung their helmets when they marched. Most of the armour would have been stained black to prevent

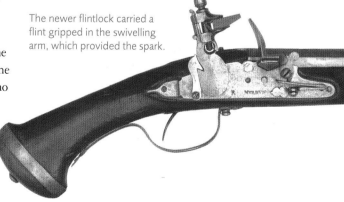

The newer flintlock carried a flint gripped in the swivelling arm, which provided the spark.

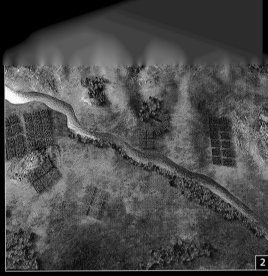

rusting. The only exception was the polished metal armour of the wealthiest officers, who had someone else to do the hard work for them.

Missed opportunities

On the morning of 27 October the royal forces awoke to find themselves in the process of being surrounded, threatened from behind as well as from in front. The king rapidly reorganized his army to fight in two directions. By 3 p.m. Waller's Parliamentarian outflanking force was in position to the west. The plan was for this encircling group to fire a cannon when it was ready to attack, and then both forces would advance simultaneously from west and east.

Unfortunately the limitations of 17th-century communications meant that when the cannon was fired, only Waller's forces advanced. His men made good progress. But still Manchester did not attack. He may not have heard the cannon. He may have heard it but refused to believe it was Waller's because he did not expect the

A contemporary illustration of the elaborate set of actions in a pikeman's drill.

Newbury 1644: surrounded

1. 26 Oct. The Parliamentarian army (right) catches the king with smaller forces at Shaw House (centre), Donnington Castle (top left) and south of the river (bottom left). Two-thirds of Parliament's army moves off northwards to sweep around behind the king's forces.
2. 27 Oct, 3 p.m. The Parliamentarian encircling force (top left) arrives behind the king's army. The king rapidly deploys a force (centre left) to meet it.
3. 27 Oct, 4p.m. The encircling force attacks (left), firing a cannon as a signal for the rest of their army (right) to attack the king at Shaw House (centre). But it fails to react for an hour and launches its assault from the east only at dusk.

outflanking force to be ready so quickly. Whatever the reason, only after Waller's men had been fighting for an hour did Manchester finally attack the Royalist stronghold of Shaw House. There was half an hour of daylight left. Although the Royalists were hard pressed from both directions, nightfall saved them from being crushed by the enemy's superior numbers. One Royalist officer removed his coat so that his men could see his white-shirted figure fighting in the growing dark. His effort to rally his troops had a quite unexpected effect on the enemy: the Parliamentarians thought he was a ghost and fled in terror.

That night the king realized that another day of fighting would lead to the annihilation of his army, so he withdrew to Oxford. Again, the Parliamentarian command missed a golden tactical opportunity. The king's line of retreat was left open by the Parliamentarians. His entire army escaped over a small bridge in the village of Donnington, which could easily have been blocked. The Roundheads woke up in the morning to find that the king's army, which they thought was trapped, had escaped.

Cromwell pleaded to be allowed to take the cavalry and chase the retreating Royalists, but was refused. He was furious, and had no doubt that the battle had been thrown away by a vacillating and divided leadership. He was convinced that victory could only be achieved after a radical shake-up.

The New Model Army

Cromwell now demanded of Parliament a complete overhaul of the Parliamentarian war effort. He envisaged a centrally funded, national army; existing local armies would be replaced by a single force. And he insisted that it should be commanded by professional officers, not by powerful regional magnates such as the earls of Essex and Manchester. Parliament was persuaded: it passed 'the New Model Ordinance', which created a single army of 22,000 men. No longer would Parliament have to rely on unwilling London militiamen; now it would have full-time professionals. They would be paid eight pence a day. From then on, although pay was often in arrears, soldiers in the New Model Army were better and more regularly paid than their Royalist opponents. Its command structure was more professional, too. Sir Thomas Fairfax was appointed 'captain general'. Nicknamed 'Black Tom' because of his long black hair, he was a tough Yorkshireman, a veteran of Continental warfare and many battles in the Civil War. He proved an excellent choice. His commander of infantry was Philip Skippon, another veteran of the Dutch wars, who had commanded the London militia. The two of them spent much of spring 1645 bringing the New Model Army up to strength, disbanding some regiments to supplement others and drafting men in from civilian life. In the end, about half the foot soldiers were new recruits.

The Royalists were scornful of the new parliamentary army's officer corps, whom they dismissed as low-born men of extreme Presbyterian views. There was an element of truth in this stereotype. The officer corps did have a dangerous flavour of meritocracy about it, and not all its members were gentlemen born and bred. Lieutenant Colonel Thomas Pride had been a drayman before the war, and Lieutenant Colonel John Hewson a cobbler. Parliament had to approve the appointment of all Fairfax's officers, and two colonels and 40 captains were rejected for having extreme political views. The list scraped through its final vote in the House of Lords by a majority of just one.

Supplies and arms poured in as the officers trained their new formations. Large groups of men with lighted matchcord and lots of gunpowder required careful drilling if they were to be more of a danger to their enemy than to themselves. Among the innovations was a uniform coat. For the first time all infantry would be wearing the same colour. To keep the price down they went for the cheapest dye – red. The soldiers of the New Model Army were Britain's first redcoats.

As the New Model Army took shape, there was only one element missing: Cromwell. His Ironsides were the model of discipline and training for the entire army, and he was the driving force behind the reforms, but he himself was excluded. Cromwell was an MP, and Parliament had passed legislation that prohibited any member of Parliament from serving in the army. It was a supreme irony: Cromwell was not allowed to serve in the force he had created.

Prince Rupert

The king set up court in Oxford, which became a busy garrison town. College cloisters were converted to gunpowder stores. The students enlisted in regiments and drilled in college quads rather than attending lectures. Teachers of younger boys had a job to stop them running off to join the Royalists.

Charles was ill suited to commanding an army: he was indecisive and a poor judge of character. All too often his opinion was merely that of the last person to have talked to him. His lieutenant general was his nephew Prince Rupert, a brave, larger-than-life figure loved by his men but hated by his enemies, who included many fellow Royalist commanders. Although he was only 26 years old, he was a veteran of 11 years of warfare on the Continent. Rupert did not share the general Royalist scorn for the New Model Army; in fact, he tried to introduce similar reforms in the royal forces, but without success.

Although the war was turning against the Royalists, Prince Rupert thought that with bold action they could still win. He wanted to lead one

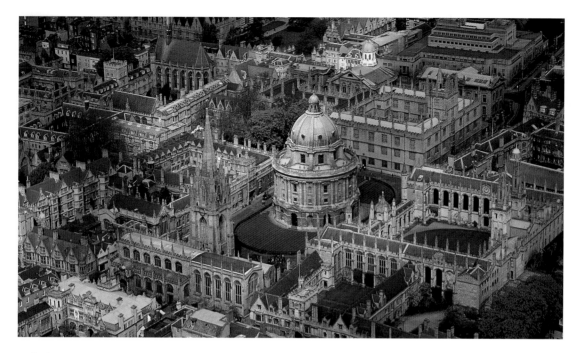

Oxford: Charles's capital. Today's picturesque academic city was a military stronghold 350 years ago.

strong army to recapture the north and perhaps meet up in Scotland with the brilliant Marquis of Montrose, who had won many victories for the king's cause. Only then did he believe that the Royalists would be strong enough to turn on the New Model Army. In an attempt to divert the Parliamentarians away from the north of England, Lord George Goring was sent to the West Country with 3,000 horsemen. Their departure was a serious blow to the strength of the royal army.

Charles and Rupert set out from Oxford in early May. They received fresh recruits from Wales and Ireland and heard that things were going well for their army in Scotland. In England the New Model Army was untested and Parliamentarian forces in the north were scattered and unsupported. At first all went well for the Royalists. Fairfax's Parliamentarian army had been tricked into following Goring to the southwest, and the north now lay at Charles's mercy. As he approached Chester, a force of

Parliamentarians broke off their siege of the city and retreated.

Success in the Midlands transformed the strategic situation. The committee in charge of Parliament's strategy responded by ordering Fairfax to besiege the king's capital at Oxford, which they hoped would force Charles back south to fight the New Model Army. Fairfax was not equipped to take Oxford because he lacked the heavy guns required to bombard its strong fortifications. Even so, the siege did have the desired

BATTLE FACT

One of Prince Rupert's most treasured possessions was his dog, Boy. The white poodle was his devoted companion until it died at the Battle of Marston Moor in 1644, the year before Naseby.

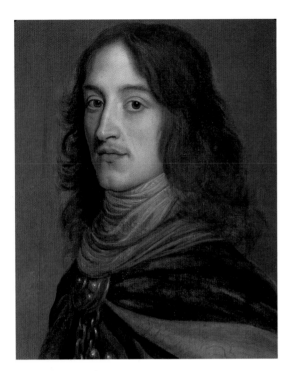

Prince Rupert of the Rhine. The ablest soldier on the Royalist side, his exploits as commander of the king's cavalry were legendary.

The net closes

After taking Leicester the Royalists plundered Northamptonshire for supplies. They had no idea that Fairfax was marching north, and the king was happy to wait a week for a convoy of ammunition. Rupert, however, was uneasy. The army had suffered 700 casualties at Leicester, and many had deserted with the booty they had taken from the sacked town. He had also ordered Goring to rejoin the army, but he had not yet arrived. Rupert learned the shocking news that his opponents were almost upon him when a Royalist cavalry detachment was caught by some Parliamentarian horsemen on 12 June near Daventry, about halfway between Leicester and Oxford. Rupert stood his men to arms all night, and at first light the Royalists left Daventry and headed north as fast as they could.

They reached Market Harborough that night, with Rupert still hoping that they could slip away to the north, but this was unrealistic: the New Model Army was so close that the Royalist supply train would be vulnerable if they tried to retreat. In fact, the fighting had already begun for one cavalry outpost in a village southwest of Market Harborough. A troop of Rupert's Lifeguard had been eating and playing games when they were surprised by a Roundhead cavalry patrol. After a brief skirmish some of the troopers escaped and galloped north to Market Harborough to warn the king that he had been surprised for the second time in as many days: the Parliamentarians were massing only 8 kilometres away, around the village of Naseby.

Cromwell returns

It was a severe shock for the Royalists. Overconfidence and disastrous intelligence about their enemy's movements had let them down badly. The Roundhead camp had a surprise that day too, but it was a pleasant one: Oliver Cromwell thundered in at the head of 600 horsemen. Delighted troops greeted his arrival with a 'mighty shout'. It seemed an auspicious

effect. Against Rupert's advice, the king and his other commanders decided to return south and rescue their beleaguered capital.

On its way the royal army stormed the prosperous city of Leicester. On 31 May three Royalist attacks were repulsed, and even when the walls had been breached, the townspeople launched a vicious street battle. The Cavaliers were furious at having to fight house to house, and sacked the city in a particularly gruesome way: it was claimed that women were raped, men butchered and 140 cartloads of loot removed. The fall of Leicester sent shock waves through Parliamentarian circles; but it also galvanized them. A week later Fairfax was given full operational control of the New Model Army. His first action was to break off the siege of Oxford and head north to seek and destroy the king's army.

omen. Fairfax had persuaded Parliament to bend the rules: he wanted Cromwell as his lieutenant general.

The news from Naseby prompted Prince Rupert and the king to hold an urgent council of war at midnight. Rupert argued against doing battle with Fairfax and Cromwell. He was for moving on north in the hope of building strength – they were sorely missing Goring's troops, who were nowhere near. But most of Charles's other commanders opposed Rupert. They believed the troops' morale was high and their opponents' New Model Army untested and ripe for defeat. The decision was made to turn and fight.

The most authoritative accounts of Naseby suggest that the New Model Army numbered between 15,200 and 17,000 men, while the Royalists' strength was only 9,500 to 12,500. The king's men were outnumbered. Would experience make up for the shortfall in numbers? The Royalist army's officer corps had on the whole seen more fighting, and its ranks contained fewer novices. But on balance there was probably not much to choose between the two armies. Both had their strengths and weaknesses: each had its elite groups of cavalry and infantry, and each had some units that had never been tested in battle.

On the morning of 14 June Prince Rupert led the royal army out of Market Harborough and headed south, showing no sign of the reluctance to fight that he had displayed at the council of war. At 8 a.m. he halted on the ridge south of East Farndon, determined to discover whether the Roundheads were as close as intelligence reports suggested. Francis Ruce, the army's scoutmaster general, was sent forward but could find no trace of them. Rupert at once set off to look for himself, perhaps believing that the Roundheads were retreating. But as he passed through Clipston, he was left in no doubt. The New Model Army was not retreating; it was forming a battle line on top of a steep ridge.

Sir Thomas Fairfax, commander-in-chief of the New Model Army. He was a straightforward soldier with no interest in politics.

'We might advance towards him'

Fairfax had brought the entire Parliamentarian army into Naseby, most probably leaving his baggage train south of the village. As soon as he saw the Royalist army in the distance, he rejoiced – his biggest fear had been that they would try to escape, and thus avoid the decisive battle he wanted. He ordered the army to deploy to meet the king: 'to be in readiness to receive him; or if not, we might advance towards him'.

Fairfax's problem was that his position was too strong. The ridge that the New Model Army occupied was very steep, and he knew that no opposing commander would risk assaulting it. Cromwell then spotted a piece of flatter ground to the west, which looked more suitable. He persuaded Fairfax, 'as though he had received direction from God himself where to pitch the battle', to shunt the entire army sideways.

So the New Model Army crabbed to the west along the top of the ridge, and the royal forces mirrored them. Rupert had sent back word to the rest of the army to make haste: he wanted to keep the initiative and carry the fight to the enemy. The Royalists marched across the fields for about 3 kilometres and then formed their ranks on a low hill facing south. Opposite them the Parliamentarians too were on a low ridge, facing north. In between the two armies was moorland without hedges, ditches, trees or walls. As Cromwell had said, it was indeed the perfect spot for a battle.

The western edge of the battlefield was bordered by the hedges of Sulby parish. At the far left of the Parliamentarian line General Ireton's cavalry were next to the hedges, while Cromwell commanded the cavalry on the right. The whole line was over a kilometre and a half wide. On Cromwell's right was a steep slope covered in gorse and rabbit warrens. In between the two wings of cavalry, Major General Skippon commanded the infantry. Five regiments containing up to a thousand men each made up the front line, with three regiments in the second line and one in reserve. In each regiment musketeers stood in the middle, with pikemen on the edges.

Each company within the regiment had its colours, a 2-metre square of painted silk. They were a powerful symbol of the regiment's honour, and it was considered a disgrace to lose them. The colours said a lot about the particular virtues of the colonel who had selected them. One contemporary manual says, 'Blew signifieth Faith, Constancie, Truth, Affection or Honourable Love; Black signifieth wisdom and sobriety, toogether with a sincere correction of too much ambition.' A so-called 'fieldword' had been issued to the troops, so that in the confusion of battle they could tell friend from foe. The Roundheads' was 'God is our strength.' As a further aid to recognition, some of the troops wore white linen or paper in their hats.

Psalms and beanstalks

Fairfax ordered his army to walk back 100 paces, which took them back behind the ridge and out of sight of the enemy. He probably did not want the Royalists watching his inexperienced infantry forming their ranks. It would also save his raw recruits from being intimidated by the sight of the Royalist army for longer than was absolutely necessary. Once they were drawn up, the men listened to sermons – in true Puritan style. During a previous battle a chaplain had ridden from rank to rank with a Bible in one hand and a pistol in the other, exhorting soldiers to do their duty. Some regiments of the New Model Army were

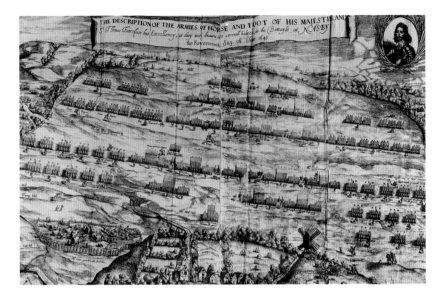

THE DESCRIPTION OF THE ARMIES OF HORSE AND FOOT OF HIS MAJESTIE AND
Sr Thomas Fairfaxe his Excellency, as they were drawne into severall bodies at the Battayle at NASBY
the Foverteenth day of   1645

Left: Streeter's contemporary plan of the opening positions at Naseby. Cromwell's cavalry in three lines on the right face an inferior number of Royalist horsemen.

Below: 14 June. The battlelines at Naseby, with infantry in the centre and cavalry on the wings. The Royalists are at the top, with Rupert's cavalry (top left), close to the Sulby hedges. The New Model Army (bottom) faces them across a shallow valley.

ready to sing psalms as they advanced; others had more worldly concerns. Equipment was checked over and over again. Musketeers blew on glowing matchcord to keep it alight and made sure that the 'serpent', the curved arm for the matchcord on their muskets, would place the burning end of the cord straight into the priming pan. Cavalrymen loaded their pistols with powder and ball. This had to be done at the last minute: if pistols stood loaded for too long they would fail to fire.

Some 800 metres away, across the dip between the armies, Rupert was finalizing his deployment. He himself commanded the cavalry on the Royalist right wing. In the centre he placed the infantry under the stocky, 66-year-old veteran Jacob Astley, and on his left, facing Cromwell, he placed Marmaduke Langdale's horsemen. In contrast to the Roundhead army, Rupert placed small groups of cavalry among the infantry and some musketeers with the cavalry. He wanted to shore up his outnumbered infantry and to give supporting musket fire to the cavalry. The king, dressed in full plate armour, commanded a third line. It was a mixture of horsemen and infantry, including his own Lifeguard and Rupert's elite Bluecoats. The troops

had marched across beanfields, and many had put beanstalks in their hats. The 'fieldword' for the Cavaliers was 'Queen Mary'.

Meanwhile, Cromwell had spotted an opportunity. He saw that the Sulby hedges over to his extreme left would provide perfect cover for a detachment to harry Prince Rupert's right flank. The men he chose for the job were dragoons, a hybrid of cavalry and infantry. Their horses were inferior to the regular cavalry's and they were not expected to fight on horseback. They used their mobility to capture bridges and raid hostile areas. Cromwell told their commander, Colonel Okey, to ride forward on the far side of the hedges and disrupt Rupert's cavalry as much as possible. Okey led his

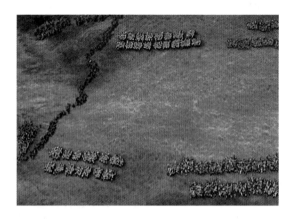

14 June, mid-morning. The first clash came when Colonel Okey's Parliamentarian dragoons (bottom left) were ordered up behind the Sulby hedges. They moved alongside Rupert's cavalry (top centre) and fired at them through the hedges .

Rupert's cavalry charges were legendary. Before the Civil War, cavalry had advanced towards an enemy and then stopped short, firing carbines and pistols to inflict casualties. Rupert had abandoned this practice. His men were told to charge in among the enemy, keeping their swords in their hands and not using firearms until they had scattered them. Rupert relied on shock action rather than firepower to break an enemy, and until now he had always succeeded.

Rupert's troopers broke into a full trot, riding three ranks deep with just a metre between each rank. In the first rank rode the veterans, 'the best and ablest men'. Each man's legs touched those of the rider next to him, and each man's sword was wrapped around his wrist with a cord in case he should drop his blade in the mêlée.

Ireton's men knew better than to receive this charge standing still, and began to advance down the hill on to the flat. Over the last few metres both sides broke into 'full career' and, seconds later, crashed into each other.

The fighting was fierce. One of Ireton's regiments was scattered by the charge and became trapped on the far left by rough ground dotted with deep, boggy holes. Other Roundhead units repulsed the Cavalier attackers. Ireton even managed to regroup his regiment and attack the advancing Royalist infantry on his right. It was a brave move and he paid for it. His horse was shot from under him, his thigh run through with a pike and his face cut by a halberd. In this parlous state Ireton was taken prisoner.

The Roundhead cavalry had lost their commander, and when Rupert's second attack thundered towards them they broke. The majority of Rupert's horsemen raced after them – some Roundheads retreated as far as Northampton, 25 kilometres away. After their victorious charge the Royalist horsemen abandoned all discipline and Rupert lost tactical control of them as they raced off after fugitives or sought the Roundhead baggage train. He had no chance of recalling

men, ten abreast, into the field behind the hedges. Then nine out of every ten men dismounted, leaving one man to hold ten horses. They ran to the cover of the hedges and fired through them at Rupert's cavalry. The Royalists had seen the threat coming and fought back.

The first shots of the Battle of Naseby had been fired. Rupert's next move was almost certainly hastened by this scuffle on his right. His desire to get away from the irritating musket fire from behind the hedges propelled him forward.

Between ten and eleven o'clock the trumpets and drums on both sides sounded the advance and the troops moved forward, led by their colours. Fairfax did not want his men to abandon the high ground; they moved to just behind the brow of the hill. Some, however, must have been able to see their enemy because we are told that as they saw each other, both sides 'with mighty shoutes exprest a hearty desire of fighting'.

'The best and ablest men'

On the right wing Rupert led the advance himself. After escaping the disruptive fire of Colonel Okey's dragoons, he stopped and reorganized his horsemen. Then he gave the order to attack.

Prince Rupert's Royalist cavalry begin their charge.

Ireton's Parliamentarian horsemen advance to meet them.

them in any numbers to influence the growing struggle in the centre of the battlefield.

Infantry mêlée

Astley's men in the Royalist centre advanced as they saw Rupert's charge pressed home. They were the target of some Parliamentarian artillery fire, but its effect was minimal because the balls flew over the Royalist heads. The Roundhead infantry were still just behind the brow of the hill, and only became visible to the Royalists at the last minute as they toiled up the slope. With only 50 metres between the two sides, the Parliamentarians brought the three rear ranks alongside the forward three to fire one mighty volley. Thousands of matchcords were plunged into pans, and thousands of lead balls were sent tearing towards the Royalists.

This volley should have been devastating. But many of the raw recruits in the New Model Army had either gripped their muskets too lightly or aimed too high. Inexperienced troops tend to shoot high, and these men were no exception. The wind blew the acrid smoke back into the faces of the Roundheads. With no time to reload, they could only lower their pikes and wait for the Cavaliers.

The Royalist pikemen were tightly packed to create an impenetrable block, which advanced in unison to a drumbeat. Each pike had steel strips or 'cheeks' that ran back 60 centimetres from the top to prevent it getting hacked off. A wall of steel pikeheads coming towards the Roundheads must have turned the new recruits' stomachs to jelly, but they met it with their own massed lines of pikemen and managed to stand their ground. The Royalists launched a second attack. This time units of cavalry among the infantry made life even harder for the Roundheads. The infantry got close enough to hit out at each other. Many pikemen dropped their pikes and used swords instead, hacking and slashing in the confined spaces. Musketeers used their guns as giant clubs, cracking enemy skulls as they swung the butts.

BATTLE FACT

The demand for equipment was so acute during the Civil War that all manner of firearms were pressed into service. This resulted in so many different sizes of bore that some musketeers had to bite pieces off the bullets to make them fit the barrel.

Novice pikemen of the New Model Army await their first encounter with the more experienced Royalist forces.

'At push of pike': the moment the two infantry frontlines clashed in the centre. The Royalists soon had the advantage.

'Their foot in great disorder'

The slope the Roundheads were defending contained a dip where it was easier for the royal troops to attack. The shallow gully also had the effect of packing the Cavaliers into a fearsome wedge shape, which brought overwhelming force to bear on one section of the Parliamentarian line. The line buckled and collapsed. Sir Edward Walker, watching events from the Royalist side, 'saw their colours fall and their foot in great disorder'. Three Parliamentarian regiments – Waller's, Pickering's and Montague's – broke and ran.

At the height of this clash Major General Skippon was shot in the stomach, probably by one of his own musketeers. The wound was serious, but not mortal, and he stayed with his men. It was an act that prompted the Roundhead George Bishop to proclaim that Skippon was 'worthy to bee continually in the best thoughts of truest English'. Partly through his example, another of Skippon's regiments held its ground and suffered the worst casualties of any Roundhead unit. Its commander, Lieutenant Colonel Francis, his

lieutenant and his ensign were all wounded and later died of their injuries. It was a moment of crisis for the Parliamentarians. But the Royalists had gambled everything. They had thrown nearly every infantryman into the front line and were still so outnumbered that they had not even engaged the eastern flank of the Roundhead infantry. To remedy this disadvantage Prince Rupert's elite infantry regiment, the Bluecoats, were sent forward from the reserve in a bid to clinch the victory.

The Royalists' gamble seemed to be paying off. Astley's hardened veterans smashed through the Roundhead front line and bore down on the Parliamentarian reserves. From the evidence of musket balls recovered by archaeologists, it appears that both sides now fired volleys. The musketeers stood six deep in files. The front rank would fire and then march to the back to reload, the next rank would move forward and so on: the idea was to keep up a continuous fire. It was a difficult drill, and in past battles inexperienced troops in the second and third ranks had been known to shoot their own men standing in front of them. A drummer gave them the timing: the drum was the only noise that could be heard in the din of battle. All recruits had to learn six different drumbeats by heart.

As musket balls flew, the soldiers went through the rhythmical process of reloading their muskets. There was a lot to concentrate on: trying to keep the priming pan sheltered from the wind, keeping the match alight, drawing out charges that had not gone off, and cleaning the barrel. Meanwhile, the pikemen on either flank kept any stray horsemen away from their musketeers: their pikes formed a jagged hedge of steel.

The Roundhead infantry knew this was their last-ditch defence. To their front Astley's Royalist infantry were within metres of the Roundhead second line, with pikes levelled and muskets firing continuously. To their west Ireton's cavalry had been scattered. Parliament's foot soldiers were now fighting a desperate battle and, according to an eyewitness, the officers 'fell into the reserves with their colours, choosing rather there to fight and die, than to quit the ground they stood on'. What followed was the decisive moment of the Civil War.

BATTLE FACT

It was considered more gentlemanly to carry a pike into battle than a musket. Pikes had been used by the great armies of antiquity hundreds of years before. The newfangled muskets were rather looked down upon.

A musket volley. The front rank fires while the next rank reloads.

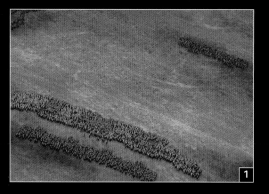

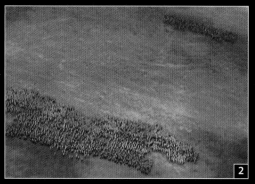

Crisis in the centre

1. With the entire Royalist infantry committed to the battle in the centre, the less experienced Parliamentarian foot soldiers are pressed back towards their own reserves (bottom left).

2. With their front line on the verge of collapse – and some units in flight – Parliament's three reserve infantry regiments are ordered into the fray.

The Ironsides

Oliver Cromwell sat on top of the ridge watching the king's cavalry units opposite him. He could not see the rout of the Parliamentarian left wing and the intense battle in the centre, but reports must have convinced him that the battle hung in the balance and that all would depend on the cavalry under his command. The horsemen opposite him, Marmaduke Langdale's, were slower to advance than the rest of the royal army. Eventually they set off, trotting towards Cromwell's men. Langdale's troopers were heavily outnumbered. Their commanders must have thought of Goring and his precious 3,000 Royalist horsemen in the West Country and cursed them for their absence. Nevertheless Langdale's cavalry valiantly charged up the incline, determined to match the success of their comrades on the other wing.

Cromwell ordered his first line forward at the trot. He had studied Rupert's tactics and knew how to tackle a Royalist cavalry charge. His Ironsides had routed their enemy in virtually every battle they had fought. To a man they were passionate believers in their cause. Fighting with the fury of crusaders, they were the best-equipped, best-disciplined and best-trained troops on the battlefield. They gripped their swords tight, stayed close to the men next to them and charged down the hill. Over months of practice the Ironsides had perfected the extremely difficult tactic of keeping their galloping horses in one solid mass. This battering ram now smashed into Langdale's cavalry.

The Cavaliers fought bravely – so bravely that the Ironsides suffered higher casualties than any other cavalry unit that day and we are told that one of their colonels 'had his coat cut in many peeces'. But Langdale was outnumbered two to one by the finest troops in Britain, and his men never stood a chance. A newspaper report told of how the Ironsides were 'like a torrent driving all before them'.

Unlike Rupert, Cromwell himself had not charged with his men. This was not because he lacked courage, but because he wanted to allocate reserves when and where they were needed most. With the enemy horsemen in retreat, he made two decisions that would now determine the course of the battle. He ordered no more than two regiments of his cavalry to chase Langdale's retreating horsemen and stop them rejoining the battle. Then he wheeled the rest of his men to the left to rescue the Roundhead infantry and the Parliamentarian cause.

Turning point

The infantry battle in the centre was still raging. Nearly every soldier on the battlefield was now committed. The outnumbered Royalists had thrown forward all their forces in their attempt to snatch victory from the Parliamentarians, and their plan looked close to success. Parliamentarian reserves were fighting a last-ditch battle against veteran royal infantry. For the king, victory appeared to be in sight. Then came the pounding of horses' hooves.

Cromwell's cavalry fell on the Royalist infantry in the centre. The men who bore the brunt of the attack were the infantry regiment of Bluecoats. They were slightly behind the Royalist front line and were now all that protected its flank and rear from the Roundhead cavalry. They stood bravely, 'like a wall of brasse' surrounded by swirling horsemen, who fired pistols and carbines into their blue ranks.

The Royalist pikemen stood in a ring so close together that we are told they were 'locking themselves one within another' to make an impenetrable wall of steel on all sides. As the cavalry surged around them, even the strongest pikemen must have been sweating, their muscles aching from holding the heavy pike at the required angle – the pikes had to be held horizontal at shoulder height because under them the musketeers fired volley after volley into the attackers. In the centre of the ring, men

BATTLE EXPERIENCE
Skill at arms

What made Cromwell's cavalry, the Ironsides, so outstanding was not just the ruthless discipline of their formation. It was the skill with which they handled their weapons as they charged into the ranks of the enemy. In those hectic moments everything depended on deft control of their sword arms. We were given a day's training by the army's Saddle Club at Larkhill in Wiltshire where they practise skill at arms by using motorbikes as well as horses. Melons on stakes were our targets, cavalry swords our weapons and motorbikes our mounts. There was no need for wild swordplay – the momentum of the charge was sufficient to slash the melon in two. As long as we held the sword steady in the hand, with a keen eye on the line to take to the centre of the target, we cleft the melon cleanly in two. The effect of the Ironsides' meticulous training was to perfect the art of making every stroke of the sword count – with lethal effect.

called ensigns held the regimental colours.

Fairfax, the overall Parliamentarian commander, had been in the thick of the fighting all day, encouraging his troops by his own example. Like all great generals, he had a knack of being present at the point of crisis, and he arrived here now, without his helmet, which had been knocked off in an earlier scuffle. He ordered his personal Lifeguards to charge the Bluecoats from the front while he took men round to the rear and cut his way into their ranks. This charge finally broke the Bluecoats, and Fairfax killed an ensign. Before he could pick up the colours, a trooper from his Lifeguard snatched it and claimed that he had killed the ensign and captured the colours. An officer moved to discipline him for this 'boasting and lying', but Fairfax intervened and told the officer to leave the trooper alone. He said, 'I have honour enough, let him take that for himself.'

Just as Cromwell's cavalry crashed into the Royalist foot soldiers, the Parliamentarian infantry was staging a rally. Even men who had run away were shepherded back into battle by their officers, while other units no doubt took

courage from the sight of Cromwell's horsemen riding to their aid. The Royalist army slid from the brink of victory towards defeat.

The king was still at the back with his reserves. Seeing the battle swinging decisively against him, he must have prayed that Rupert would return to the field before all was lost. But he did not. Many Royalist units were surrounded. Some surrendered, some fought to the end. We are told that Irish Catholic troops, who faced hanging if captured, 'chose to die in the field'. Musket balls have been found stretching back across the meadows marking the line of retreat. A particularly large concentration on some high ground behind the Royalist army's original position suggests a valiant last stand. But the battle was lost, and further resistance was futile.

The king watched the collapse with what was left of his horsemen. Lord Carnwath dissuaded him from making one last suicidal charge, grabbing the king's bridle and shouting, 'Would you go upon your death?' The king had no choice but to flee the field. Fairfax's forces chased the king's army relentlessly. 'Happy was he that was best mounted,' wrote a survivor.

1. Cromwell's Ironsides have routed Langdale's Royalist cavalry, and he now wheels most of his horsemen to the left – sending only two of his regiments in pursuit of the fleeing Cavaliers.

2. The Ironsides bear down on the exposed flank of the Royalist infantry in the centre.

3. The Royalist foot soldiers (centre), on the verge of victory, reel under the shock of Cromwell's onslaught (right).

Royalist humiliation

The Parliamentarians captured the entire Royalist baggage train. Of the hundreds of women who had been following the army, some were killed and others had their faces slashed. There was chaos as baggage was looted and fought over. Coins are still found on the spot today.

The king's correspondence was captured, and found to contain highly damaging revelations about his promises to the Irish and French in return for support. But that was not the severest damage to his cause. From a force of up to 12,500 Royalists, fewer than 4,000, some severely wounded, were to reach safety. The king's army had been destroyed. Naseby was not the last battle of the Civil War, but it was the beginning of the end. Never again would Charles command an army of the quality of the one that nearly triumphed in June 1645.

After the battle Royalist prisoners claimed that the Parliamentarians would have lost the day if it had not been for Cromwell's horsemen. This may well be so. But it was more the fault of Rupert, who had risked all on smashing the Parliamentarian left and centre. His gamble failed

Cromwell's cavalry surround the beleaguered Bluecoat regiment. The elite Royalist unit makes its last stand fighting in a tight square.

and Langdale did not have enough horsemen to deal with Cromwell. Rupert has been blamed for being hot-headed and not keeping control of his men, as Cromwell did: his critics argue that he should have reined them in and swung them against the Parliamentarian centre rather than let them gallop off and attack the baggage train. In his defence, restraining his horsemen in full

Musketeers at sunset. The Civil War went on for some time after Naseby, but the Royalists lost so much in this battle that they never recovered. The New Model Army had come of age.

The execution of Charles I. The king wore two shirts to shield him from the cold in case he appeared to shiver from fear.

charge would have been a nearly impossible talk. But Rupert's defeat was also due to the fact that, because he was outnumbered, he was forced to commit all his reserves from the start and had nothing left to counter the Parliamentarians with when they threw in their reserves later.

The Cavaliers had underestimated the New Model Army. It had more experience than its name suggested, and its infantry did not break at the critical point but stood bravely under heavy pressure. Fairfax, Cromwell and Skippon had shown personal bravery, strategic judgement, imagination and, when it counted, restraint. Above all, their New Model Army had entirely vindicated the time and effort put into its training.

Within a year of Naseby, Parliament had completed its victory and Charles was a prisoner. In 1649 he was tried for treason in Westminster Hall, condemned to death and beheaded. The country became a republic and Oliver Cromwell its head of state.

The monarchy was eventually restored, but the war had changed Britain for ever. No future ruler would dare take arms against Parliament again.

1690: THE BATTLE OF THE BOYNE

No battle in British history has cast such a long shadow over the centuries as the Battle of the Boyne. It was a ferocious struggle between two kings that ended in triumph and immortality for one, defeat and disgrace for the other. For several hours on 12 July 1690 tens of thousands of men scrambled shoulder-deep through a fast-flowing river under point-blank musket fire. Minutes after the first order to advance into the water, the river ran red with blood. And by the end of the day the fury of the fight had earned the Boyne its haunting place in history. It had a lasting impact on the people of Britain and Ireland, and it still has echoes in the religious tension that persists in Northern Ireland today.

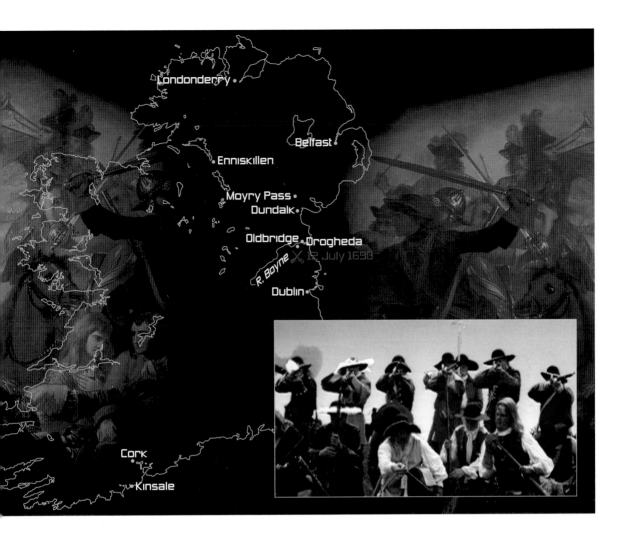

In the folk memories of many of Northern Ireland's Protestants King Billy, the Protestant hero, was out to crush a rebellion that would have subjected Ireland and the rest of Britain to the Church of Rome for ever. But the Battle of the Boyne was part of a much wider conflict. King Billy was William III, and his opponent was James II, the last of the Stuart kings. James was fighting to reclaim the British crown, which William had seized from him two years earlier. And James had the support of the most ambitious ruler in Europe, the Catholic king of France, Louis XIV, whose expanding empire threatened Britain and his other neighbours.

Much, then, was at stake as the two armies, one Protestant, one Catholic, lined up on either side of a river that cuts through the heart of Ireland. It was to be the last time two men crowned king of England were to face each other in battle, and the result would do much to decide the shape of Britain's politics and faith to this day.

James – the Catholic champion

It was an extraordinary chain of events that led to the battle on the river Boyne. Until two years earlier Britain had been through nearly a century of erratic rule by the Stuart family. James II had succeeded his brother Charles II to the throne in 1685.

JAMES II

An unprepossessing fellow, James displayed those louche Stuart features that betrayed a weak and feckless character. Like his dynastic predecessors, he was devoid of any measure of political wisdom that might have given him a respected role in the running of the country. But he was no coward: he had a stout record of fighting in battles on the Continent.

James II. In his short reign (1685–8) James succeeded in becoming one of Britain's most unpopular monarchs.

He had one fierce passion that caused deep anxiety to Britain's ruling class: late in life he had become a fervent Catholic, and was determined to restore the influence and, if possible, the predominance of that faith.

Britain was overwhelmingly Protestant by the end of the seventeenth century, but now here was a king resolved to turn the religious balance of power upside down by promoting the few remaining Catholics to all the top jobs – judges, army commanders, the higher echelons of government. Britain's Protestants became increasingly alarmed with their new king. To them Catholicism meant one thing: control by a foreign pope and domination by France, the leading Catholic power in Europe. Their only consolation was that James was getting old and had no male heir. When he died the crown would pass to his daughter, Mary, who was – to the relief of most people – a Protestant.

But then came the bombshell that would plunge the country into crisis and Ireland into war. In 1688 James announced with delight that his second wife, Mary of Modena, was pregnant. A few months later the Protestants heard the news they were dreading: the queen had given birth to a baby boy. And with the insensitivity that was often a Stuart hallmark, James proudly declared that the child would be baptized a Catholic and that the pope had agreed to be the child's godfather.

William, the Protestant superhero

It was the last straw for Britain's Protestant establishment, which was already seeing its hold on power diluted by James's promotion of Catholics. It took drastic action to stop this new Catholic dynasty from becoming entrenched. In June 1688 seven Protestant politicians sent a letter to William, Prince of Orange – the Dutch hero of Protestant Europe and husband of James's daughter Mary – inviting him to secure Britain for the Protestants. He jumped at the chance. On 5 November 1688 he landed at Torbay in Devon with a force of 10,000 men and headed for London.

Almost overnight James's reign collapsed. His troops defected and he himself fled. Parliament declared that he had abdicated and

William III ruled for 13 years, from 1689 to 1702, after deposing James, who was his uncle – and father-in-law.

WILLIAM III

William was 38 years old at the time of the Battle of the Boyne. Despite his heroic image in parts of Northern Ireland today, he was short and hunch-backed, pockmarked and asthmatic. There were also rumours of homosexuality. But he was a respected and popular military commander, and therefore the ideal champion for England's Protestants. Previously he had been fighting to protect his small country, the Netherlands, against Louis XIV's expansionist France.

that his daughter Mary should be queen. William, however, demanded the throne himself. Two months later William and Mary were crowned king and queen. It looked like the end of the Stuart dynasty, and the triumph of the Protestant House of Orange.

James fights back

But James was not finished. He crossed to France and sought the help of the man who represented everything William hated, Louis XIV. Louis welcomed the opportunity to unsettle his rival, and was quick to provide James with a force of French infantry and cavalry. James's fight to reclaim the British throne was about to begin. But the battlefield would not be in England; it would be in Ireland.

James was no convert to Irish nationalism, no champion of Irish rights; he saw Ireland merely as the back door to the restoration of his power in

Louis XIV, king of France from 1643 to 1715. Louis spent a lifetime fighting for French supremacy in Europe. His megalomania helped make Ireland a battlefield too.

James and his French allies land at Kinsale. He marched from here to Dublin unopposed.

Britain. His plan was to use Ireland and its predominantly Catholic population as his base. With 22 ships and 2,000 elite French troops under General Lauzun, James landed at Kinsale on Ireland's southern coast on 12 March 1689 and was greeted, in his own words, 'with all imaginable joy by his loyal Catholic subjects'. Among them was Lord Tyrconnell, the Catholic lord lieutenant of Ireland, whom James himself had appointed when he was still king.

The siege of Londonderry
But Ireland was not his for the taking. Much of the country was indeed Catholic, and over most of the island James was greeted with enthusiasm; in the north, however, the news of his arrival had a mixed reception. A resolute and growing group of Protestant settlers had been planted there over the previous century. New arrivals in a Catholic country, they had developed a fortress mentality, and erected a set of strongholds called 'bawns' from where they expanded their hold on the best land. They were determined to protect their livelihoods – and their faith – and in the previous year they had made a bold stand in defiance of James and his Catholic supporters, known as Jacobites from *Jacobus*, Latin for James. It was a clash that would pass into Irish folk memory and would lead inexorably to the battle

between the two kings on the river Boyne.

A regiment of Catholics, the famous Red Shanks – so called because their lower legs were often red after wading through many a freezing river – was sent to replace the garrison of the city of Londonderry (originally Derry, it had been renamed by the settlers). But a group of young Protestant apprentices took the law into their own hands and slammed the gates of the city shut. Shortly after his arrival in Ireland, James rode up to the gates of the city in person and demanded its surrender. The response was a fusillade that killed two of his companions. James immediately began a siege that lasted more than 100 days. He ordered a boom of logs to be stretched across the river Foyle to stop any supply ships reaching the beleaguered garrison, and the Protestant defenders became so desperate that they began eating dogs that had been fed on the human remains of attackers killed outside the walls.

William to the rescue

In London King William was so impressed by the resistance of the Protestant people of Londonderry that he sent a fleet of ships to break the boom on the river Foyle. Supplies poured in, Londonderry survived and Protestants still celebrate the lifting of the siege. It was a serious reverse for James.

Jacobite cannon bombard the Protestant stronghold of Londonderry from Windmill Hill.

The city's walls, which are still visible today, were stoutly defended.

The siege of Londonderry. News of the city's determined resistance had a powerful impact on Protestant opinion in the rest of Britain and Europe.

The Duke of Schomberg. A Dutch mercenary who had fought for Portugal and France, he switched allegiance to William when Louis XIV forced Protestants out of his army.

William decided to send an army to Belfast to put an end to James's Jacobite rebellion once and for all. The man he put in command was a fellow Dutchman, the 73-year-old Duke of Schomberg, a veteran of military campaigns all over Europe.

BATTLE FACT

James had trouble equipping his new army in Ireland. He was so desperate that his wife, Mary of Modena, pawned her jewellery to buy 2,000 flintlock muskets.

Schomberg landed in July 1689, but conducted a lacklustre campaign which failed to bring James to battle. His army was hit by disease and desertion, and by autumn his mission had run into the ground.

William was so exasperated at Schomberg's failure that the following June he crossed the Irish Sea himself with a large fleet and reinforcements that he hoped would match any force James could put together. His army was composed of a remarkable mixture of nationalities: his own Dutch Guards, several battalions of Danes, a large force of Huguenots – French Protestants bitterly opposed to Louis XIV and his ally James – and English troops, many of them commanded by trusty foreigners hotfoot from William's Continental campaigns against Louis. King William was so angry at what he saw as Schomberg's dithering and lack of spirit that, when he landed, he swept straight past his army commander. William said he was determined not to 'let the grass grow' under his feet, and within days he and his forces were marching south. Along the route reinforcements joined him from Protestant strongholds, such as Londonderry and Enniskillen.

James's strategy was to hold as much of Ireland as he could. He had to settle on a line of defence north of the capital, Dublin, and his first choice was the chain of mountains that run along today's border between north and south, just above Dundalk. He marched his army to Dundalk and his troops ambushed an advance party of William's army moving through the Moyry Pass. A few hundred Jacobites pounced, killed some of William's men and captured a Captain Farlowe. The prisoner told his captors a deliberate lie – that William had a huge army of 50,000 troops marching on James. When James heard further intelligence that William had sent another force around to the west to outflank the Jacobites, he decided to retreat. But where to? There was only one other obvious line of defence north of Dublin: the river Boyne.

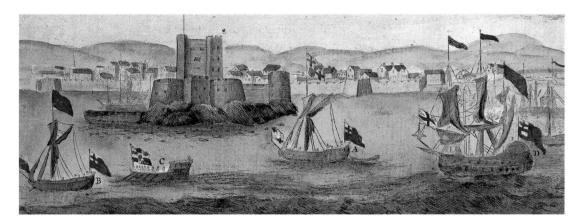

William landing at Carrickfergus in Belfast Lough on 14 June 1690.

To the banks of the Boyne

The Boyne flows out to the sea 50 kilometres
north of Dublin: on the face of it a natural barrier,
a formidable defensive position. It is a fast-
flowing, wide river with hills rising up on both
banks. James crossed it on 29 June and decided to
concentrate almost his entire force on the south
bank around the tiny village of Oldbridge, 8 kilometres from the sea, where the river was shallow
enough for an enemy to ford. Lauzun and some of
James's other commanders pointed out that the
river was fordable elsewhere too: they advised him
not to do battle on the Boyne, saying it could be
crossed in many places. But James reckoned it the
only defensible line north of Dublin, and he was
determined not to give up more ground than he
had to. He was the king, not a guerrilla
commander; he would defeat these Protestant
rebels and protect his capital, Dublin. He would
fight his battle to reclaim the throne on the banks
of the Boyne.

On the slopes behind his infantry James placed
his crack cavalry from Ireland and France, lent to
him by King Louis. There was another ford across
the river – at Rosnaree, 6 kilometres west of
Oldbridge. In case William tried to cross the
Boyne there, James sent a detachment of 800 men
to guard it. That same evening, William and his

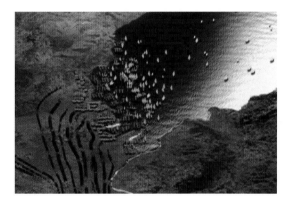

William's army disembarks in Belfast Lough and moves south.

As William heads south, he is joined by reinforcements from
other Protestant strongholds.

James's troops take up position on the south bank of the river Boyne in and around the village of Oldbridge.

advance guard arrived on a hill north of the Boyne near Drogheda and took in the situation at a glance. He could see James's army encamped on the south bank around Oldbridge, and ordered his commander to set up camp opposite Oldbridge on the north bank but well back from the river.

James had around 29,000 men; William had 36,000. William had the more professional, seasoned force. Discipline was tight – with all those different nationalities, it had to be.

Two Danes were shot for mutiny; soldiers were hanged for deserting; and any looting from civilians was severely punished.

Religion underpinned both sides. James's was largely a Catholic army, and he was dismayed when he found out that some of the troops Louis had sent him were German Protestants. Many of William's men had first-hand experience of the bitter religious war in Europe and hated Catholics. When one Frenchman in a Huguenot regiment was seen praying with rosary beads he was immediately shot by a Danish soldier.

William's Danes and his prized Dutch Guards were armed with the new flintlock muskets and revolutionary new weapons called grenades. But most of James's army, like his father's at Naseby, depended on the old matchlock muskets. Many of his troops did not even have these and some Jacobite regiments were armed only with scythes and clubs. In March 1690 Tyrconnell complained that powder was in such short supply that two-thirds of his men had never fired a shot, and he lacked 20,000 muskets. The Frenchmen's weapons were in poor repair, too, because Louis' minister of war had never approved of his king's enthusiasm for the expedition.

James was also very short of artillery. His weakness in cannon had been one reason for his failure at Londonderry. He had 16 field guns at the Boyne and he regarded them as so precious that he sent most of them back to Dublin rather than risk them falling into William's hands. This left William with more big guns on the banks of the Boyne by the time battle was joined.

One striking characteristic of both armies was how difficult it was to tell them apart. Each camp was a great palette of many colours, each regiment on either side had its own uniform, each officer his own personal attire. Units often looked more like troops on the other side than their own. The only way to distinguish friend from foe was to wear some sort of emblem in their hats. The Williamites were told to wear a sprig of green, the colour of the Dutch and their Spanish allies; the Jacobites wore the traditional French white cockade. It was not always enough, as the next day's battle was to prove.

A close shave

There was no doubt that William's biggest challenge would be to cross the river quickly and in force while under fire. The day before the battle he arrived to reconnoitre the riverbank himself, only 50 metres or so across the Boyne from the Jacobite front line in the village of Oldbridge. From where he stood, he could have been in no doubt that James, with his infantry all along the south bank, was in a powerful position. But he was also convinced that this spot, where the river was fordable, was the place to make his assault.

You might have expected William to waste no time loitering in that exposed spot. But, ignoring the danger, he decided to sit down with his

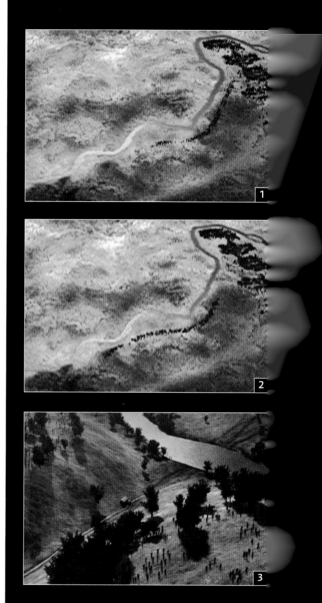

James's defence

1. The majority of James's army masses on the south side of the Oldbridge bend.
2. He despatches 800 men southwest on a 6-kilometre march (moving towards bottom left) to guard the ford at Rosnaree.
3. They arrive and prepare to defend the steep slopes on the south side of the ford at Rosnaree.

commanders and take some refreshment. He was spotted by some Jacobites on the opposite bank. They quietly hauled up a couple of cannon and, after waiting for William to make himself even more visible by leaping up on to his horse – in full uniform, which he had a reckless habit of wearing wherever he went – they loosed off two shots at him. One hit the riverbank, bounced up and was seen to hit the king. A wave of excitement swept around the Jacobite camp: they thought William was dead, and there was great cheering and shouting. But the cannon ball had only grazed his right shoulder. He had the wound dressed, and joked that it might have come a lot nearer. That evening he rode around his camp with his arm in a sling, chatting to his men and reassuring them that he was fit and ready for battle the next day. He even had a portable wooden house carried about so he could sleep amongst them. He was, for a relatively dour man, a canny commander, who knew that leadership depended on being visible and in touch with his men. They respected him for it.

As for James, on the opposite side of the river, he was doing no such morale-boosting – he lacked the personality to give his men confidence in his leadership. He had been quick to leave the riverbank and retire up the hill at the first cannon shots from the other side. Moreover, he had no bold plan: his overall strategy was to wait and see what William's first move would be.

William's battleplan

That evening, William called a council of war at Mellifont Abbey in the woods north of the Boyne. He asked his commanders how they would recommend tackling James's forces. Opinion was split. First, from the old warrior Schomberg, came the recommendation not to plunge straight across at Oldbridge where James was heavily entrenched, but to divert west to Rosnaree, cross the river there and march against James's left flank. Crossing at Oldbridge was urged by the Dutch general Count Solmes. William preferred the latter option: it was more daring, and he wanted to snub Schomberg after his handling of the last year of campaigning. But he could see Oldbridge was riskier, and he settled for a compromise. He would keep most of his army at Oldbridge, but would send a sizeable force under Schomberg's son to make an early crossing at Rosnaree.

That night soldiers on both sides quietly prepared themselves for the battle ahead. Fortunately, it had been one of the hottest months on record, so the men could bed down under the stars; the luckiest ones found straw to make themselves more comfortable. But before they could sleep there was important work to do. On the march down to the Boyne they had stripped lead from everything they could lay their hands on. Now they melted it down to make musket balls. Then they prepared cartridges: rolls of paper into which they poured gunpowder. The paper was folded down until the bullet was needed in the heat of battle. It was then that the soldiers would draw the bullets from their bandolier and bite off the top of the paper cartridge to release the gunpowder.

The ford at Rosnaree

Early the next morning there was great bustle in the Williamite camp on the north side of the river. It was foggy at 5 a.m., and through the gloom James's sentries on the southern bank could hear a noise. It was troops on the move. To some of the

Jacobite sentries it sounded like an entire army. The news was reported to James: the Williamites were moving westwards towards Rosnaree. What was he to do? Was William planning his main attack across the river at Oldbridge or at Rosnaree? If the latter, James had planted only 800 men there. He risked being outflanked and cut off from the road to Dublin behind him.

He made a bold decision: he would lead the bulk of his army to Rosnaree and leave a smaller force under Tyrconnell to defend Oldbridge. Off he went with more than half of his troops, including his most seasoned soldiers, the French infantry, to stop what he thought was William's main attack at Rosnaree. He knew he was racing against time to reach the ford before the enemy could cross.

The 800 Jacobites already at Rosnaree felt they were in a strong position to hold the crossing until reinforcements arrived. True, they had only three small field guns on the surrounding slopes, but they had taken up a very strong defensive position and were led by a commander said to have the heart of a lion – Sir Neill O'Neill. His men were devoted to him, and their task was to hold off the Williamites until James's reinforcements arrived from Oldbridge. Their combined force should be enough to stop William's men from crossing the Boyne.

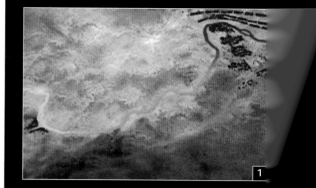

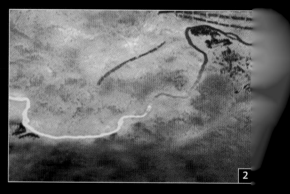

William's attack

1. On 30 June William concentrates his army (top right) just north of the Oldbridge bend.
2. At dawn the following morning he sends 10,000 men southwest (centre) to force a crossing of the Boyne at Rosnaree (bottom left).

The heavy tramp of the Williamite column marching to Rosnaree tricked the Jacobites into believing William's entire army was on the move.

View of the Boyne at Rosnaree from the top of the steep slope on the south side of the river.

The Williamites cross the ford at Rosnaree, where they have the Jacobites (bottom) massively outnumbered.

Some time before 8 a.m., William's troops reached Rosnaree and prepared to cross. Although under fire from O'Neill's cannon, they massively outnumbered his men: old Schomberg's son, Count Meinhard Schomberg, had a force of 10,000 infantry and cavalry. The first men ordered into the water were the Dutch dragoons – elite mounted infantry. The moment they were in the river they came under concentrated musket fire from the Jacobites. Even for such battle-hardened troops, it must have been a fearful ordeal: they had to spur their horses through the current, keeping their weapons and powder as dry as they could. And when they reached the other side they had to fight their way up a muddy bank before they had any chance to load their muskets and fire back.

Gradually the determination of those crack units at the front and the sheer weight of the infantry that followed forced O'Neill's men back. They were driven up a heavily defended defile that led from the water's edge to higher ground. At the height of the battle for the ford at Rosnaree O'Neill himself – fighting valiantly and exposing himself to enemy fire as much as any of his men – was shot through the thigh. Suffering huge loss of blood, he was carried away from the fighting and died a week later. Without the continued inspiration of his energetic leadership that day,

his men lost heart, and the ford at Rosnaree was in Williamite hands before James's reinforcements could arrive.

Stand-off at Roughgrange

After trudging 5 kilometres through the hills, and long before they were anywhere near O'Neill and his beleaguered force, the Jacobite reinforcements found themselves on the edge of a boggy ravine called Roughgrange that cut straight across their front. On the other side they saw the Williamites, who had advanced along the south bank after their successful crossing at Rosnaree. Both armies were anxious to get to grips with each other, but this gully was to prove an insuperable obstacle. James and his French commander, Lauzun, on the one side, and Meinhard Schomberg on the other, knew that whichever army attacked across the boggy bottom of the ravine risked losing all. And so these two forces, not more than a few hundred metres apart, could only glare across at each other.

Suddenly a messenger ran up and told James the horrifying news that the main Williamite

Opposite: Sir Neill O'Neill, the Jacobite commander who made a courageous attempt to defend the ford at Rosnaree. He was a Gaelic chieftain and dressed not in a colonel's uniform but in his traditional robes.

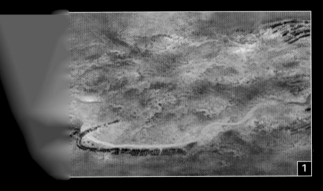

Roughgrange

1. The Williamites, having forced their way across the ford at Rosnaree (bottom left), march east to confront James, who is moving a large force (bottom right) to meet them.
2. The Williamites (top left) arrive at the ravine at Roughgrange, where they can only glare at the Jacobite army (bottom right) on the other side.
3. The ravine at Roughgrange today. The boggy ground made battle impossible.

attack had now begun at Oldbridge, where James had left only a fraction of his army. The Battle of the Boyne had started in earnest, and James and the best of his infantry regiments were not even there. They had wrongly interpreted the movements they had heard at dawn, believing that William had taken his main force to Rosnaree. Perhaps if Meinhard Schomberg's sweep to the west had led to a decisive breakthrough, William would have exploited the opportunity and perhaps reinforced it, but it had always been intended to distract attention from the main advance at Oldbridge. And it had worked better than he could ever have hoped. But even so, the main encounter was to be fiercely fought by both sides.

The Oldbridge crossing

James had left barely 6,000 foot soldiers and only three regiments of cavalry at Oldbridge. William, on the other hand, had 25,000 men there. For two hours William's cannon pounded the village. At around ten o'clock the troops who were to form the first wave of his assault emerged from a wooded ravine on the north side of the river – still called King William's Glen today – and plunged into the river. They were William's prized Dutch Guards – dressed in splendid blue uniforms, and singing the now legendary song 'Lilliburlero' accompanied by their fifes and drums. It had been written only months earlier to make fun of James's lord lieutenant in Ireland, Lord Tyrconnell, whom James had left in command at Oldbridge. Two thousand of them waded in eight to ten abreast, almost damming the Boyne as they crossed it in their tight ranks. William had timed their crossing to catch the tide at its lowest, but the water still rose almost to their chests. The current was swirling past them, and the bottom was an unstable mixture of mud and stones. The Guards had to struggle to keep their footing, and all the time they had to hold their muskets and their powder pouches above their heads to keep them dry.

Suddenly, as the Guards reached the middle of the stream, volley after volley of shots rang out from the other side. The Jacobites facing them at Oldbridge were two of James's Irish infantry regiments, Antrim's and Clanrickard's, and they had the cover of the houses, trees and hedges along the riverbank. Their shooting was not very effective because they were inexperienced and poorly trained: they tended, as beginners do, to let the muzzles of their muskets bounce up when they were fired, making their shots go too high. Only one or two Dutch Guards were seen to stagger and fall in the water.

The first Jacobite to meet the Guards face to face was a Major Arthur Ashton, who ran forward and plunged his pike into one of the first officers to climb up out of the water. But Ashton himself was despatched by the dead man's comrades a moment later. The first Dutchmen across were the grenadiers, each armed with a new weapon that was to transform infantry tactics. The grenadiers were some of the fittest and ablest men in William's army, each carrying three of the new grenades. These prototypes of the weapons that have become essential to every infantryman today consisted of a lethal canister of gunpowder, cased in iron, wood or ceramic material, which was ignited by a slow fuse lit just before it was thrown.

The Guards scrambled out of the river, formed two ranks on the bank, and, with the help of their artillery on the north bank, slowly pushed the defenders, whom they heavily out-numbered, out of the village and on to the high ground behind Oldbridge. This gave the Williamites a vital foothold on the grassy meadows on the southern banks of the Boyne. A hundred Dutchmen had died in this first fierce confrontation; in return they had killed 150 of the Irish infantry. However, the Guards' struggle had only just begun. They might have made the infantry retreat, but they now faced attack by the pride of James's army: his cavalry.

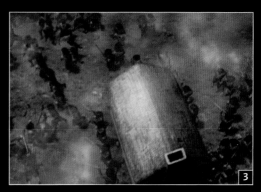

Oldbridge

1. The first wave of William's troops, the Dutch Guards, plunge into the Boyne and fight their way out of the river.
2. The Jacobites prepare to attempt to hold them back, taking cover in and around the buildings at Oldbridge.
3. The Dutch Guards flush the Irish infantry out of Oldbridge. William has his first foothold on the south bank.

Cavalry charge

1. The Jacobite cavalry, under the command of the Duke of Berwick, charge at the Dutch Guards, who have quickly formed up on the south bank of the river.
2. The Jacobite horses shy away from the rows of Williamite bayonets facing their charge.
3. The Williamite infantry form tight lines and squares to resist the Jacobite cavalry.

Berwick's cavalry

Most of these horsemen, like William's best veterans, had fought in many battles on the Continent. They were led by some of the best cavalry officers in Europe, two of them bastard sons of James himself. James Fitzjames, Duke of Berwick, James's illegitimate son by Lady Arabella Churchill, led 1,000 horses in the charge. He had a considerable reputation as a soldier – much like his cousin, the Duke of Marlborough – and was, at 19, the youngest cavalry general of the day. At his side was his 17-year-old brother, Henry Fitzjames. Their assault on the Guards had William watching anxiously from the other side of the river. Three times he was heard to say, 'My poor Guards.'

But the elite Dutch troops lived up to their reputation. One observer gave a vivid description of their resistance:

> *At the first push the first rank only fired and then fell on their faces, loading their muskets again as they lay on the ground; at the next charge they fired a volley of three ranks; then at the next the first rank got up and fired again, which being received by a choice squadron of the enemy, consisting mostly of officers, they immediately fell upon the Dutch as having spent all their front fire; but the two rear ranks drew up in two platoons and flanked the enemy across and the rest screwing their swords into their muskets received the charge with all imaginable bravery and for a minute dismounted them all.*

The 'swords' referred to here confirm that the Dutch Guards were at the forefront in the evolution of infantry tactics: they were using bayonets that would soon completely replace long, cumbersome pikes. Used by disciplined troops, they were to prove the most effective way of deploying a line of steel points to frighten off charging horses.

The Guards were among the best, if not *the* best troops in Europe, but William said that he had never seen infantry do what his men had done

The ford at Oldbridge today. This was the point William's Dutch Guards had to struggle across to reach the south bank.

that day. He breathed a huge sigh of relief at their successful defence of the bridgehead, but he knew that he had to take the pressure off them by putting more troops across the river.

'A la gloire!'

To widen the front William ordered a second crossing slightly downstream from Oldbridge, at Grove Island. This time he ordered his French Huguenots, together with his Protestant Irish and English infantrymen, across the river. Their assault led to fighting even fiercer than the struggle still going on at Oldbridge.

They were met by Jacobite Irish infantry, who soon broke. Their commander, General Hamilton, found himself abandoned in midstream and, waving his sword, begged his men to stand firm. In desperation, he rallied some nearby cavalry and led them against the four regiments of Williamite troops to drive them back into the river.

There was a fierce fight for half an hour, during which nothing could be seen but smoke and dust, and nothing heard but continual firing. This was the bloodiest fighting in the battle and resulted in the most severe Williamite casualties in the whole Irish war. Suicidally brave Jacobite cavalrymen charged into the river and slashed at the terrified infantry. It was a critical moment. The two

Huguenot regiments were stalled midstream and nearly broke. Unlike the Dutch, they were not armed with bayonets and had little effective protection against the ferocious cavalry charges. A regimental commander, Colonel de la Caillemotte, was mortally wounded. He was carried back to the north bank shouting: '*A la gloire, mes enfants, à la gloire!*' – 'To glory, my children, to glory!'

William's commander-in-chief himself, the Duke of Schomberg, charged into the river on his horse, drew his sword and bellowed at the Huguenot troops, reminding them of their suffering at the hands of the French Catholics: '*Allons, Messieurs, voilà vos persécuteurs!*' – 'Come on, men, there are your persecutors!' The appeal worked and they rallied. On the other side the tireless Jacobite cavalry were utterly fearless in

BATTLE FACT

Cannon could fire 15 rounds an hour. But when the barrels got too hot to touch, the rate of fire had to be reduced to 10 an hour, otherwise the barrels would explode.

 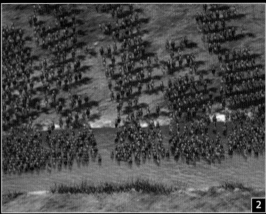

The Duke of Schomberg is fatally wounded at a critical phase of the battle. Jacobite cavalry attacks are threatening to drive the Williamites back into the Boyne.

1. Anxious to widen his front, William orders his English
   and Huguenot troops to cross Grove Island in a second
   crossing (left), and the Danes to make a third crossing
   a few hundred yards further east (right). Jacobite
   cavalry (bottom) race to defend the south bank.

2. The Danes cross the river successfully but they still
   have to face the cavalry.

3. Both crossings are met by ferocious cavalry
   counter-attacks.

their determination to destroy this second crossing.
Berwick's horse was killed under him. A trooper
swept him off to safety, and Berwick was soon
back on a new horse at the head of his men. One
cavalry commander, John Parker, led 400 men in
a charge at the Williamite bridgehead and only 40
survived unscathed; Parker himself was seriously
wounded but survived.

An old warrior's death

Old Schomberg was less lucky. Slashed by a Jacobite
cavalryman's sword twice and then shot through the
neck, he fell and died instantly. The old warhorse
whom William had sent to subdue Ireland the year
before, and whose campaign had so disappointed his
master, was dead. William did not say a word when
he was told the news, but laid a finger on his lip to
make a sign to the messenger not to let the word get
around and dismay his troops. His commander's
death and the fierce resistance met by the troops in
the second crossing confirmed William's judgement
that the battle was far from won.

At 11 o'clock, an hour after the first crossing at
Oldbridge, William ordered the Danes across in a
third crossing. Twelve thousand of them – carrying

their general, the Duke of Württemberg, on their
shoulders – waded across to extend the front even
further. The tide had now turned: the water was up
to their armpits and even, at one stage, up to their
necks. It was touch and go … If the Danes made
it across, they would still have a steep hill to climb
and the fearsome Jacobite cavalry to face.

The infantry defending the bank against them
quickly turned and fled, but the Jacobite cavalry
attacked, and the troops in this third crossing were
soon in a savage struggle to establish a foothold.
Eyewitnesses on William's side heaped superlatives
on the Jacobite cavalry: the resistance they put
up that day became legendary. William now determined to strike his final blow.

King Billy into the fray

The fact was that, after four hours of fierce
fighting, his original plan had stalled: the
Jacobites still had his men pinned down only
metres from the riverbank at all the crossing
points. He now hoped a fourth and final crossing
further downstream would stretch the Jacobite
line to breaking point. Before the battle he had
promised to be 'among the thickest of them'.

BATTLE EXPERIENCE
Fording the Boyne

Dan was given the task of wading across the river Boyne to test what the crossing must have been like for King William's soldiers. Peter gave Dan the end of a strong rope to tie himself to – for safety's sake, in case the current swept him away – and a sack of dry sand to represent the powder pouch every soldier had to carry across. He would have to hold it well above his head to prevent it getting wet.

Dan is nearly 2 metres tall, probably a full 30 centimetres taller than the average solder at the Boyne, but he still had quite a struggle to cross the swift-flowing river with that bag above his head. On 12 July 1690 he would have had to lug not just the powder but an 11-kilogram musket as well, and he would have had to keep both dry.

The rock, loose stones and mud of the river bed made Dan's footing very uncertain, but he managed to scramble across the stream without going under. Peter emptied Dan's sack of sand and found it dry. So the Boyne is fordable today, and you can still keep your powder dry wading across it. But imagine if you were a lot shorter than Dan and under deadly fire from the opposite bank.

Dan crossed at Rosnaree, the site of the first crossing of the river on the day of the battle. We checked the remaining crossing points as well – Oldbridge, and the others further east – and it is clear that you could still ford the river at all these places today.

King William III leads his forces in the fourth and final attack across the river Boyne.

The previous day he had been reckless in exposing himself to the enemy's cannon fire. Now he was to show real leadership and bravery at the pivotal moment of the battle and lead the crossing himself. Once again, he made no attempt to disguise who he was: the decorative star and garter he wore on his chest marked him out clearly to anyone within eyesight. His shoulder wound did not appear to bother him, but he could not wear his customary breast plate and at one stage he was forced to hold his sword in his left hand.

Just after noon William led his Dutch, Danish and English cavalry down to the riverside. He had chosen the most difficult place to cross, where the banks were deep and muddy. It was to be a tough ordeal for a slight, asthmatic man with a shoulder

wound. William was an accomplished horseman, but getting across the Boyne proved too much for him. His horse got stuck in the mud, and when he tried to free himself it brought on an attack of asthma. One of his men, a sturdy soldier from Enniskillen, lifted the king on his shoulders and carried him to the opposite bank. William was so exhausted by the effort of struggling up the bank that he had to lie down for a while.

Two thousand cavalrymen struggled across the river with William. Now he had nearly his entire army on the southern bank, fighting the Jacobites on a front some 2.5 kilometres long. Once recovered, William was again encouraging his troops and fighting alongside the best of them. At last his superior numbers began to tell and James's horsemen were so severely overstretched that the Jacobite line broke. But the apparently indefatigable Jacobite cavalry charged again and again to shelter their scattering infantry, many of whom were throwing away their weapons as they fled.

Two of those Jacobite infantrymen fighting desperately for survival, William Mulloy and his 17-year-old nephew Charles, owed their lives to a lucky family tie. By sheer good fortune Charles's father and William's brother, Theobold, was a captain of the Williamite dragoons opposing them. The story goes that Theobald saw his brother's horse shot under him and gave him his own, and that when Charles was captured Theobold managed to secure his release at the end of the battle.

Last stand at Donore

It was at this point, with James still absent along with half his army at Roughgrange, that Tyrconnell recognized the hopelessness of the situation. He ordered General Hamilton to do what he could to hold William while he left the field to organize a retreat to Duleek, a village on the river Nanny a few kilometres south. Hamilton's only hope was to make a stand on a piece of high ground – the hill at Donore, which looks down on the Boyne with slopes on all sides. Today the only sign of the village is a ruined church on the very top of the hill. The beleaguered Jacobites fled up the steep slope with William's soldiers in hot pursuit. Most of the Irish infantry had now deserted the field and were trying to escape to Dublin. Again, it was the Jacobite cavalry that bore the brunt of the assault. It was a desperate last stand for them; and for William's leadership it was a final test.

The dust and smoke surrounding this last encounter made it one of the most confused and bitterly fought of the whole day. Many soldiers no longer had their green or white emblems, and in the chaos it was harder than ever to tell who was on which side. A man from Enniskillen, one of the most stalwart Protestant towns in the north, had

lost his sprig of green and was about to be speared by a Huguenot. He was only saved when he shouted, 'I'm an Enniskillener!'

William rode up to the nearest cavalry regiment, which happened to be the Enniskillens, and shouted, 'What will you do for me?' In the smoke he was not recognized and several of his troopers raised their pistols at him. But in the nick of time someone spotted the star and garter on his chest and cried, 'It's the king.' Amid loud cheers William stood up in his stirrups and declared, 'Gentlemen, you shall be my guards today. I have heard much of you. Let me see something of you!' The hardy Enniskilleners, fighting for their homes and religion, roared their support and followed him up the hill into concentrated Jacobite fire.

William had another close escape when a bullet scraped against his boot, taking the heel off and wounding a horse next to him. Another bullet grazed his pistol. As if that were not enough, a little later one man, who could not tell friend from foe so close was the combat, pulled a pistol on a soldier in front of him without realizing it was the king. He was about to shoot when William calmly said, 'What? Are you angry with your friends?'

Again and again Hamilton's Jacobites threw themselves at the advancing Williamites. At one point in the chaotic mêlée the Duke of Berwick was about to order a group of Jacobite musketeers to fire on his own horsemen, but just in time realized his error. The redoubtable Hamilton was injured and captured. William himself intervened to save his life from the rough troopers who had captured him, and even instructed his own doctor to tend to him. The king asked Hamilton whether he thought the Jacobites would charge again. 'Upon my honour,' came the reply, he thought they would. 'Your honour?' rebuked William. He was reminding Hamilton that he had originally gone to Ireland at William's command to persuade Tyrconnell to come to terms, but he had actually urged him to fight. In spite of this, the king spared Hamilton and he was later returned to the

Jacobites in a prisoner exchange.

For 30 minutes this final battle hung in the balance, but in the end William had the numbers to overwhelm the final resistance of the remaining Jacobites. The surviving cavalry finally turned and followed the infantry into retreat.

Retreat to Dublin

At two o'clock James learned that the troops he had left at Oldbridge were in headlong retreat. He was still at that impassable ravine at Roughgrange, suffering the appalling frustration of not being able to join battle with the inferior force of Williamites opposite. Now he heard that, on top of his own blunder in leading off the best part of his force on a wild goose chase, the forces he had left behind had suffered a catastrophic defeat. Utterly disheartened, he took Lauzun's advice and hurried off to Dublin.

The retreat of his army rapidly got out of hand. One infantry regiment was moving in good order down a sunken lane to Duleek when the men were charged by their own cavalry. Some of the horsemen even fired their pistols. The infantry scattered, and orderly retreat soon became panic-stricken flight. Regiments got mixed up with each other and the hillside was soon covered with abandoned weapons. Men threw away any encumbrance

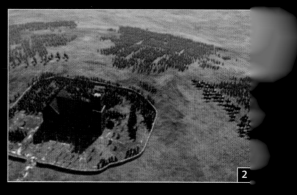

Last stand

1. The Jacobites retreat to the hilltop church at Donore to face the final assault.
2. William surrounds the Jacobites on three sides and attacks.

The final savage hand-to-hand fighting in the graveyard.

Jan Wyck's painting (c.1690) of a cavalry skirmish at the Boyne.

they could to get out of the way even faster. Arms, ammunition, coats, hats and shoes were discarded by the Jacobites as they fled. To make matters worse, the doling out of the brandy ration had been confused that morning and certain regiments had drunk a lot more than was wise before an important battle. So between the corpses and the wounded lay the drunk. One Jacobite reported later:

It was certainly an unparalleled fright that caused our own horse to ride over the greatest part of our first line of foot and break ten or twelve of our battalions, firing upon them as enemies ... I thought the calamity had not been so general till viewing the hills about us I perceived them covered with the

soldiers of several regiments all scattered like sheep flying before the wolf but so thick they seemed to cover the sides and the tops of the hills. The shame of our regiments' dishonour afflicted me before; but now all the horror of a routed army just before so vigorous and desirous of battle and broke without scarce a stroke from the enemy, so perplexed my soul that I envied the few dead and only grieved that I lived to be a spectator of so dismal and lamentable a tragedy.

Around 1,000 Jacobites died at the Boyne and only 500 Williamites. The Jacobite toll would have been higher if William had ordered a full-scale pursuit of the defeated Jacobite army, but he preferred to let them go. He had already won a decisive victory.

James flees Ireland

King William had fought alongside his men until the battle was won. King James had seen no fighting at all, and was in Dublin by dusk. He was quick to blame his army rather than himself for his defeat. One story – possibly invented by the contemptuous Williamite victors – is that James arrived in Dublin Castle at about nine o'clock that evening and was met by Lady Tyrconnell. He told her, 'Your countrymen, Madam, can run well,' and she was quick to reply, 'Not quite so well as Your Majesty, for you have won the race.'

Early the next day James told some of his leading supporters that the Irish had played him false: 'When it came to a trial they basely fled the field and left the spoil to the enemy ... henceforth I am determined never to head an Irish army and do now resolve to shift for myself, and so, gentlemen, must you.' He also said that he would never again use Irish troops to fight the English, and mocked their lack of basic training and equipment. Within five days James had reached the south coast and boarded a ship for France, still bitterly blaming the Irish for his failure to regain the throne.

William made no attempt to stop him. He reckoned that capturing James would be more trouble than it was worth. And William was in the end generous to his former comrade in arms Schomberg, who had failed him earlier but had died trying to rally the Huguenots at the second crossing. He summoned Schomberg's son, Meinhard, who had led the successful crossing at Rosnaree, and told him, 'I deeply lament your father. I shall never forget his services or yours. I owe this day to you and will remember it all my life.'

Aftermath

Superior numbers and weapons, and William's good tactical judgement, won him the Battle of the Boyne. His opponents had brave and resourceful cavalry: only 16 of 200 men in Berwick's regiment remained unscathed after the battle. But the Jacobite army suffered from poor equipment and weak and uninspiring leadership. William's diversionary attack on Rosnaree had succeeded in luring James from Oldbridge with a large part of his force. Had the French been left to guard the ford at Oldbridge it might have been a lot harder for the Williamites to cross. In the main battle William had kept the initiative throughout, with successive crossings of the Boyne that had stretched the Jacobite line until it broke. And at the end he had led his men from the front with great courage.

After the Battle of the Boyne it was no longer a question of whether the Protestants would win, but when. The fight between the Jacobites and the Williamites rumbled on in Ireland for another year. Then, in 1691, the Jacobite cause was destroyed, and with it Catholic hopes of supremacy in Ireland, in the far bloodier slaughter that took place at the Battle of Aughrim. Irish Catholics who fought for James blamed him for their downfall, nicknaming him James the Shit.

James lived out the remaining 11 years of his life in France on a pension from King Louis XIV. The Boyne was not only a defeat for James's bid to win back the British throne. It also represented a major defeat for his ally Louis, who would have been delighted to see the downfall of Britain's new Protestant king.

Protestant Britain went on ruling Ireland until the Catholic south broke away and was recognized as a separate state in 1921. In the new Irish Republic the religious feud rapidly became an irrelevance as Protestants shrank to a tiny minority. But Northern Ireland still has a Protestant majority, who remain deeply conscious of the religious divide to this day. For many of them the commemoration of William's victory on the Boyne is the most colourful and evocative event of the year. Three centuries later, the echoes of those fierce 12 hours of fighting on the Boyne still resound as loudly as the beat of the drums in the marching season.

1746: THE BATTLE OF CULLODEN

A ragged army of rebels was assembling on the moor on the morning of 16 April 1746 as the icy wind blew sleet into their faces. Most of the front-line men were from the Highlands of Scotland. They were a breed apart, recognizing no law but their own. Above all, these 'Highlanders' were warriors. The unkempt, wild-looking men, carrying anything from French muskets to simple clubs, were without question the best fighters in Britain. Shrieking pipes called the clans into position. Each clan chief barked orders in a tongue no Englishman could comprehend. He wore a tartan jacket, a waistcoat and an eagle feather in his hat. From his belt hung two bulky pistols, and he held a long, heavy clansman's sword.

Across the heather to the east another army fanned out: well-drilled foot soldiers, nearly all dressed in red coats, three ranks deep, with two flags flying taut above each regiment – the Union flag of Britain and the regimental flag. Some of them bore a Scottish thistle: there would be Scotsmen on both sides in this battle. Each man in this British army had a Brown Bess musket and 24 rounds of ammunition in a waterproof leather cartridge box or pouch. They had been ordered to the Highlands by the king in London to put down a rebellion, and they would not leave until they had destroyed it and the clan system that made it possible.

The rebel leader was Charles Edward Stuart, known as Bonnie Prince Charlie, intent on seizing back the throne of Britain for his family, the Stuarts, who had ruled the country from 1603 until 1714. The leader of the redcoats was his cousin, the Duke of Cumberland, who was determined to defend his father, George II's, hold on the crown. Many of their followers neither understood nor cared about this dynastic dispute. They were about to fight because their homes would be burnt or they would be flogged or hanged if they did not. The Battle of Culloden, the last to be fought on British soil, was as savage and pitiless as any that had gone before.

The king across the water

Bonnie Prince Charlie was a man with a sense of destiny. His grandfather James II, Britain's last Catholic king, had lost his throne in a Protestant coup 57 years earlier. Charles's father, James, known as the Old Pretender, had made several attempts to seize back the throne, but he and his Jacobite supporters in Britain had always failed. Now he had largely given up and lived in Rome, leaving his son Charles to pursue the Stuart family's claim.

By 1745 Charles, the Young Pretender, had grown impatient. He decided to head for Scotland, where he thought he could exploit the Scots' distaste for the Union with England and its Hanoverian monarchy. His Scottish supporters were less confident; they begged him not to come without French military support.

Charles acquired only some modest private backing in France and left there in June 1745

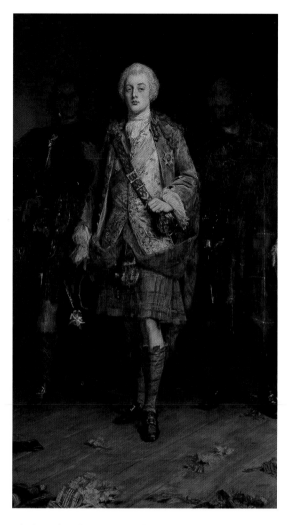

Charles Edward Stuart, the Young Pretender, had little Scottish blood in his veins but took pains to dress like a Highland chieftain and learn Gaelic.

BONNIE PRINCE CHARLIE

Charles was tall, handsome and charming, but hardly a Scot. Born in Rome in 1720, he spoke mostly French and Italian, and had never set foot on Scottish soil before his landing in 1745. But he threw himself into the role of Highland leader with great energy. He marched on foot with his men, even through deep snow, and 'could seldom be prevailed upon to get on horseback to pass a river'. But his enthusiasm for military operations was not matched by experience. In times of crisis he was unable to control the bickering of his subordinates.

with two ships, some gold and 700 men. But on 9 July his ships were spotted by HMS *Lion* off Cornwall, 160 kilometres west of the Lizard. Charles watched helplessly as the *Lion* and the ship that was carrying his troops exchanged broadsides, damaging each other so badly that both vessels only just managed to limp home. Charles sailed on alone, and reached the Outer Hebrides on 23 July.

'I am come home'

When Bonnie Prince Charlie arrived on the island of Eriskay he and his seven companions were hardly the army that English and Scottish Jacobites had hoped for. Most people in his position would have returned to France, but Charles was driven by the same obsession with his hereditary rights that had driven his great-grandfather Charles I to the scaffold and his grandfather James into ignominious exile. A local chieftain told Charles to go home, but he replied, 'I am come home.'

He headed for the mainland, where he began a desperate round of negotiations. For a month he held meetings with clan chiefs and bribed, begged and cajoled them into joining the rebellion. Many refused. Clans such as the Campbells, Monros and Sutherlands were prospering under the current regime; they rejected Charles, and their clansmen would even fight against him. Others sat on the fence. The last major Jacobite uprising, in 1715, had ruined many, and they had no stomach for more government reprisals. Charles swung some by promising that the French would send troops if a rebellion took place.

On 19 August Charles decided to force the clan chiefs into the open. At 1 p.m. he arrived at Glenfinnan, a natural amphitheatre at the head of Loch Shiel, and raised the royal standard. It was a public call to arms. Charles waited with about 400 Macdonalds and a handful of others until four o'clock, when the sound of bagpipes was heard to the east. Then 800 Camerons led by Donald Cameron of Lochiel streamed over the crest of a hill. It was a defining moment. Charles now had an army and the support of one of the most respected lairds in the Highlands.

Cameron had agonized over whether to join the rebellion, but once he had made up his mind, the men he brought with him had no choice. The chiefs had the power of life and death over their clansmen. Anyone who ignored the call to arms could expect to be beaten and have his house burnt down or worse. The Rev. James Robertson from Ross-shire watched Highland recruits being 'dragged from their plows … one I did see myself overtaken by speed of foot, and when he declared that he would rather die than join the rebellion, was knocked to the ground by the butt of a musket and carried away all bleed'.

Glenfinnan. The spot at the head of Loch Shiel where Charles raised his standard is marked today by a column topped by an unnamed Highlander.

BATTLE FACT

Charles was taken to Scotland in the warship *Doutelle*, owned and skippered by Antoine Walsh. He was the grandson of Philip Walsh, whose ship had taken Charles's grandfather James II to France after his defeat at the Battle of the Boyne.

To Edinburgh

The government of King George II in London was shocked. All summer it had been fearing a French invasion. British troops were fighting France on the Continent, and in July the prime minister, Henry Pelham, lamented, 'We have not troops left enough in this country to mount guard over the royal palaces nor to quell an insurrection or smuggling party of one hundred men.'

The king's commander-in-chief in Scotland, Lieutenant General Sir John Cope, was ordered to crush the rebellion. He set off with 1,400 troops into the Highlands, but Charles dodged Cope's army completely and headed straight for Edinburgh. With the rebels advancing unopposed on Scotland's capital, the government in London recalled its ten best battalions from fighting the French in the Low Countries.

Cope's slow-moving army, disastrously wrong-footed in the Highlands, now embarked by sea from Aberdeen. But it was too late to beat the Jacobites to Edinburgh: on 17 September the city was in Charles's hands. Only the garrison of the almost impregnable castle refused to surrender. Charles proclaimed his absent father King James VIII of Scotland, and a crowd of 60,000 cheering townspeople watched the 'bonnie' prince process through the city. 'Great numbers of old women on their knees' kissed his hand, and windows were full of ladies clapping and waving their handkerchiefs.

The Battle of Prestonpans

Cope had arrived in Dunbar, the nearest port to Edinburgh, on the same day that the capital fell to Charles. He marched west and on the 20th arrived at Prestonpans. It was an ideal position: flat, open ground with the Firth of Forth to the north and a boggy morass to the south. It was not the terrain Highlanders were used to. Cope drew up his men, about 2,500 of them, facing Edinburgh and the advancing Jacobites. Here on this stubble-covered cornfield, with cavalry and six cannon, he felt there was no danger of the ambushes he had feared

The government redcoats under General Cope march towards Inverness to track the rebels down.

Meanwhile, Charles and his Highland army slip through the mountains and march on Edinburgh.

in the Highlands. He was certain he could finish off the rebellion in one stroke.

When the Jacobites arrived they found Cope in this strong defensive position and immediately seized the high ground that overlooked the government army from the south. So Cope wheeled his army round 90 degrees to face his enemy across the bog.

LORD GEORGE MURRAY

By the age of 50 Murray had seen action in two previous Jacobite uprisings, but had taken advantage of an amnesty to return home, where he had lived in peace until he joined Prince Charles in 1745. He had a gift for strategy and was always vigorous and courageous in the execution of plans. Unfortunately he was also, even according to his own aides de camp, 'proud, haughty, blunt and imperious ... Feeling his superiority he would listen to no advice.' His rows with William O'Sullivan, Charles's chief of staff, were a constant source of tension throughout the rebellion.

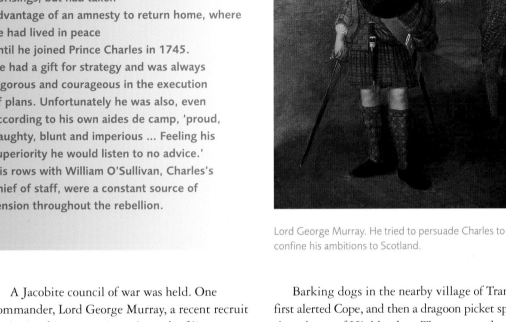

Lord George Murray. He tried to persuade Charles to confine his ambitions to Scotland.

A Jacobite council of war was held. One commander, Lord George Murray, a recent recruit to the Jacobite army given the rank of lieutenant general because of his military experience, suggested marching around the bog and attacking the redcoats from behind. Then a local wildfowler told them of a secret but difficult short cut through the marshes. By following this track the army would be able to threaten Cope's rear in a much shorter time. The Jacobite column set off at 4 a.m. on 21 September.

Cope's camp was illuminated by great bonfires; even so, the Jacobites had difficulty finding their way through the marsh. It was taken as a bad omen when the prince fell while leaping over a ditch, but he and his army were clear of the marsh by first light. They formed up to attack the redcoats.

Barking dogs in the nearby village of Tranent first alerted Cope, and then a dragoon picket spotted the column of Highlanders. The commander-in-chief reacted with speed, wheeling his army round yet again to face the Jacobites, who were assembling to the east. Cope's infantry were drawn up in a line about 200 metres long, flanked on either side by a regiment of dragoons on horseback. During a last-minute inspection of his forces, he was disturbed to see that the dragoons had not bothered to draw their swords, an indication of their poor morale. A battery of artillery on his right was operated by only two experienced men with four invalids to help them. The two men ran from one gun to the next, firing them one by one. They did not get a chance for a second volley because out of the dense morning mist the Highlanders attacked.

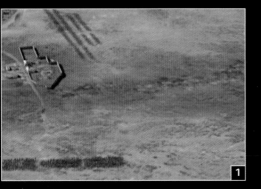

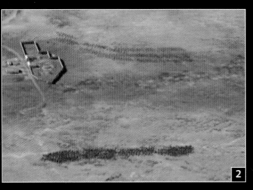

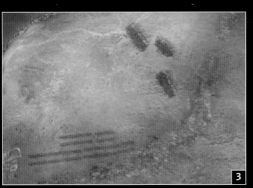

Prestonpans

1. With the redcoat lines (top) facing west, Charles's Jacobites (bottom) arrive from Edinburgh and threaten their left flank.
2. Cope swings his redcoats south to face them, with a bog to his front and the walls of Bankton House on his flank.
3. The Jacobites surprise the redcoats by appearing to their east (right) after slipping though the bog overnight. Cope has to wheel again to face them.

The Highland charge

As Cope's cannon started firing, the Highlanders charged. Wearing loose clothing and unencumbered with packs or other loads, they were able to move quickly. In the first rank were the officers of the clan, the family of the clan chief and other men of means. They could afford the classic Highland array of weapons – the broadsword, the dirk, pistols, a musket and a target, a small circular shield about 50 centimetres in diameter. Their tactics meant that battles were extremely violent and short. There were no lengthy exchanges of musketry: the clans closed immediately with their enemy and fought hand to hand. It was an age-old tactic, out of place in a world of musket volleys and cannon fire, and much of its impact was psychological. The sight of a charging clan was enough to break the morale of poorly trained troops.

The Macdonalds made up the Jacobite right wing, their place of honour since the days of Robert the Bruce. Now they howled their war cry and charged the redcoats. But the two armies were not properly aligned. The Macdonalds had crossed the marsh first and strayed so far north that they had outflanked the government left wing. Instead of hitting the redcoated infantry as intended, they smashed into the inexperienced dragoons. The Highlanders on the left, led by Murray, charged at the same moment. Two Jacobite spearheads 150 metres apart bore down on the government line. When they were 50 metres away those with muskets fired, then hurled their guns to the ground. Drawing their swords, they sprinted the remaining distance.

The dazed redcoats, who had only just woken up, saw two columns of Highlanders hurtling out of the morning murk. They knew their fearsome reputation. Many on the government side had never seen action before. The dragoons had not even completed their training. Now this novice redcoat army was faced with an onslaught of howling clansmen.

The front rank of a Highland charge. The shrieking clansmen aimed to unnerve their enemy before they even came to grips with them.

At the northern end of the government line, the main weight of the Highlanders' charge fell on Hamilton's dragoons. The government infantry in the centre could only watch as musket balls tore through the ranks of men and horses. The dragoons wavered. When they saw their commander, Lieutenant Colonel Wright, pinned to the ground beneath his mount they turned and fled in headlong retreat, abandoning the infantry to their fate.

The Highlanders on the other, southern, wing got so close before they fired their volley that the wads from their powder charges went flying into the government ranks. Then they too flung down their muskets and charged home with broadswords. A contemporary account says they were 'like a torrent and carried all before them'. The government's cannon were overwhelmed, and the dragoons on this flank also fled when their

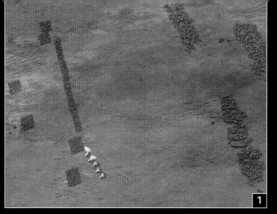

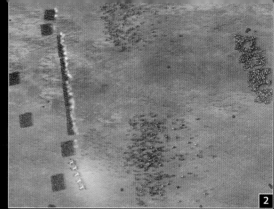

Redcoat infantry – with bayonets fixed – face the Highland charge. Each rank was trained to fire a volley and then reload while another rank fired.

lieutenant colonel had his left arm shattered by a musket ball.

By a quirk of poor light and an unintentionally bungled deployment, the Highlanders had routed both flanks of the government army and left the infantry in the centre relatively unscathed. Now they turned and fell upon the redcoats, trapping them in a giant pincer movement. One of their commanders, Colonel Lascelles, tried to hold his men together, but they had seen the Highland charge and their spirit was broken. He later remembered them 'crouching and creeping gently backwards'. They were no match for the clansmen, experts at close-quarters fighting. A French eye-witness wrote, 'Having once got … into the ranks of an enemy … the fate of a battle is decided in an instant, and the carnage follows; the High-landers bring down two men at a time, one with their dirk in their left hand and another with the sword.' Some fought against the odds. Colonel Gardiner, disgusted that his regiment had fled, grabbed a half pike and fought on until a massive blow from a Lochaber axe sent him crashing to the ground.

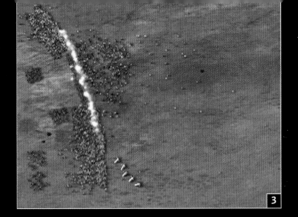

1. The redcoats (left centre) have now wheeled east to face the three groups of Highlanders. Cope has his infantry in the centre, and cavalry on the flanks. His cannon (bottom) open fire.

2. The two Jacobite wings charge towards the flanks of the redcoat army.

3. The horsemen on the redcoat flanks flee, leaving the infantry in the centre under attack from both sides and from Charles's third group of Highlanders, who now attack them head on.

Fifteen minutes after the first cannon had fired the redcoats broke, and the Highlanders chased them. Some government troops were trapped against the 4-metre perimeter walls of the estates of Preston and Bankton Parks and were cut down mercilessly. Three hundred of Cope's men were killed, and only 25 Jacobites. Fifteen hundred government troops were taken prisoner, and Cope himself fled to Berwick.

The battlefield was a gruesome spectacle, for the hacking, slashing and stabbing of the medieval-style weapons had dealt horrific wounds. The dead were described as so 'butchered and mangled as scarce to be known'. All of this enhanced the psychological impact of the Highland charge – even if it was, strictly, an outdated tactic. What mattered was that it had won Charles a stunning victory. The British army in Scotland had been destroyed and the government presence reduced to a few isolated garrisons. Charles spent the night in a mansion at nearby Musselburgh; it belonged to the secretary of state for Scotland, who only days earlier had put a bounty of £30,000 on Charles's head.

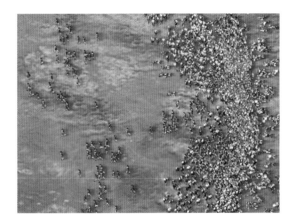

The government lines collapse. But many of those who ran did not make it to safety. They were trapped against the walls of the Bankton Estate off to the left and were cut down mercilessly.

BATTLE FACT

More Scots fought for King George II's government in 1745–6 than served in Bonnie Prince Charlie's army.

The invasion of England

Prestonpans had an electrifying effect on the government in London. It ordered eight of its best regiments home from the Continent and sent 10,000 men north to Newcastle. The government now feared the French would seize the chance to launch a cross-Channel invasion. And no sooner had Charles returned to Edinburgh after his victory than he urged the immediate invasion of England. For Charles, Edinburgh and the Scottish crown were not enough; he would not stop until the Stuarts were back on the throne in London.

On 10 October the Jacobite high command had a particularly acrimonious council of war in the Palace of Holyrood. The clan chiefs, led by Lord George Murray, begged Charles not to embark on an invasion of England. They had no interest in the English crown; in fact many of them had joined Charles because they hoped to see an end to the union of the two countries. They wanted to stay in Scotland to consolidate their successes and to crush clans such as the Campbells, who remained loyal to the king in London. Charles argued passionately that the English would rise up and support him if he invaded, and he promised that the Jacobites would receive French support. Speed and momentum were everything. Take the fight to England, he argued, and they might unbalance the government and topple the Hanoverian dynasty. After a bitter dispute, Charles won the debate – by one vote.

On 5 November the Jacobite army, 5,500 strong, crossed into England. New recruits had been pressed into service and the army now contained a large proportion of Lowlanders. The rebels were in Carlisle on the 9th, Preston on the 20th and Manchester on the 28th. The English cities put up no more of a fight than Edinburgh had. The only snag was the disappointing number of English Jacobite recruits.

To stem Charles's advance the Duke of Cumberland, son of George II and Britain's best general, was summoned back from the Low Countries. He assembled an army as fast as he could in Lichfield in the west Midlands. The Duke of Devonshire raised a militia regiment in Derbyshire but complained, 'I have no notion of an army being able to march at the rate these fellows have come.'

From 4 a.m. until 11 a.m. on a frosty, snowy 3 December the Hanoverian army was drawn up for battle on a field in Staffordshire. But there was no sign of the enemy. The Jacobites had tricked Cumberland into going the wrong way, and were now heading flat out for London.

Disinformation

On 5 December Charles's army reached Derby, just 200 kilometres from London. The townspeople were friendly, but only three recruits joined the Jacobite ranks. Charles and his commanders debated their options at Exeter House in Derby. Murray used the absence of any serious French or English support to press for an immediate withdrawal to Scotland. Charles again insisted that the French would help and that a bold march to London would

DUKE OF CUMBERLAND

William Augustus was the second and favourite son of King George II. At the time of Culloden he was a hard, brutal young man, who was vicious to enemies of the Hanoverian regime. After retaking Carlisle Castle on 30 December 1745, he complained to London that he had not been allowed to kill all the Jacobite garrison. He was a competent commander and a good administrator, and his campaign against the Jacobites was well organized if uninspired.

The Duke of Cumberland. His ruthless campaign in Scotland was to earn him the nickname 'Butcher Cumberland'.

topple George II's Hanoverian regime. But a well-dressed man called Dudley Bradstreet arrived in Derby that day with news for the council. Claiming he was a wealthy Jacobite sympathizer, he reported that an army of regular government troops was blocking the road to London at Northampton. This swung the debate; even loyal Cameron of Lochiel was now for going home.

It was a tragic moment for the Jacobite troops. They reacted with glee as they left Derby the next morning, believing they were off to chase Cumberland's army; but when they realized it was a retreat 'nothing could be heard throughout the army but rage and lamentation'. London had been tantalizingly close. Had they known then what they learned later, they would have been even more upset by their commanders' about-turn. The fact was that London was in a state of panic and the stock market had collapsed. Henry Pelham, the prime minister, said, 'credit was sunk so low that I doubted whether we should be able to raise enough money to carry on the common business of this country'. Worse, there was no government army in Northampton. Dudley Bradstreet was a spy paid by the crown to mislead the Jacobites. Moreover, the French had indeed been poised to invade. Cannon and supplies were loaded at Dunkirk on 7 December. On the 20th the French commander was in a position to embark, but he was discouraged by news of the retreat from Derby. By February the invasion had been cancelled.

Retreat to Scotland

As quickly as they had come south, the Jacobite army slipped back into Scotland. An attempt to regain the initiative failed. They were unable to take Stirling Castle, and a battle at Falkirk with a British army that was now getting wiser to the Highland charge ended in stalemate. Some redcoats fled before it, but others stood their ground, firing withering musket volleys and forcing the Jacobites to run.

The Jacobite high command was torn apart by disagreements. Murray wanted to retreat to the Highlands to consolidate and regroup. Charles feared that this would prompt his army to dissolve. The Lowlanders would desert, the Highlanders would go home to stash their booty and see their families. But he was outvoted and the Jacobites retreated into the Highlands. They marched in horrific weather: one storm left icicles hanging on their eyebrows and beards.

Cumberland was sent back to Scotland to crush the rebellion before it could consolidate its hold on the Highlands and attract more French support. He stayed in Aberdeen for just over a month while supplies of food came in and 1,000 soldiers rejoined their regiments from field hospitals. In order to be sure of victory, his battered redcoats would need some rest and retraining.

They also had to be taught how to resist the Highland charge. Thirty dragoons and 30 infantrymen from regiments that had run away at Falkirk were hanged. But Cumberland was not just relying on fear to force his troops to fight. He also trained his men to combat the charge by using their bayonets. Soldiers were taught to lunge not at the opponent immediately in front of them but at the next one along to the right. In theory this opponent would be vulnerable to a bayonet thrust as he raised his sword. How effective or realistic this was is open to debate. But the training did bolster soldiers' morale and rebuild trust between men in the ranks.

BATTLE EXPERIENCE
Musket drill

When Cumberland rested his tired and demoralized army in Aberdeen he put his men through some rigorous retraining, in the belief that firepower was the key to defeating the dreaded Highland charge. Ever since Marlborough had commanded the British army 40 years earlier, it had had the reputation of firing muskets as rapidly as any army in Europe. Cumberland practised his soldiers in musket drill until it was second nature to them, and this gave them the confidence to fire volley after volley at the charging Highlanders rather than turn and run away from them.

We were taken through musket drill at Culloden. There are dozens of actions to firing a musket, and the drill covers every detailed movement of the fingers. That way an entire regiment could reload simultaneously in tight ranks without anyone poking, stabbing or butting the man next to him. We found the drill difficult to master in just one session, and the speed with which we could fire and reload did not match up to the 18th-century standard of three shots per minute. After dealing with misfires, powder burns and interventions by the safety supervisor, we developed a healthy respect for the redcoat infantrymen in Cumberland's army.

The windswept, heather-covered moor at Culloden, which straddled the approach to Inverness.

'Not proper for Highlanders'

On 8 April, when he heard that the river Spey was low enough to ford, Cumberland left Aberdeen. The beleaguered Charles waited for him in Inverness. The Jacobite army was now paralysed by a shortage of money: since the men could not be paid, many deserted. A small reserve of oatmeal had been built up in Inverness, and abandoning both the city and these supplies of food would have led to the disintegration of the army. There was no choice; retreat was not an option.

Knowing they had to make a stand, Jacobite leaders had a lively debate as to where to fight the battle. Murray suggested some boggy ground which the prince and others, such as Charles's Irish chief of staff, Colonel O'Sullivan, rejected. Instead they selected the featureless, heather-covered moorland next to a mansion called Culloden House. The moor cut across Cumberland's route from Aberdeen to Inverness. Murray wrote afterwards: 'I did not like the ground; it was certainly not proper for Highlanders.' O'Sullivan was adamant that the army needed an open space like Prestonpans, where they could get to grips with

the enemy, but the unexpected success of the Jacobite army there had blinded him to the realities of 18th-century warfare. Battles were decided by firepower. The flat, open ground of Culloden Moor would favour the musket and cannon over the sword and dirk.

As the Scottish and English regiments of Cumberland's force approached Inverness, the Jacobite army was woefully under strength. Some clans had gone home to raid or to protect their glens from government supporters, such as the Campbells. An expedition to Sutherland and Caithness had reduced the army by 1,500 men. But Charles had made up his mind to fight. It was beneath the dignity of the Prince of Wales and Regent of Britain, Ireland and her colonies to slink around the Highlands like a brigand. So on 15 April the remnants of Charles's hungry, grumbling army lined up on Culloden Moor to do battle.

The night march

All day they waited. Nobody had arranged for any food to be brought out from Inverness. The troops started scouring around for something to eat, and a large group set off back towards the town. But the Jacobite command had other ideas.

Realizing that Cumberland's army had been given a day off to celebrate his 25th birthday, Murray hoped that the enemy would be drunk and vulnerable to a surprise dawn attack. It was a high-risk strategy, but Murray was keen to avoid a pitched battle at Culloden. So the Jacobites were rounded up and sent off at night in a long column towards Cumberland's camp 13 kilometres away to the east.

Murray led the way with the Highlanders, followed by the Lowland troops and the French detachments that had made it to Scotland. The moorland was difficult terrain: it was dark and foggy, and soon the Highlanders had left the other troops behind. Stone walls and dykes made progress slower than expected. The unfed men lacked the energy to march the distance in time. The intended night raid was turning into a shambles. When Murray and the advance guard arrived at a farm about 5 kilometres from

Cumberland's camp he sent a message back to Charles, advising him to abort. Charles was livid. He replied that Murray was to attack with whatever forces were available.

Murray haughtily refused and marched back along the Inverness road to Culloden. When Charles heard this he had a tantrum, shouting, 'I am betrayed!' Interestingly, the rest of the army did reach their starting positions for a raid on Cumberland's camp, and had started to deploy before they realized that Murray had gone. Had Murray waited, the Jacobites might have fought on better terrain and better terms than they would now do at Culloden. But with Murray's Highlanders gone, the other divisions had no choice but to trail back as well. At first light the Jacobite army was spread out along the road to Inverness. They were cold, starving, exhausted and in low spirits. Meanwhile, in Cumberland's camp, 12 scarlet-coated drummers beat the call to arms, while bagpipes roused those Highland troops who were fighting for the government.

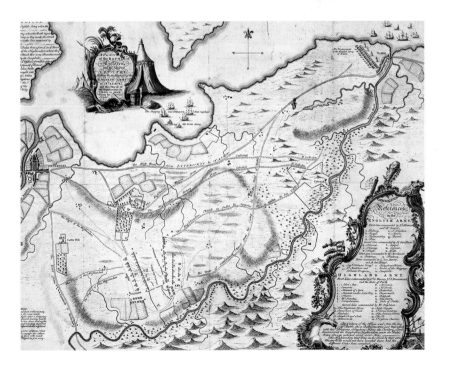

An 18th-century map showing Inverness (left), the battlefield (bottom centre), and Cumberland's camp at Nairn (top right).

Advance to Culloden

The men of the British army were not drunk as Murray had hoped. The previous night they had been given brandy to toast their duke's birthday, but had then settled down to a good night's sleep in ridgepole tents, neatly set out along the Inverness road. As the men were called to arms, subaltern officers collected their valuables for safe-keeping and checked each man's weapon and ammunition. Then the troops turned out in the cold rain to hear morning prayers and general orders, which stated the penalties for cowardice and desertion.

At 5.15 a.m. on 16 April the drums beat again and the army formed columns. Three contained five infantry battalions, one behind the other; the fourth was made up of cavalry. Bayonets were fixed, since the enemy was known to be close. Muskets were carried, with the metre-long barrels pointing down in order to stop rainwater soaking the powder. This made marching difficult because the bayonets tended to dig into the rough ground. As the rain turned to hail, soldiers tugged down their tricorn hats, each emblazoned with the white horse of Hanover, no doubt cursing their ill-fitting double-breasted coats of heavy scarlet for not keeping them warmer. In no time their gaiters were soaked through. They trudged through the sodden heather at 75 paces a minute, the Highland troops leading the way, and behind the troops the supply wagons.

The army swung from column into line when they reached Leanach Farm, about 400 metres from the Jacobite force, which was drawn up to the west. The redcoat infantry stretched out in long lines – regiment by regiment, 500 men each, in three ranks. A pair of cannon was manhandled into each gap between the regiments in the front line. Every gun had a pile of 1.4-kilogram balls placed beside it.

Cumberland's cavalry was placed on both wings, the Duke of Kingston's Horse and Cobham's 10th Dragoons guarded his northern flank, and Lieutenant General Hawley's dragoons the south. Hawley led his men around the southern flank of the battlefield, taking advantage of some dead ground that allowed his men to keep below the skyline. He also took some Highland infantry, led by Captain Colin Campbell of Ballimore. After they had escorted him some of the way, he sent them back to the main force: he did not want their Highland dress to result in any friendly fire incidents. But the Campbells could not resist staying up front, and they hid behind a wall that lined the southern end of the battlefield. Here they would have a chance to get to grips with their Highland opponents in the Jacobite ranks.

Cumberland now said a few words to his troops. Tricorn hat in hand, he rode along the line on his large grey horse, golden tassels bouncing on his saddle. He exhorted his 'brave boys' to stand firm and promised, 'Your toil will soon be at an end.' The troops cheered him and he took position behind the regiment of Royal Scots, most of whom were Highlanders.

Fathers, sons and brothers

Across the heather the pipes were again calling the Jacobites to arms. The last of them had trailed back from their night march at 6 a.m. They had thrown themselves on the heather to get some sleep or wandered off to find scraps of food – there were still no supplies from Inverness. Now, worn out and dejected, they trudged into place for the battle that would decide the outcome of the rebellion.

Charles rode amongst his men, telling them to be brave and testing sword edges. But his confidence was not shared by those around him. Murray was in a state of pessimistic resignation. The French ambassador, the Marquis d'Eguilles, had gone on his knees to implore the prince not to fight a battle. Against over 8,000 men in the government army the Jacobites could muster fewer than 5,000. They had some artillery, but nearly all the trained gunners had deserted or been killed.

The relationship between Jacobite commanders had almost totally broken down. The prince was furious at Murray for aborting the attack the previous night. The Macdonalds were angry because Murray had insisted on giving the place of honour on the right wing – traditionally the Macdonalds' – to his own men from Atholl.

Three thousand, eight hundred men stood in the front line and it stretched for a kilometre, but it was not parallel to Cumberland's. In the south the two sides were only 400 metres apart, but in the north the Macdonalds found themselves 500 metres from their enemy. The men were bunched together in their clan groups: the clan chief acted as colonel, his immediate family as officers. Boys as young as 14 joined their grandfathers. Fathers, sons and brothers stood together so that none would waver or lose heart. The most prominent families stood in the front line, and the poorly armed sub-tenants in the rear.

The only regular troops in the Jacobite army were in the second line – the few French soldiers who had slipped through the British government's blockade. One regiment, the Royal Ecossois, was made up of Scottish exiles in France; they were well trained, but numbered only 300 men. Another 150 Franco–Irish troops stood on their flank. Scottish Lowland formations also stood in the second line, ready to plug any gaps that opened in front of them.

This was a civil war, and there was more at stake than a change of king. The Macleans were less concerned about the Stuart dynasty than the fact that the Campbells fought in the other army. The Campbells had recently raided Maclean homes on Mull while the men were away, burning houses, stripping the women naked and slaughtering their cattle. The Macleans were at Culloden for revenge.

As in all civil conflicts, families were split, fighting for both sides. Lord Kilmarnock commanded a regiment in the prince's second line, while his son fought with Cumberland. Old MacIan, chief of the Chisholms, was playing both sides so that whatever the outcome his lands and titles would not be stripped from him. His youngest son, Roderick Og, led the clan for the

Culloden battle lines

1. The Jacobite army (left) face the redcoats (right) 400–500 metres away. The government troops have also seized the ground behind the Leanach walls (in a T shape at the bottom).
2. The Highlanders await the order to charge. Nearly all are on foot; a few senior officers are mounted.
3. The redcoats stand three ranks deep, with two cannon between each regiment.

rince, while his other sons, John and James, were officers in the Royal Scots regiment, standing just in front of Cumberland.

The Jacobite army had no standard uniforms. While the French troops fought in blue, Charles had ordered the clans to be in kilts. These came in a variety of colours and there was even the odd red coat in the ranks as deserters from the British army lined up against their former comrades. The clan MacNeill tucked seaweed into their bonnets because it fertilized the barren earth of their Western Isles. All the troops had one defining mark, however: the white cockade of the Stuarts had been stitched into their jackets or plaids by seamstresses from Inverness to Wakefield. Now they all stood and roared their defiance at the redcoats. The British army remained silent.

Deadly bombardment

The most reliable estimate is that the Jacobite artillery started firing at one o'clock. The firing was erratic as inexperienced Highlanders fired and reloaded their 2- and 3-kilogram guns. Six men in Colonel Fleming's regiment were wounded, and

Cumberland had a lucky escape when a cannon ball killed two men in front of him; but the gunfire did not seriously threaten the redcoats.

It was a different story when the government gunners responded. They were the most professional arm of Cumberland's force. Officers in the infantry or cavalry could buy promotion, but in the artillery advancement came strictly through technical competence and seniority. Their guns could fire three 1.4-kilogram solid lead balls into the Jacobite ranks every minute. This was an impressive rate of fire which required an experienced team to ram, sponge, prime and aim with great precision. The balls tore through the dense Jacobite ranks six to ten men deep.

This bombardment did not cause a massacre, but it was deeply unnerving for those rebels who had never faced artillery before. The prince's standard came under heavy fire; Charles's groom, Thomas Caw, was killed. After only eight or nine minutes his men were furiously asking why they were not being given the order to charge instead of standing still under the hail of cannon balls, but it seems that a courier carrying the order from

1. The Highlanders wait with growing impatience and fury as their ranks are thinned by the cannon barrage.

2. Without waiting for an order, the exasperated clansmen begin their charge. The Highlanders at the northern end of the charge had further to run to get to grips with their enemy.

3. When the charging clansmen are within 300 metres the government artillerymen switch to canister.

the prince to the front line was killed. Eventually the Highlanders took matters into their own hands and charged. The battle that followed must have seemed to last an eternity to those who fought it but it was in fact over remarkably quickly.

The charge

The story has it that the MacIntosh clan charged first. Without waiting for orders, they surged forward. Clans to the left and right followed their lead and joined in, roaring their battle cry. Frustration and anger changed what should have been an orderly walk towards the enemy, followed by a musket volley, into a mad, confused sprint. Many discarded their new French muskets without even firing a shot. Clans bunched together to avoid cannon fire or boggy areas, and to an eyewitness it looked as if there were 'three large bodies like wedges' heading towards the government line. The clansmen's faces twisted with rage and hatred as they hitched up their kilts and ran. Because the land was flatter and drier on the south side of the field, the Atholl men, the Camerons and the MacIntoshes made quicker progress than the men to the north.

The Macdonalds in particular, still smarting from the dishonour of being placed on the left flank, were the last troops to charge and faced the boggiest ground, which slowed their progress. But, according to a government soldier opposite them, Alexander Taylor of the Royal Scots regiment, the Highlanders still ran at them 'like troops of hungry wolves'.

The Highlanders charged ferociously in their rush to close the gap with the cannons, but worse was to come. When they were 300 metres from the British line, the artillerymen changed from round shot to canister. Popularly known as grape shot, canister consists of a linen or paper bag filled with musket balls that bursts on firing and turns each cannon into a giant shotgun. The cannon spewed hundreds of musket balls at the hapless Jacobites as they laboured across the moor. Historian Stuart Reid has calculated that in the 90 seconds it would have taken a fully armed man to cover the 300 metres to the government ranks each cannon would have been able to fire four or perhaps five rounds of canister. If a single round knocked out eight to ten men, he estimates that 60 to 80 men were killed or disabled every 20 seconds.

A high proportion of the casualties were from the top ranks of the Highland forces because they were leading from the front. Cameron of Lochiel had both his legs shot through; Alexander Macdonald of Keppoch was killed as he encouraged his reluctant men to charge. An eyewitness saw Colonel Lachlan Maclachlan mortally wounded: 'His guts were laid out over his horse's neck.' An officer in Clan Chattan, Angus MacIntosh of Farr, died while his 14-year-old son watched the battle from less than 2 kilometres away. Murray's Atholl men got squeezed against the wall of the Leanach enclosure by clansmen desperate to avoid the canister fire and trying to stick to the firm ground. This caused severe bunching of the Jacobites at the southern end of their charge.

As the Highlanders got within musket range, they could finally see the redcoat ranks. John Grant of Clan Chattan remembered seeing nothing through the smoke until he caught sight of a long line of legs, white-gaitered to the thigh, with black buttons running down the calves. At 100 metres out the Highlanders met a crashing volley of musket fire. It is amazing that any Jacobites at all reached the British line; the fact that they did is a testament to their extraordinary courage and determination. It was to the south, where the ground was driest and the gap between the armies smallest, that the great bunch of Jacobites who had survived the cannon fire and musket volleys crashed into the redcoats. One battalion took the brunt of the impact of this swirling, disorganized mass of Highlanders: Colonel Barrel's 4th Regiment of Foot.

They did not run, as had so many other regiments in past battles, but stood their ground and fired one more musket volley at point-blank range. Nonetheless the Highlanders' momentum carried them forward into the redcoat line. Now at last they could use their swords and axes to good effect. In just a few minutes Barrel's regiment lost 17 killed and 108 injured out of a total of 373 men.

Barrel's regimental flag. The commanding officer had his hand cut off trying to prevent the flag from being seized.

The flag of Lord Ogilvy's Jacobite regiment. The motto reads 'No one will do me harm and get away with it'.

Captain Lord Robert Kerr was cleft from crown to collar bone by Gillies MacBean of the MacIntosh regiment. Barrel's commanding officer, Lieutenant Colonel Robert Rich, tried to save the regimental colours but had his left hand cut off, his right arm removed below the elbow, and six cuts in the head. But the men of Barrel's were veterans; they fought ferociously and after the battle 'there was not a bayonet but was either bloody or bent'.

Barrel's regiment was pushed back bit by bit, temporarily losing one of its colours. Some of the Highlanders then turned on the two cannon between Barrel's and Munro's regiment to its north. They over-ran Sergeant Bristo's gun detachment, but not before he got off a round of canister shot at a range of 2 metres which, we are told, caused 'dreadful havoc'.

Then Munro's regiment came under attack. An elite grenadier company wearing tall mitre hats guarded the flanks of each regiment, and the rage of the Highlanders was now directed against the grenadiers on the left flank of Munro's regiment. Munro's men had run away from the Highlanders at Falkirk and now they were going to win back their honour. It seems that the front rank fought hand-to-hand with bayonets fixed, while the second and third rank kept up a stream of musket fire over their heads straight into the Highlanders. Redcoat survivors were proud that they had proved the Highlanders' broadswords to be not 'so terrible as they had flattered themselves'. In this kind of close fighting bayonets could be wielded in far less space, and a veteran with a bayonet found he could get the better of a man with a long sword. Nevertheless, Munro's lost 14 killed and 68 wounded, including John Tovey, 55 years old and 'born in the army', who had his jaw shot away.

'Never saw a thicker field of dead'

In the north of the field the Macdonalds and Chisholms were still struggling across the moor, through water that was almost up to their knees, while the redcoats poured fire into their ranks. Fusilier Linn, facing them, said, 'I never saw a thicker field of dead.' But with Barrel's regiment fast disintegrating and Munro's putting up a desperate resistance there was a critical opportunity at the southern end of the line. If the Jacobite commanders could control their men, they might exploit and widen the breakthrough.

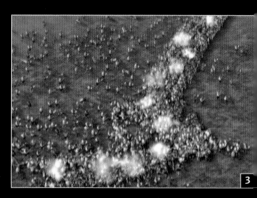

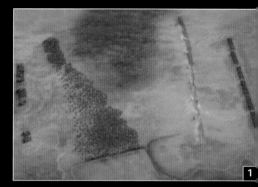

The clash

1. As the Highlanders charge (left), those on firmer ground to the south have less far to run to reach their enemy.
2. The redcoats (right) fire musket volleys but fail to stop the Highlanders at the southern end of the charge getting closer and closer.
3. The Highlanders crash into Barrel's regiment and begin to break through.

However, the Highlanders were pouring through the hole in the government front in total disorder. And the bravery of Barrel's and Munro's had given time for the commander of the redcoats' second line, Major General Huske, to organize a counter-attack. With great urgency, he brought forward Semphill's 25th regiment from Edinburgh, Wolfe's 8th Foot and Ligonier's 59th. They formed a giant semi-circle of nearly 1,100 muskets plus officers and non-commissioned officers. Then, with Wolfe's firing into the Highlanders' flank and the other two regiments directly facing them, they opened up a withering musket fire. Rank after rank of redcoats fired and reloaded, fired and reloaded: biting the cartridge, priming the pan, ramming the ball, firing at the beat of a drum three times a minute. The Jacobites had thrown away their muskets and could brandish only their swords as thousands of musket balls came lashing at them from front and side.

They were an ideal target: a mass of men 20 or 30 deep. Stuart Reid has made another calculation. By now Bligh's regiment had come to the support of Munro's, so it seems that while the front ranks

stood with bayonets fixed, there were 1,200 muskets in the second and third ranks firing at close range into the Jacobites. A corporal in Munro's regiment reckoned that he fired his musket nine times. In the second line a captain in Wolfe's regiment believed his troops fired five or six times. Reid assumes that as little as one round in ten hit its target. But even his cautious calculation suggests that at least 700 Jacobites were killed or wounded in the space of two or three bloody minutes. In a feeble gesture some Highlanders threw stones at the redcoats. But only minutes after they had charged across the moor the hopelessness of their position was obvious and the surviving Highlanders turned tail and fled.

'All is going to pot'

It had finished in the north even before it was over in the south. The Macdonalds, Macleans and Chisholms had seen their officers killed, and they were literally bogged down still 100 metres away from the government line. They faltered and Cumberland, sensing an opportunity, galloped up to Cobham's dragoons and 'clapping some of

1. With the redcoats reinforced, the Highlanders face overwhelming odds. Three other government regiments have advanced to assist Barrel's and Munro's.

2. The critical moment. The Highlanders, outgunned and outnumbered, realize that all is lost and turn to flee.

3. In their attempt to escape they also come under fire from behind the walls on their left.

them on the shoulders' told them to fall upon the wavering Jacobites.

In the south Murray's horse was killed in the assault and his coat riddled with canister and tattered by bayonet thrusts. He ran back across the field of corpses to find reinforcements from the second line. But only the blue-coated Royal Ecossois stood where he had left them; the rest had gone to guard the flank from Hawley's cavalry, who had threatened to cut off the Jacobite army's retreat. Before Murray could organize any reinforcement the fleeing Jacobites started to stream past him. His Highland army had disintegrated.

The Royal Ecossois stood their ground and fired volleys of musket shot to cover the headlong retreat of the Jacobites. But they had not reckoned with the Campbell Highlanders of the Argyll militia, who were hidden behind the stone walls along the southern end of the battlefield. They had stayed there, sniping at the rebel Highlanders as they charged up past the walls, and then retreated past them again. When the Argylls saw the Royal Ecossois they leapt out from behind

their wall and drove them back until they were forced to surrender.

Prince Charles was trying to rally his troops in the centre of the battlefield. O'Sullivan rode up to his entourage and shouted, 'You see all is going to pot. You can be of no great succour.' One eyewitness says that O'Sullivan had to grab the harness of the prince's horse himself to stop him racing off to lead his troops in a futile attack. It was an exact replay of his great-grandfather Charles's last-minute gesture of bravery after the catastrophe at Naseby 101 years before. In both cases, their obstinate determination to fight a stronger enemy had led to the slaughter of their followers and the destruction of their cause.

The prince was persuaded to leave the field and escape. He was accompanied by some troops, mainly from the second line, who fled before Hawley's dragoons from the south and Cobham's dragoons from the north enveloped the field. What followed was a massacre.

Cumberland's horsemen scoured the battle-field, killing the living, finishing off the wounded and trampling the dead. Cameron of Lochiel

The redcoats' new bayonet drill pays off as they stand firm before the Highland charge at Culloden.

escaped the slaughter only because four loyal clansmen carried him off the field. Macdonald of Keppoch was carried off too. A wounded Macdonald clansman was being helped off the field by his son when he saw Keppoch carried past and ordered his son to leave him and tend to their chief, as his first duty was to the head of the clan rather than his father. The vast majority of wounded were not as lucky as Macdonald of Keppoch. The cavalry hacked and slashed fleeing Jacobites on the moor, in the park of Culloden

House and on the road to Inverness. Back on the battlefield the Duke of Cumberland rode down the line thanking each regiment. The redcoats grounded their muskets and cheered. A couple of kilometres away Prince Charles heard the cheers and dispersed what remained of his army. 'Do as you wish,' he said, 'only for God's sake let us go now.'

On the battlefield the redcoats played macabre games amongst the corpses, 'dabbling their feet in blood and splashing it about one another'. John and James Chisholm, who had fought for Cumberland, found the body of their Jacobite younger brother surrounded by the remains of almost all their clansmen. They straightened his limbs, cleaned his face and stood guard over the body all night to protect it from mutilation. General Hawley rode amongst the troops exhorting them to kill the Jacobite wounded and bayonet corpses just in case. Many who had come to watch were indiscriminately killed by the dragoons, including some women and a boy of 12.

BATTLE FACT

Wounded redcoats were hauled away by their female followers, who themselves risked life and limb by bringing water and aprons full of cartridges to the troops in the thick of battle.

The Jacobites lost about 1,500 dead and wounded on the field of Culloden, while the British army officially suffered only 50 dead and 259 wounded. A recent survey by the University of Glasgow identified a mass grave in the so-called 'Field of the English', a rectangular plot measuring 50 or 60 metres long by 10 metres wide. This suggests that more government soldiers died than reports at the time admitted. Even so, it was an overwhelming victory for the British army: they had crushed the rebellion in less than 20 minutes. Today the mass graves of the clans on the battlefield are a poignant reminder of the bloodshed and the devastation that Culloden wrought on the clan system.

'Howlings and lamentations'

The '45 rebellion was over. Charles immediately recognized this fact, and two days later finally disbanded his army with the words, 'Let every man seek his own safety the best way he can.' He knew that he could not pay, feed or equip an army any more, and after the overwhelming defeat at Culloden there was no longer any hope of French intervention. When Charles's message was read to the surviving Jacobite Highlanders they apparently 'gave vent to their grief in wild howlings and lamentations'.

Unfortunately for them, worse was to come. Ignoring Cumberland's offer of an amnesty, some of the clan chiefs decided to keep fighting. This phase of the rebellion achieved nothing except to make Cumberland launch massive punitive raids into the Highlands. All signs of resistance were crushed. Houses were burnt, people were killed and cattle confiscated on the mere suspicion of Jacobite sympathies. This brutal repression was accompanied by a legislative crackdown. The kilt, pipes and weapons of the Highlanders were outlawed in August 1746. Many chiefs also lost their lands, and a few their heads. Some, such as Cameron of Lochiel and Murray, were forced to flee into exile. Over 1,000 clansmen were banished to the New World. Soon the lairds lost their independent judicial powers over their clansmen, and the ancient clan system was destroyed.

Charles had a lengthy and romanticized escape through the Highlands and eventually arrived back in France. For the rest of his life he travelled throughout Europe, drinking heavily and suffering from violent mood swings. He died in 1788, enraged that the pope had refused to recognize him as Charles III, 100 years after his grandfather, James II, had been driven off the British throne.

In the Highlands Charles was remembered as 'the Bonnie' and Cumberland as 'the Butcher'. But in London Cumberland became a hero of polite society: he was 'our dear Bill'. Handel composed 'See the Conquering Hero Come' in his honour, and the plant Sweet William was named after him. But he went on to have an undistinguished military career and was soundly beaten by the French in the Low Countries.

Britain had endured its last civil war. The rebellions of the 18th century ended with Culloden. After this last land battle Britain became united and could now turn its attention to empire-building abroad. Only ten years after Culloden, the same clans who had died on the bayonets of the British army on the moor were to provide soldiers for some of its finest regiments. The Highlanders would march again.

A stone marks the mass grave of the Cameron clan where they died on the field of Culloden. It is not unusual to see people leaving flowers here, even today.

1940: THE BATTLE OF BRITAIN

The morning of 15 September 1940 began fine and crisp. A little mist here and there would clear later, giving perfect visibility for hundreds of German bomber crews to identify their targets in London. Perfect too for the hundreds of Royal Air Force fighter pilots out to intercept them. All over southern England observers in their sandbagged lookouts, radar operators in their huts below the tall masts, sector controllers ready to scramble their crews, all awaited the day's first alert – the news of the first big build-up of raiding bombers casting its shadow over Kent.

None of them knew that this day would be the climax of the Battle of Britain. But the outcome of that Sunday's struggle between a few hundred pilots on either side was to have a decisive impact on the course of the Second World War. Each aerial encounter, each dogfight, would be a testament to the skill, courage and sometimes sheer luck of the pilots on each side. Each would be an element in the desperate game of wins and losses that would decide whether Hitler could knock Britain out of the war – by bombing if possible, by invasion if necessary.

For that essentially was what the Battle of Britain was all about. When Hitler's armies smashed their way through the Low Countries in May 1940, invaded France and sent British troops racing for home from the beaches of Dunkirk, total victory appeared to be within Germany's grasp. Britain alone stood between Hitler and the total domination of Europe. But the Führer told his high command that only if the German air force, the Luftwaffe, had air superiority would he contemplate a massive seaborne invasion of southern England. The Battle of Britain, the struggle for control of the skies, was to last three months from July to September 1940. This is the story of the ups and downs of that battle for survival and how near Britain came to losing it.

'We shall never surrender'

In June 1940 Hitler believed that Britain, his only opponent left in western Europe after the fall of France, would have no alternative but to make peace with him. But he had not bargained for Britain's new prime minister, Winston Churchill, who did his best to disabuse him: 'We will fight them on the beaches, we shall fight on the landing grounds, we shall fight in the fields and in the streets, we shall fight in the hills; we shall never surrender,' he told the House of Commons on 4 June.

Six weeks later Hitler issued his Directive No. 16: 'Since England, in spite of her hopeless situation, shows no sign of coming to an agreement, I have decided to prepare and if necessary to carry out an invasion of Britain.' The grand plan was christened Operation Sealion, preparations were to be completed within a month, and the RAF 'must be so reduced morally and physically that it is unable to deliver any significant attack against the German crossing'. Already the Luftwaffe had begun to bomb British ships and ports. In mid-July these raids became one of Germany's top strategic priorities. The only restricted target was London: no attacks must take place there, Hitler ordered, without his explicit consent.

Against the odds

Germany's air force was at least twice the size of Britain's, in both fighter and bomber numbers. Bombers were destructive, but they were slow and highly vulnerable to enemy fighters; so it was the

Hitler discusses plans with his air force commander Goering (left) and his chief of staff Keitel (right). The Führer always reserved the big strategic decisions for himself.

fighters that mattered most. The RAF had around 530 fighters serviceable out of a total of over 600. The Luftwaffe had twice as many. Germany had no shortage of fighter pilots either: some 800 new pilots were coming out of training each month, whereas in Britain there were only 200. Fortunately, Churchill had appointed Lord Beaverbrook minister of aircraft production: his energy and enthusiasm were to transform Britain's output and soon leave the Germans behind in the manufacture of fighters.

The battle to produce Europe's most lethal fighter was already well under way. There were three leading contestants: the single-seater British Hurricane and Spitfire, and the German Messerschmitt 109. If most pilots, British and German, reckoned the Spitfire the best, it was only by a small margin. Both the Me109 and the Spitfire could achieve speeds of around 560 kph (350 mph) at over 4,500 metres altitude; the Hurricane was around 50 kph (30 mph) slower. All three were far more agile than any other aircraft.

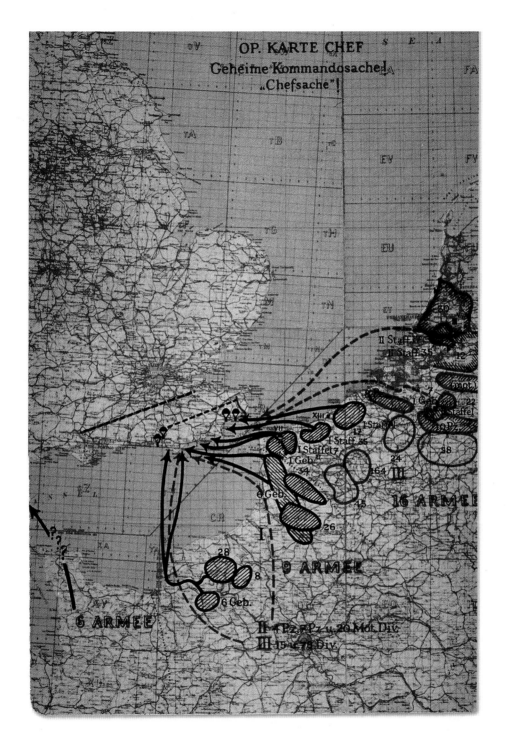

Unternehmen Seelöwe (Operation Sealion). The plan by the German high command provided for German units in France and the Low Countries to fight their way into southeast England in two phases shown by the dotted lines.

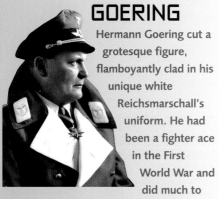

GOERING

Hermann Goering cut a grotesque figure, flamboyantly clad in his unique white Reichsmarschall's uniform. He had been a fighter ace in the First World War and did much to promote the astonishing growth of the Luftwaffe in the late 1930s. His was one of the fastest promotions to high rank of any figure in German history. During the course of the war he amassed a huge collection of looted art. Condemned to death at the post-war Nuremberg War Crimes Tribunal, he took poison before he could be hanged.

DOWDING

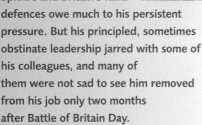

The reserved and dour 'Stuffy' Dowding was tireless and painstaking in pursuing his obsession: the needs of his fighter force and its pilots. The development of the Spitfire and Britain's radar defences owe much to his persistent pressure. But his principled, sometimes obstinate leadership jarred with some of his colleagues, and many of them were not sad to see him removed from his job only two months after Battle of Britain Day.

But the Me109 could out-dive the two British warplanes. Its direct fuel injection system allowed it to swoop into a dive without pausing; British aircraft had normal float carburettors, and a sudden plunge from the horizontal into a dive would interrupt their fuel flow.

But the most important difference between British and German aircraft was their armament. The Spitfire and Hurricane had eight 8-millimetre machine guns in their wings. The Me109, on the other hand, had two machine guns mounted in its body, and in its wings two powerful 20-millimetre cannon – three times the calibre of British guns. Very few RAF planes were equipped with cannon until after the Battle of Britain. None of the three planes had enough ammunition to last for more than 15 seconds of continuous firing. This seems like nothing but Peter Brothers, who flew a Hurricane in 1940 with 32 and 257 Squadrons, says that in practice he never had the opportunity to fire bursts of more than two or three seconds in the gap between arriving within range of an opponent and having to swerve to avoid him.

All three planes had a very limited range: they could fly for little more than an hour without re-fuelling. This was a particular disadvantage for the German Me109: unlike its British rivals based in southeast England, it had to cross the English Channel before it saw action and fly back over it afterwards. When it had to escort German bombers as far as London, for example, it could spend only ten minutes there before having to turn back. If the Germans had put drop tanks under the wings of their Me109s to increase their range, it would have reduced their performance. Rightly or wrongly, they made the decision not to fit them.

Goering versus Dowding

The Battle of Britain was conducted on both sides by commanders whose names are now an indelible part of history. There was one man apart from Adolf Hitler who was mainly responsible for the astonishing growth of the German air force in the late 1930s – Hermann Goering. Hitler appointed Goering a Reichsmarschall when he had far less seniority and experience than most of his contemporaries, but it was Goering's drive and influence with Hitler that helped make the Luftwaffe Europe's most powerful air force. Goering's appointment of the two air force Generalfeldmarschalls, Albert Kesselring and Hugo Sperrle, who were to lead the onslaught on the RAF, was also a wise decision. Each in his own way was a capable commander. But, as the Battle of Britain developed, the flaws in Goering's personality and judgement were to become a serious and eventually a disastrous handicap for the Luftwaffe. Any admiration his pilots had for the swaggering self-confidence with which he prophesied triumph in the skies over Britain was soon to turn to doubt and disillusionment.

The British airman in charge of the battle was the commander-in-chief of Fighter Command, Air Marshal Sir Hugh Dowding, nicknamed 'Stuffy'. His withdrawn personality was in glaring contrast to that of his bombastic German opponent. But he was single-mindedly committed to building Fighter Command's strength. He made his mark for stubbornness early, before the fall of France, urging the government not to send any more of his fighters to France. It would have been a futile gesture, he asserted, to save a cause already lost, and those fighters were desperately needed to defend Britain's homeland. He was right, but he won only grudging acceptance from the cabinet.

Scramble!

The people Dowding led, the pilots and the crews who serviced and prepared their aircraft, now embarked on an extraordinary three months that none of them were sure they would survive. For the aircrews it was a combination of bouts of whirlwind activity – risking their lives in the air, dodging ferocious German attacks on their bases – and long periods of anxious waiting for the alarm to sound. All would risk death or terrible injuries. Pilots such as Peter Brothers and their back-up teams would

require awesome reserves of courage and stamina.

It was the pilots rather than the aircraft that would decide most contests. You had to out-fly an opponent to get him in your sights; you then had to make your shots strike him. Both called for daring and skill. Around 80 per cent of the 'kills' in the Battle of Britain were made by only 10 per cent of the pilots. The 'aces' were on the whole the ones who scored, and it was the aces with their greater experience who stood the best chance of survival.

Dowding's defences were designed to concentrate RAF power as near to the German threat as possible. He arranged his fighters in four groups, each composed of several squadrons of 12 aircraft each. By far the largest, 11 Group was located in

A German Luftwaffe pilot boasts about how he achieved a 'kill' by swooping down on his victim from behind.

the southeast of England. It comprised seven 'sector' airfields: each sector controlled a number of air stations. By August 1940 there were 25 squadrons based at 11 Group airfields from Tangmere in west Sussex across to Manston in northeast Kent and up to bases such as North Weald in Essex. Another 9 were in 10 Group in the southwest, 14 in 12 Group in the Midlands, and a further 15 squadrons in 13 Group in the north. Each group had a headquarters – 11 Group's control rooms at Uxbridge, from where it scrambled its squadrons to meet each reported raid, can still be seen today.

Air Vice Marshal Keith Park commanded 11 Group, while Air Vice Marshal Trafford Leigh Mallory commanded 12 Group at Watnall near Birmingham. Dowding himself had an operations room giving him an overview at Fighter Command headquarters at Bentley Priory near Stanmore in Middlesex. Each of these centres had a so-called 'filter' room, where the news of approaching 'bandits' was fed in: the raid's progress was then plotted in an 'operations' room – before the days of computer screens – by staff with long cues, who

The makeshift operations room at Bentley Priory before it was moved to an underground bunker in the summer of 1940.

pushed mounted symbols around on a huge flat map. Park, Leigh Mallory and their teams then had only to make a phone call to an air station to get the pilots leaping out of their armchairs, grabbing their kit and running to their aircraft.

Timing was everything. Squadrons took minutes to get airborne, and once airborne they used vital fuel. So the trick was not to scramble

The far more sturdy ops room 20 metres under the ground at RAF Uxbridge. Moveable wooden blocks represented German raids and RAF squadrons, which scrambled to meet them.

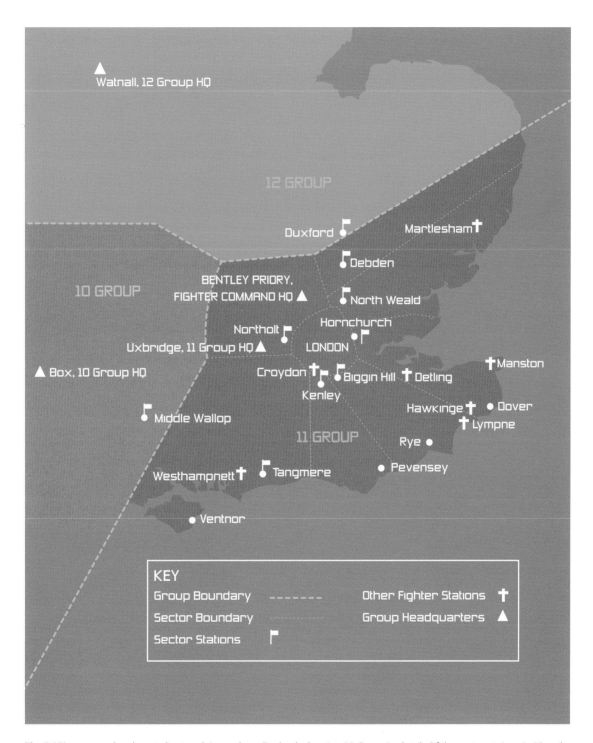

The RAF's command and control network in southern England, showing 11 Group in detail. Of the sector stations in 10 and 12 Group, we have shown only Middle Wallop and Duxford.

them until the threat was identified as a real one. Often the Germans would send out dummy raids of one or two aircraft in an effort to tempt squadrons into the air prematurely so that they would be low on fuel when the real raid crossed the Channel. This made group commanders hesitate to commit, but their understandable caution prompted some sector stations to complain that they got too little notice of the real raids and so lost vital seconds in their race to intercept.

The most important intelligence came to the ops rooms from the radar stations. These were the brainchild of a team of scientists who had successfully tested the first radar detection of an aircraft only four years previously. Since then, some 20 huge radar stations had been built around the east and south coasts of Britain. The transmitters were a trio of towers 100 metres high, the receivers 80 metres high. The transmitters bombarded the space 80 kilometres in front of them with radio waves and, if they located an aircraft, the receivers recorded the 'blip' of a returning signal bouncing back from the plane. From this it was possible to determine its distance, direction and altitude. This innovation made it unnecessary to run wasteful and inefficient fighter patrols.

Target: Shipping, 10 July–11 August

The Battle of Britain began in earnest, with the first really big raid by the Luftwaffe, on 10 July 1940. In this opening phase of the battle the Germans were out to destroy Britain's seaborne supply line, so their targets were mainly convoys and ports. That Wednesday morning a British convoy codenamed 'Bread' was steaming through the Strait of Dover when it was spotted by a German reconnaissance aircraft escorted by Me109s. Spitfires from Manston airbase in Kent were scrambled. They damaged two of the German planes, but the Dornier reconnaissance plane managed to limp home and report the course of the convoy.

Just after 1.30 p.m. the radar screens at Dover reported the biggest build-up of enemy 'blips' over Calais that the British controllers had ever seen. Air Marshal Park and his team at 11 Group head-quarters plotted some 70 aircraft heading across the Channel and immediately telephoned a scramble

A typical chain home radar station. The taller towers transmitted a radio signal that was reflected by planes back to the smaller receiving aerials (on the right). It was the first air defence radar system in the world.

order to around 30 Spitfire and Hurricane pilots at Manston, Biggin Hill, Kenley and Croydon. They caught the German raiders – bombers escorted by fighters – attacking the convoy, and a massive dogfight followed. The fight for control of the skies, the Battle of Britain, had now begun in earnest.

Some of the British fighters – 111 Squadron from Croydon – used spectacularly daring tactics: they attacked the approaching bombers head-on. Peter Brothers said he often had to do this when there was not enough time to get above and behind the enemy – the conventional position – before an attack. 'Attacking head-on gives you an easy sight on the enemy: you don't have to aim off [fire in front of the enemy plane to allow for its speed], and the chances are he'll pull up frantically to avoid colliding with you.' The RAF's counter attack was hugely successful. The German bombers were distracted by the attacking fighters and their formation broke up. Their coordinated attack on the convoy became a shambles and the raiders dispersed. Only one ship was hit. But the squadron paid for its courage with the loss of Flying Officer Higgs and his Hurricane, which collided with a Dornier: both exploded.

There were two other big raids that day, on the ports of Falmouth and Swansea – it is a myth that the Battle of Britain was confined to the southeast and London. In the first three weeks alone German bombers raided Southampton, Plymouth, Swansea, Glasgow, and even as far north as Aberdeen. A Welsh wing commander was so frustrated at the RAF's response to one raid on Swansea that he leapt into the only plane he could find, an unarmed one, and fired off his Verey signal pistol at the attackers.

Critical to the morale of either side, and to the measurement of success or failure, was the level of pilot and aircraft losses. The problem was that each side immediately knew the extent of its own losses, but not that of its opponents'. Two – or even more – pilots might claim to have shot down the same aircraft, and however rigorous their

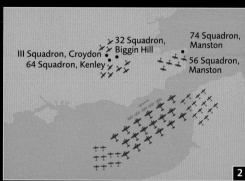

10 July

1. 1 p.m. A large convoy codenamed 'Bread' passes Dover. Seventy German aircraft – bombers and escorting fighters – approach from France.

2. Alerted by radar, RAF fighters scramble from four airfields to break up the raid.

Three Me109s in tight formation near Dover. In combat they would have flown in fours and much further apart.

assessment of claims, neither side could be sure. Only when the war was over and the world had access to the records of both sides could the truth be known. We now know that on that first big day the British had the better of it. Two planes and two pilots were lost, against the Germans' 10 aircraft lost and over 20 crew killed. But the pendulum was to swing in both directions: nine days later the British lost eleven aircraft and the Germans only four.

There was little to choose between the pilots on either side. The German pilots of the Luftwaffe were, on the whole, better trained and more experienced: many had fought during the Spanish Civil War of 1936–9. But they suffered from one severe drawback. They had to cross the Channel and then do battle over enemy territory: if they were forced to bail out, they risked drowning at sea or spending the rest of the war in a British prison camp.

Hitler's change of policy

Day by day it went on: frantic duels in the sky between a few hundred pilots on either side. By the beginning of August both protagonists were hurting severely. Neither side was winning the battle for British airspace; both sides were taking heavy losses in pilots and aircraft. The US ambassador in London, Joseph Kennedy, father of the future president, was warning the Americans, who were not yet in the war, that he doubted the British could win it.

In Germany Goering oozed confidence, but when he asked one of his top fighter aces what he most needed he got the cheeky reply: 'Spitfires.' Operation Sealion, Hitler's planned invasion, was postponed to mid-September, and on 1 August he issued a new directive. From now on the Luftwaffe's main target was to be the RAF itself. *Adlertag* (Eagle Day) was earmarked for a mass

A German machine gunner in a Heinkel bomber sets his sights on a RAF Spitfire.

attack on England's air defences, and it would take place within a week or two.

Hitler's switch of strategy was long overdue, but Goering's over-confidence was already giving rise to serious misjudgement in the German high command. He said he believed the RAF had only around 450 fighters left and that a couple of weeks should be enough to clear the air for a German invasion. He was wrong on the first count: the RAF had over 700 fighters. But the battle for control of the air would be a very close-run thing.

Blind the RAF: 12 August

Adlertag was fixed for 13 August, but German pressure was building well before it. On the 11th the RAF lost 27 aircraft, and on the next day, a fine Monday, Britain took the full force of Hitler's new strategy. First, German bombers hit the radar towers at Dover, Pevensey and Rye. Then, around

midday, a large force of no fewer than 220 bombers and fighters crossed the Channel further west. Some went for a Spitfire factory and other targets on the mainland, but 15 bombers under Johann Volkmar Fisser peeled off and attacked the radar at Ventnor on the Isle of Wight. Fisser's was one of the ten Junkers bombers shot down, but the damage he did to the radar was severe: it was out of action for weeks.

And this was only the start. With the radars desperately struggling to keep their 'eyes' open through the bombing attacks, the Germans used Britain's temporary blindness to send raid after raid against the fighter stations in Kent. When the bombers swooped on Manston it was lunchtime, and 65 Squadron were still on the ground. But most fighters managed to get airborne – the Germans did not even spot them as they took off – and the damage to Manston's all-grass airstrip was easily repaired. Lympne and Hawkinge, however, were severely cratered, and two hangars and several other buildings at Hawkinge were badly damaged. Even so, five battle-scarred Hurricanes under Squadron Leader Mike Crossley, who were too low on fuel to make it back to Biggin Hill a little further northwest, managed to make a landing at Hawkinge, miraculously ploughing through the damage there. It was patently clear that the attacks on the radars and the air stations threatened the very existence of the RAF. Would they continue? Remarkably, the Germans, deceived into believing that Ventnor was still working and discovering that the Dover radars were soon operational again, decided it was not worth persisting with attacks on the radars. Within days Goering was to make another critical mistake. Insisting that fighters stick close to bombers to protect them at all times, he banned the free-ranging flights his fighter pilots had made over southern Britain which frequently caught the RAF's fighters unawares. But the Luftwaffe's attacks on RAF airfields were to go on, and to become more and more effective.

Eagle Day: 13 August

Adlertag dawned foggy and drizzly. Goering ordered a postponement, but Oberst Johannes Fink was already leading an early-morning bomber raid on RAF targets in Kent. Fink returned, complaining he had no fighter cover. Goering's orders had held them back, and it was not until 3.30 p.m., when the weather cleared, that the British radars picked up wave after wave massing on their screens and heading across the Channel – some of them for Kent, others for destinations further west. There were raids on fighter stations in all areas, and savage dogfights between British fighters and German fighters and bombers.

A flight of six Hawker Hurricanes. Although less manoeuvrable than Spitfires, they were still highly effective at breaking up German bomber raids.

The pattern was nearly always the same. Pilots trying hard to catch a wink of sleep or play a quick game of cards at the fighter stations were scrambled time and again. 'Seventy-plus bandits approaching from south. Angels 15.' 'Angels' meant height in feet; so the 'bandits', the 70 or more enemy planes, were at 15,000 feet – about 4,500 metres. Every second of warning counted, for each time they had to gain the altitude and the angle to make an attack. It took seven minutes for a Spitfire to climb to 4,500 metres. Seven vital minutes in which the 'bandits' would have flown nearer the British coast. The leader of the dozen or so planes in the squadron or of the 'flight' of six aircraft would spot the enemy, shout 'Tally-ho' into his radio and lead his aircraft into the attack.

But from then on it was every man for himself. As the German bombers were attacked, their escorting fighters keeping watch above them would swoop down on the tail of the British fighters. 'And when you have a 109 on your tail,' says Peter Brothers, 'you forget about the bombers. You put everything into outflying the fighter, turning more sharply than he does and getting behind to destroy him.' Brothers made a habit of crabbing his Hurricane slightly sideways as he flew, so that any Me109 coming down from behind, believing his target was heading forward

in a straight line, would aim dead ahead of the Hurricane and miss it.

The outcome of *Adlertag* was a heavy toll for both sides, with the Germans suffering more losses than the British. But although the Germans had their strategy right – striking at the RAF itself – the detailed targeting had been imprecise and ill directed. They failed to concentrate their attacks on the vital sector airfields that were the RAF's backbone.

'Utter shambles'

It was not long before the Luftwaffe began to do just that. Over the next three weeks, from mid-August until the first week in September, the relentless pressure of the raids began to sap the RAF's strength. The Germans' aim was now focused on the airbases that mattered: sector stations that controlled whole areas, such as the airfields at Biggin Hill, Tangmere and Kenley. On 15 August German aircraft made 2,200 separate sorties (flights), and on the 16th they made 1,700. The damage the raids did to Kenley airbase forced the RAF to remove one of the three squadrons operating there, and compelled the operations room to relocate to the local butcher's shop.

After serious damage to the sector station at Tangmere in Sussex, Sandy Johnstone, who commanded a squadron at nearby Westhampnett, drove over to take a look. He describes the scene in his book *Enemy in the Sky*:

> I found the place in an utter shambles with wisps of smoke still rising from shattered buildings. Little knots of people were wandering around with dazed looks on their faces, obviously deeply affected by the events of the day .... The once immaculate grass was littered with personal belongings which had been blasted from the wing which had received a direct hit. Shirts, towels, socks, a portable gramophone, a little private world exposed for all to see. However the bar had been spared and was doing a brisk trade.

German raid on Kenley airfield, 18 August. This picture was taken from a Dornier bomber attacking at low level. A still undamaged Spitfire stands in a blast pen (centre).

In his book *Spitfire on My Tail*, German pilot Ulrich Steinhilper describes his raid on Manston airfield on 19 August:

> At first my heart was hammering in my chest, but when we pushed the noses of our aircraft down for the attack, I calmed down. My mates who followed me in confirmed that I was doing well. I aimed at a fuel tanker which was filling a Spitfire, then at two Spitfires one after the other. The tanker exploded and everything began to burn around it. My other two Spitfires began to burn on their own. Only now do I realise what power is given to a pilot with those four guns.

On the threshold of defeat:
30 August–6 September

It was Steinhilper's side that was now winning, with the Luftwaffe turning the knife in the wound that was seriously debilitating Dowding's Fighter Command. The major sector station at Biggin Hill suffered three days of raids, from 30 August to 1 September. There were four attacks on the 30th alone. The worst of these was at 6 p.m., when, the station diary reports:

> A low level bombing attack was carried out by the enemy and very serious damage was done to buildings and equipment. The raiders dropped 16 big HE [high explosive] bombs, estimated to weigh 1000 lbs [450 kilograms] each, of which six fell among the buildings rendering completely useless and unsafe workshops, transport yard, stores ... and the Airmen's married quarters ... The total casualties were 39 killed and 26 wounded.

On the German side, plans for the invasion of Britain proceeded apace. Orders were sent from the army's high command to the 16th Army in northern France to prepare to launch themselves across the Channel from 15 September. 'The Army's landing forces will first win local bridgeheads. Then its first operational objective will be a line from the Thames estuary through the heights south of London to Portsmouth. Further task: to defeat enemy forces still holding out in southern England, to occupy London and to mop up the enemy in southern England.' The RAF secured its own confirmation of these plans with aerial pictures of barges concentrating in Channel ports and supply dumps being set up.

BATTLE EXPERIENCE
The dogfight

Surviving a dogfight in the Battle of Britain depended on the ability of pilots to react in split seconds. Dan was given a taste of the challenges of aerial combat and the stresses this puts on the body by former RAF fighter pilot Andy Cubin. He took Dan up in an Xtra 300, a purpose-built stunt aeroplane.

First of all Dan was taken through the gruelling G turn. In 1940 if pilots had an enemy on their tail, all they could do was throw the plane into a tight spiral until the G force became unbearable. If they did not turn sharply enough, they would be shot down; if the turn was too sharp, they would black out and lose control of their plane. Andy took Dan in a series of turns at up to 7G (seven times the force of gravity), in each of which Dan slowly lost his vision and then consciousness.

He learnt how to resist the G force by clenching muscles in the lower half of his body to stop the blood rushing down to his legs. By now exhausted, he was shown the dangers of the pilot's blind spot as another plane swooped down out of the sun: its glare made it impossible to see the attacker until he was just metres away. Finally, in a mocked-up dogfight, Dan experienced the split-second reactions a pilot needed to make a head-on attack and learnt the art of deflection shooting – how to aim slightly ahead of the target in order to hit it. When safely back on the ground, Dan staggered out of the plane, his clothes soaked through with sweat, exactly like the fighter pilots of 1940. And he had to fly only once! In late August 1940 pilots sometimes had to scramble as many as six times each day.

Dowding was now under very severe pressure. Each week he was losing 120 pilots, and only 65 were coming in from training. Some of the newcomers had trained for only a handful of hours on Hurricanes or Spitfires. The gap between British and German losses was closing: in the critical two weeks between 26 August and 6 September the RAF lost 273 fighters and the Germans 308. Earlier the gap had been wider. British aircraft losses were now outstripping the pace of their production, and 231 pilots were lost in the worst single week – between 24 August and 1 September. Grave damage had been done to five forward air stations and six of the seven sector stations in Park's 11 Group, whose pilots were taking the greatest strain. He wrote later: 'By September the 5th the damage was having a severe effect on fighting efficiency.'

Dowding's pilots were now suffering from extreme exhaustion: tiredness is a pilot's greatest enemy, and most of them were seriously deprived of sleep. Another tragic reality was that, as the demand on pilots grew, the death toll was far higher among the new, barely trained pilots who were thrown into the conflict with very little battle experience. Sandy Johnstone recalls in his diary: 'Everywhere the strain is beginning to show. I notice people are becoming edgy and short-tempered and one wonders for how long the lads can go on taking it. Yes things are tough. There is little doubt that Hitler is preparing to launch an invasion.'

The Germans were within sight of victory in the Battle of Britain – victory that would only be a few weeks away if they stuck to their strategy of striking at the RAF's airfields. If …

Target: London – Hitler's strategic switch

At this critical moment Hitler made a dramatic decision to change his strategy. It was a radical change that shifted the Luftwaffe's sights from the RAF to London. He believed that this would be the *coup de grâce*: the RAF seemed all but defeated, and a few bombs on the capital would bring the

BATTLE FACT

Goering spent much of the Battle of Britain touring around in his luxurious personal train loaded with good food and crates of wine. On one occasion, in an effort to show his pilots he was one of the lads, he tried to squeeze into the cockpit of a Me109 but found he couldn't fit.

nation to its knees and leave Britain's beaches wide open to invasion.

Hitler may have intended to bomb London all along, but the precise timing of the change in strategy appears to have been partly the result of an accident. Up to now the Thames estuary and Britain's ports and docks were fair game, but London was off limits – Hitler had vetoed it. He had, however, allowed free-ranging German bombers to find what targets they could over Britain by night. And this may have contributed to what happened on the night of 24–25 August. A large force of German bombers was directed at targets on the Thames east of London. Some pilots may have been confused about their positions and a number of them dropped their bombs on residential areas, mainly in the East End. Nine civilians were killed on that first night, 58 injured and 100 made homeless. By design or not, it was the beginning of the Blitz, and Churchill ordered immediate retaliation against Germany's capital, Berlin. The raid the following night by 50 Wellington and Hampden bombers was about as inaccurate as the German one had been. It appears that only two people in Berlin itself were injured; most of the bombs fell outside the city.

What mattered was the effect of this raid on German morale and on Hitler himself. An American journalist in the German capital reported that Berliners were dumbfounded. They had been told by Goering that nobody would be able to bomb their city, and now the impossible had happened. Hitler reacted with fury: 'If the British declare that they will attack our cities, we will erase theirs.' From now on, Germany's main target was to be London.

'A seething cauldron of aeroplanes'

It took two weeks for the switch in strategy to become effective, and when it did it came as a surprise to the RAF, who were fighting to preserve their airfields against increasingly shrinking odds. Until, that is, the afternoon of 7 September. It was a warm Saturday which started quietly, and it was teatime before the first indication of Hitler's new plan showed up on the radar screens. At five minutes to four the plotters at Fighter Command headquarters moved their first counter on to the map: 20-plus 'bandits' over Calais. Within minutes Dowding and his team knew they were facing the biggest raid in history. Only half an hour earlier Goering himself had watched more than 1,000 aircraft – 350 bombers and over 700 fighters – flying over Cap Gris Nez near Calais straight for the English coast. They were packed into one massive, multi-layered formation advancing on a 30-kilometre-wide front at heights of between about 4,500 and 7,500 metres.

The British had no idea where these planes were heading – yet. Goering knew exactly where they were going: they were making for London, at the extreme end of the range of their protecting fighters, but with the advantage of surprise and a huge total bombload. Goering had told his top commanders of Hitler's plan four days earlier. Sperrle had urged that it be reconsidered: the current strategy of attacking RAF airfields, he argued, was working, and should be given just a week or two more. Kesselring slapped him down: the Führer had spoken and the die was cast.

By 4.15 p.m. nearly every fighter squadron in the south of England had been scrambled. There was some initial hesitation about where exactly to direct them. Were the fighter stations the target? Or was it somewhere else? It was soon clear that this gigantic air armada, hundreds of square kilometres in extent, was headed for London, and the next hour saw a desperate battle in the air with Britain's fighter pilots struggling to dent the threatening mass of bombers.

Sandy Johnstone, leading his squadron of Spitfires into battle, wrote in his diary:

> I have never seen so many aircraft in the air all at the same time. The escorting fighters saw us at once and came down on us like a ton of bricks … the squadron split up and the sky became a seething cauldron of aeroplanes swooping and swerving in and out of the vapour trails and tracer smoke. A Hurricane on fire spun out of control ahead of me while above to my right, a Me110 flashed across my vision and disappeared into the fog of battle before I could draw a bead on him. Everyone was shouting at once and the earphones became filled with a meaningless cacophony of jumbled noises. Everything became a maelstrom of whirling impressions – a Dornier spinning wildly with part of its port mainplane missing. A stoutly built German floating past on the end of a parachute, his arms held above his head in an attitude of surrender …

Johnny Kent attacked a German aircraft and was fascinated by what he described as the pretty sight

BATTLE FACT

The German Foreign Ministry suggested that attacking the East End of London and leaving the affluent West End alone would 'accentuate the breach between the classes'. Another suggestion was that the Luftwaffe should bomb Fleet Street because 'without newspapers political life in Britain will come to a stop'.

7 September. The first daylight raid on London. Much of London's industrial East End was damaged and many civilians killed.

of his tracer bullets sailing 'gracefully towards the German while at the same time his came streaming back at me like a string of gleaming red beads'. Kent won the contest when he shot the German's starboard engine to bits.

On the ground any Londoners who had not run for the air-raid shelters would have seen an astonishing firework display of vapour trails and blasts of gunfire way above them. Bombs rained down on factories and houses in and around London's docklands in the east and further west as far as Kensington. The people who suffered most were the ones whose houses were in the more deprived areas of the East End near the docks. Every fire appliance within reach was called out. Horrified Londoners would become used to these scenes over the next few months. On this day alone over 400 civilians were killed and another 1,300 were injured; 13 British fighter pilots died trying to save them.

The RAF's reaction to that first big raid was far from satisfactory. In particular, 7 September pointed up the growing and increasingly bitter argument that was now raging between Air Marshal Park at 11 Group in the south and Air Marshal Leigh Mallory at 12 Group to the north of London. Leigh Mallory – encouraged by one of the great aces of the Battle of Britain, Wing Commander Douglas Bader – believed the most effective way to counter the German raids was with large formations of three to five squadrons plunging in together – the Big Wing, as it became known. Park argued that he had no time to allow his squadrons to form bigger formations, and he complained that when he asked Bader's Big Wing to assist him quickly it was often too late. Park complained that the wing spent valuable minutes forming up over its airfield when he was desperate for the support of any fighters that were airborne, even if they were only in squadron strength.

A Heinkel 111 bomber over the Isle of Dogs. The tell-tale bend of the river Thames around the heart of London's Docklands gave German navigators an unmissable landmark.

The dispute became so fraught that Dowding summoned the two men for a dressing down, but he still failed to resolve the controversy.

The Battle of Britain was now entering its final phase. The Germans had around three weeks – the rest of September – in which to launch their invasion before the chancy autumn weather settled in, three weeks in which finally to crush the RAF and so demoralize the British that German armies would gain a firm foothold in the south of England. Some say that Hitler had already given up hope of this, but his orders remained clear:

the invasion force must be ready to move from 15 September.

Holding their breath

When Britain woke up on Sunday, 8 September, prospects had never looked more bleak. Londoners awoke to the first of many mornings with streets and families shattered by the night's bombing. The human and material resources at the severely damaged RAF bases were almost at breaking point. And intelligence reports indicated that a German seaborne invasion was imminent. It was actually set for 21 September, but that did not prevent false alarms on the English coast. Church bells, to be used only to signal the final alert, rang out over parts of southern England, and many expected to see German tanks on the beaches. But nothing happened.

Over the next few days RAF commanders held their breath. Had Hitler really called off the attacks on fighter bases to concentrate on London? And would that suddenly transform the Battle of Britain from a struggle they were in danger of losing to one they could win? The answer to both questions – it quickly dawned on them – was: Yes. The raids on the airfields were indeed virtually abandoned. The RAF was now able to reconstruct its bases and build up its strength, freed from the constant anxiety of having to protect its planes against surprise attack on the ground. It was now able to throw all its efforts into combating the German raids on London. It was even able to take the battle decisively across the Channel and attack the invasion forces as they built up in the Continental ports.

On 11 September there were successful British bomber raids on Calais, Boulogne, Le Havre and Dunkirk. A hundred German barges were destroyed. More raids two days later included one on Antwerp and wrecked another 70 barges designed to carry the invaders across the Channel. At home, squadrons found they had time to give their newly arrived pilots a few hours' training in the cockpit; a week earlier that would have been unthinkable. The average daily loss in the week following 7 September was 16 planes; this was now being equalled by the output of the aircraft factories.

In Germany too the prospects suddenly looked very different. Hitler had a meeting with his chiefs of staff on 13 September, and the man who was his Luftwaffe adjutant throughout the war, Nicolaus van Below, wrote later that 'nobody believed in the [Sealion] operation any longer'. Although Hitler told them he was not calling the invasion off for the present, there was now a clear sense

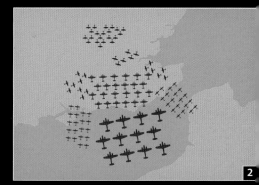

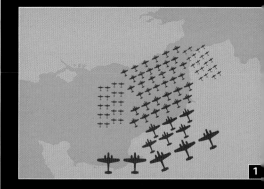

7 September

1. 4 p.m. The largest German raid yet. The bombers stretch several kilometres wide and are several layers high. They know their target is London: the RAF does not.

2. 4.15 p.m. With the Luftwaffe now clearly heading for London the RAF scramble to protect their capital. Help comes from 12 Group in the north – in the form of a 'Big Wing' of more than one squadron grouped together. But it arrives too late to affect the outcome.

that, unless it could achieve a spectacular break-through in the next day or two, the Luftwaffe would fail to secure the clear skies that would allow it to go ahead. But it would make one last major effort to crack the RAF, and pilots such as Ulrich Steinhilper still thought they could do it; he says that in mid-September they were gathering their strength for 'what must surely be the death throes of the RAF over Britain'.

Battle of Britain Day: 15 September

The climax came on 15 September. From then on, this day was to be known as Battle of Britain Day. It started fine – fine enough for Goering to give the green light to two of the biggest raids ever. The first showed up on British radar screens at 11 a.m. At 11.30 the first wave crossed the English coast, but Park and Leigh Mallory were ready for them. Ten squadrons were scrambled by 11 Group in the southeast, and in 12 Group Douglas Bader had his Big Wing of no fewer than five squadrons in the air in one big formation – around 60 Hurricanes and Spitfires under his immediate command.

Peter Brothers was told to fly his Hurricane to what they called the Maidstone line in Kent to meet the raiders. He climbed desperately. The sky was black with what he described as 'this phalanx of stuff coming straight at me'. Enemy bombers at 4,500 metres, fighters 600 metres higher. He had no time to get above them and had to confront them head-on. That was when he destroyed Wilhelm Raab's Dornier 17. Brothers' frontal attack set Raab's engines on fire; the Hurricane then swung round behind the bomber and finished it off with a further burst, killing two crewmen and only just allowing Raab to parachute to safety – and captivity. Brothers recalls that Raab contacted him after the war to describe the carnage the Hurricane had caused among the Dornier's crew. 'He told me I'd killed his gunner and navigator,' says Brothers, but 'by then there were no hard feelings.'

Paddy Barthropp, a pilot officer at the time,

tells us he was scrambled no fewer than five times that day. Each flight averaged around 40 minutes: much more than that and pilots risked running out of fuel and ammunition. He says he 'set one or two Heinkel bombers on fire, but I cannot be sure I shot them down'. RAF pilots always tried to attack the bombers and avoid the fighters if they could: it was the bombers, after all, that could do the most damage.

By the time the first huge raid reached London, just before noon, the bombers had been met by several fighter squadrons head-on and by the Big Wing from the side. Many of the bombers scattered; the German fighters, at the limit of their range and struggling to protect their fast-dispersing flock, fought hard for a while but soon had to head for home. The bombers were forced to swing away from their main targets and drop most of their loads over southern London. Two fell on Buckingham Palace but failed to explode: the king and queen were not there at the time. Another British pilot, Raymond Holmes, says he deliberately collided with a Dornier bomber after running out of ammunition. He sliced off the Dornier's tail, destroyed both aircraft and survived to watch the engine of his Hurricane dug up near Victoria Station in 2004.

But this was only the beginning. An even larger bomber raid was picked up on the radars after lunch and was approaching London by two o'clock. Churchill himself was at the 11 Group operations room watching Park send every plane he could find into the air. Park had to tell the prime minister not to light up his cigar as the bunker was a smoke-free area. Churchill had to be content with clenching the unlit cigar between his teeth. 'How many fighters have you got in reserve?' the prime minister asked Park. 'None,' came the reply. This time, however, the combined effect of the 11 Group squadrons in the southeast and the Big Wing from 12 Group was devastating. Over 150 Spitfires and Hurricanes met the raiders over Kent, and battled it out mainly with the massive escorting formation of German fighters.

Peter Brothers remembers that in this second big battle of the day he had time to gain the right height:

I went down to attack a Ju88 bomber. The Junkers has guns facing backwards. I was caught by three of the bombers: the one I was attacking and its two companions to either side. I dived away after destroying the Junkers in the middle but I was not fast enough. In the vicious crossfire from all three aircraft I had a shot through my aileron cable in the left wing and the aileron jammed up. That sent my plane spiralling off to the left and I nearly abandoned it. I had the cockpit open but decided not to jump in the end: I was too frightened of parachuting. Most pilots tend to roll the aircraft over and fall out underneath: that works particularly well if you are on fire. But I managed to straighten up by raising the other aileron and made it to Biggin Hill. I then telephoned my base at Martlesham and just managed to stop the adjutant there sending a telegram to my wife Annette saying I was missing in battle.

The German fighters were so battered in this second big battle on the 15th that when the Big Wing fell on the bombers further north, the fighters were too disorganized to protect them. The bomber formations were so severely broken up that they dropped only a few bombs on militarily important targets. As the Germans desperately jettisoned their bombs where they could and turned for home, Churchill sent a message to Dowding: 'The Royal Air Force cut to rags and tatters separate waves of murderous assault upon the civil population ...' The following morning the British press claimed the RAF had shot down 175 enemy aircraft. It had actually despatched 56 German planes for the loss of 27, but the effect was still decisive. Germany had lost the Battle of Britain.

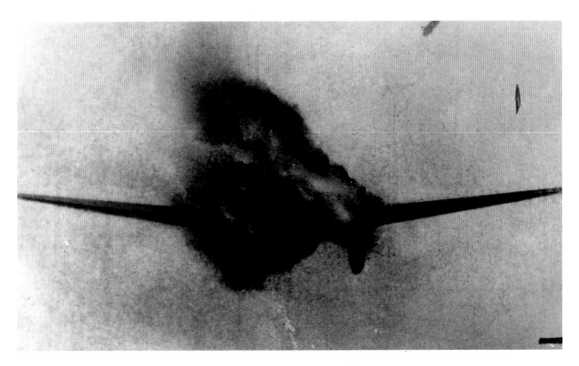

A Heinkel 111 disintegrates as its engine, fuel tanks and fuselage burst into flames.

Battle of Britain Day
This time hundreds of RAF fighters, forewarned of another huge raid on London, surround and pick off the Luftwaffe bombers. German fighters, with their fuel running low, abandon the bombers and head home. Many will have to ditch in the Channel.

'Postpone Sealion indefinitely': 17 September

It took days, even weeks, for the outcome to become apparent to either side. But the critical event was the final postponement two days later, on 17 September, of plans for Operation Sealion. An entry in the German naval staff diary for that date states baldly: 'The enemy airforce is by no means defeated … The Führer has therefore decided to postpone Operation Sealion indefinitely.' The relentless death toll among Goering's fighter and bomber pilots was having its effect on German strategy and on pilots' morale. Steinhilper says, 'Given that we spent 60 per cent of our time over hostile territory and that London was invariably our target necessitating maximum range penetration, the odds were well and truly stacked against us. Time was now against us and time was running out.' He remembers one raid in which:

> *One after another the [German] fighters ploughed into the Channel or rose in a last desperate search for height before the pilot baled out. Our track across these wild waters became dotted with parachutes, pilots floating in their life jackets and greasy oil slicks on the cold water showing where another 109 had ended its last dive. Our air sea rescue people tried their best but it was hard to locate the men in the high waves. Most that were located were already dead, victims of exposure or drowning. The next day I was privileged to see a secret memorandum which reported 19 pilots drowned.*

Victory

The war was to go on for another four and half years, and many thousands of people were to die in bombing raids on cities all over Britain. But by the end of September 1940 the Germans recognized they had lost the battle to control British airspace, and Hitler's grand strategy for winning the war turned eastwards – to Russia.

The RAF victory in the Battle of Britain was not just due to its pilots and technicians; it was as much a product of German failure. Goering's aircraft and pilots were a match for the British; but their intelligence, communications and, above all, leadership were greatly inferior. Bombers and fighters in the air could not talk to each other: bombers could communicate only in morse code, fighter pilots by radio. German intelligence was slow to clarify which were the critical fighter stations for the raiders to target, so a lot of time and munitions were wasted on unimportant RAF facilities. British radars were left almost unscathed after the early half-hearted attempts to blind them. British runways were cratered, but then left alone to be quickly repaired by the RAF. Ironically, in the Falklands war 40 years later the Argentines were to demonstrate how quickly a runway could be back in operation after an RAF attack.

Leadership on the British side was consistently strong from the top right down to the pilots themselves; on the German side, while the pilots were the equals of the British, they were let down by their high command. At the very top Goering

These Polish pilots of 303 Squadron are a reminder that many Allied airmen flew with the RAF in the Battle of Britain.

became increasingly fanciful, and Hitler himself conducted a strategy that was fundamentally flawed. He made his key mistake in early September – to switch from targeting the airfields to bombing London. Churchill wrote that if the strategy had not changed on 7 September, the whole intricate organization of Fighter Command might have been broken: 'Goering should certainly have persevered against the airfields … By departing from the classic principle of war he made a foolish mistake.'

We can only guess what would have happened if the Germans had not made this blunder. The Royal Air Force would probably have had to pull back to the Midlands, and that would have left the south coast largely unprotected. The weather might then just have allowed Sealion to go ahead. Churchill might then have had to fight the battle on the beaches, for which he had prepared the country.

As it was, the invasion was put off, and when the Americans joined the war in 1941 Britain was a ready-made aircraft carrier, anchored just off the shores of the Continent that the Allies were determined to liberate. The Allies' version of Sealion – in reverse – had to wait for D-Day in June 1944. But the key turn of the tide and the first big lift to British spirits since the war began had been the achievement of the pilots of the RAF in 1940. 'Never in the field of human conflict,' said Winston Churchill, 'was so much owed by so many to so few.'

BATTLE FACT

In November 1940 'Stuffy' Dowding and Keith Park, the two commanders who had been instrumental in winning the Battle of Britain, were moved on. Park later commanded the RAF in its defence of Malta, but Dowding was retired with just a few days' notice.

This book – born from a TV series – has allowed us to tell the full stories of the characters and events that got only fleeting mention in each action-packed hour of *Battlefield Britain* on BBC2. We were inspired and greatly helped in our research for the book by the enthusiasm and judgement of the people who made the programmes. They were a brilliant team: without Sarah Hargreaves the bizarre concept of father and son, journalist and historian, explaining the great battles of British history would never have happened. Two people deserve the main credit for bringing the series to life: Executive Producer Jane Aldous and Series Producer Danielle Peck. We were incredibly lucky to work with them, and no less fortunate with the rest of the BBC team: the producers Zoe Heron, Martina Hall, Deborah Perkin, Nathan Williams, Mary Cranitch, Paul McGuigan and Ian Lilley each had a major impact on what we have written. They were ably assisted by Louisa Bowman, Renuka Chapman, Ed Hart, Kate Ereira, Stephen Douds and Phil Cairney. We owe our thanks to many others too: Emily Samson, Lynn Hyde, Emma Giles and Maximilian Brunold are the unsung heroes of the project, and the TV crews, though too numerous to mention, all cheerfully slogged after us through muddy and sometimes frozen fields and never complained.

For 18 months our office at the BBC has resembled a second-hand book stall. Dog-eared volumes piled up in unstable towers with tufts of yellow Post-it notes sticking out to mark key quotes, passages and diagrams. Certain authors deserve special mention for imposing some order on these often chaotic and sometimes obscure battles – in particular Colin Martin and Geoffrey Parker's *Spanish Armada*, Glenn Foard's *Naseby* and Stuart Reid's excellent body of work on Culloden. As for the Roman historian Tacitus, our debt to him has left its scars on the small red volume of the *Annals*, which Peter carried with him wherever we went.

What has made this book – and this TV series – unique is the contribution by Red Vision in Manchester. An extraordinarily talented team led by Pete Farrar and Pete Metelko has revolutionized the way we can explain military history. We owe them a huge debt for illustrating the stories of the battles by charting the precise movements of the troops, ships and planes in images that are as real as photographs. The lack of sources as to precise numbers or dispositions, particularly in the more ancient battles, means that our conjecture has had to take the place of firmer evidence. In all cases any mistakes are entirely our own and not those of our tireless animators.

We have received generous and energetic help from the War Studies Department at the Royal Military Academy, Sandhurst, under Duncan Anderson. Throughout the series both they and the Army, Navy and Air Force more generally were always hugely accommodating. Other indispensable help has been provided by Martin Marix-Evans whose research on the ground led us to conclude that he had settled on the likeliest site of Boudicca's final battle with Rome. Battle of Britain fighter pilots Peter Brothers and Billy Drake were two among many who provided us with unmatchable first-hand accounts of aerial warfare in 1940.

The publishing team at BBC Worldwide who worked on the book has shown ingenuity with the design and considerable patience with the two Snows. Sally Potter led the project with great creative judgement, Sarah Hopper has moved mountains in finding the pictures that tell the stories best, and Hon Lam and Paul Vater of sugarfreedesign have produced a beautiful volume. And throughout the whole process we have been guided by the thoughtful, calm and always painstaking hand of Martin Redfern: his contribution is on every page – in every line.

Thanks must finally go to our family who have light-heartedly tolerated the impact on domestic life of our expeditions to out-of-the way battle sites and our arguments about the effective range of 18th-century muskets. Special mention must go to a wonderful wife and mother, Ann MacMillan, for whom watching her husband and son going off to make television programmes, and to research this book, on the back of a small moped must have conjured up an entire range of emotions. This did not stop her reading every word we have written and cutting through much of the pomposity and confusion of the early drafts. Without her, *Battlefield Britain* could, quite literally, not have been written.

PICTURE CREDITS

BBC Worldwide would like to thank the following individuals and organizations for providing photographs and for permission to reproduce copyright material. While every effort has been made to trace and acknowledge copyright holders, we would like to apologize should there be any errors or omissions.

akg-images/Erich Lessing: 17r, 26t, 42, 55, 60; akg-images/Museum Kalkriese: 32; akg-images/Peter Connolly: 26b; Birmingham Museums and Art Gallery/www.bridgeman.co.uk: 120l; Louisa Bowman: 6, 11l; British Library, London: 62; British Museum, London: 15t, 41tl; The Blair Castle Collection, Perthshire: 171r; By permission of His Grace the Duke of Bedford and the Trustees of the Bedford Estates: 115; By special permission of the City of Bayeux/Musée de la Tapisserie de Bayeux: 58; Bundesarchiv (Federal Archives): 197; CADW: 66, 70, 84; Renuka Chapman: 41tr, 97; Christies Images/www.bridgeman.co.uk: 142r; Colchester Museums: 19; Corbis: 204–5; Courtesy of the Director, National Army Museum, London: 129t, 177; Stephen Douds: 145c; Kate Ereira: 133, 138; Edward Hart: 7, 64; Zoe Heron: 17l, 28; Hulton Archive: 100, 194–6, 203, 211; Imperial War Museum: 9, 192l, 198t, 200, 212, 215, 217; Ian Lilley: 166, 173, 174b, 179; © Don Maddox: 88; Pepys Library, Magdalene College, Cambridge: 98b; Musées Royaux des Beaux-Arts de Belgique: 93; Museo Nacional del Prado: 92; Museum of London: 44; National Gallery of Ireland: 140, 161; © National Maritime Museum, London: 90, 96r, 106–7; National Museums and Galleries of Wales: 85, 89t; National Museums of Scotland: 8, 186; National Portrait Gallery, London: 77, 89b, 94r, 126–7, 139; © Oxford Picture Library/Chris Andrews: 125; PA Photos: 192–3; Danielle Peck: 38, 53; Deborah Perkin: 67t; Photo RMN/Hervé Lewandowski: 143b; Private collection/www.bridgeman.co.uk: 146; Reproduced with the kind permission of the Trustees of the National Museums and Galleries of Northern Ireland: 113–14, 144, 145b, 147t, 158b, 164; Royal Air Force Museum: 207; Dan Snow: 152l; Peter Snow: 18b, 22b, 24b, 41b, 61, 68t, 72, 86, 102, 154b, 157, 169, 180, 191, 198, 208; Sothebys/akg-images: 143t; © Tate, London 2004: 153; The National Archives: 181; The Royal Armouries, Leeds: 54, 116t, 120r, 121, 122b; The Royal Collection © 2004, Her Majesty Queen Elizabeth II: 118b, 168r, 190; The Viking Ship Museum, Denmark/photo Werner Karrasch: 45; Ullstein Bild: 202; University of Oslo/photo Ove Holst: 48; Victoria Embankment, London/www.bridgeman.co.uk: 12; Nathan Williams: 10, 112.

Graphic stills generated by Red Vision, © BBC.

E-fits generated by Aspley Ltd, © BBC.

INDEX

Page numbers in *italics* refer to illustrations

and the Battle of the Isle of Wight 103, 104, 105
and the Battle of Plymouth 101, 102
and the Battle of Portland Bill 103
and Calais 106
and the defeat of the Armada 113, 114
and the fireship attack 106–7
Montrose, Marquis of 125
Mortimer, Sir Edmund 70, 71, 88
alliance with Glyndwr 76
and the Battle of Pilleth 72–3, 74, 85
and the Worcester campaign 85
Mulloy, Charles 162
Mulloy, Theobald 162
Mulloy, William 162
Murray, Lord George *171*, 171, 176, 178, 180, 191
and the Battle of Culloden 182, 189
and the Battle of Prestonpans 172
and the night march on Cumberland's army 181, 182–3

Naseby, Battle of (1645) 8, 9, 11, 116–17, 126–39, 189
battle lines *129*
and Cromwell 126–7
opening positions *129*
Royalist baggage train 116
see also Parliamentarian army; Royalist army
Nero, Roman Emperor 17, 37
coin *17*
Netherlands, and the Spanish Armada 92–3
New Model Army 123–4, *125*, 126
baggage train 127, 128
and the Battle of Naseby 127, 128–9, 131, 132–9
pikemen *132*, 132
Norman army 39–40, 60, 61
archers *58*, 59–60
Breton retreat 56, *56–7*, 57
cavalry stallions 40, 52, *55*, 55, 59
divisions 51–2
and preparations for battle 50–1
Northern Ireland
and the Battle of the Boyne 140, 165
and the siege of Londonderry 144–5, *145*

Odo, Bishop 43, 52, 57
Ogilvy, Lord, Jacobite regiment *186*

Okey, Colonel 129–30
O'Neill, Sir Neil 151, 152, *153*
O'Sullivan, Colonel 180, 189
Oxford, and the Civil War 124, *125*, 125, 126

Park, Air Vice Marshal Keith 198, 200, 211–12, 214, 217
Parker, John 159
Parliament, and the Civil War 118–19
Parliamentarian army
areas controlled by 119
armour 120, 121–2
and the Battle of Newbury 120–3, *122–3*
infantry 120–2, 133, *134*, 136
Ironsides 119, 120, 134–5, *135*–6
muskets 120, *121*, 121, 131
pikemen 121, *122*
uniform coat 124
see also New Model Army
Parma, Alexander Farnese, Duke of *93*, 93, 96, 97, 102, 103, 105–6, 107, 113–14
Paulerspury, possible site of battle (AD 60–1) 23–6, *24*, 29–34, *30*, *31*, *33*, *34–5*, 37
and the Celtic warriors 29
death toll 34
leaders' speeches to the troops 29–30
method of fighting 24–6
opening skirmishes 30–1
and the Roman legions 26–7, *27*
Paulinus, Suetonius 9, 17, 35, 37
abandonment of London 21–2, 23
appearance *16*, 16
and the battle with Boudicca 23–5, 27, 33
speech to the troops 29, 30
and the destruction of Colchester 18
Pelham, Henry 170, 178
Percy, Henry (Hotspur) 11, 68, 69, 71, 76
and the Battle of Shrewsbury 78, 79–81, 83
Philip II, king of Spain 91–2, *92*, 97, 114, 115
Pilleth, Battle of 8, *72*, 72–5, *73*, *74–5*, 82, 85, 89
Bryn Glas hill *72*, 72, 74
plate armour 71, 72, 73, 80
Plymouth, Battle of 100–3, *101*
Poenius Postumus 25

Portland Bill, Battle of *102*, 102
Prasutagus, king (husband of Boudicca) 15, 16
Prestonpans, Battle of (1745) 170–6, *172–4*, *175*
Pride, Lieutenant Colonel Thomas 124
Protestantism
and the Battle of the Boyne 141, 142–3, 148, 165
and the Civil War 118, 119
Protestant settlers in Ireland 144
and the siege of Londonderry 145
and the Spanish Armada 91, 92, 93
Puritans, and the Civil War 119

Radnor Castle 69
Recalde, Juan Martinez de 97, 98, 101, 103, 104, 114
redcoats *see* British (Hanoverian) army at Culloden
Reid, Stuart 185
Rich, Lieutenant Colonel Robert 186
Richard II, king 66, 68
Robert the Bruce 8
Robert, Duke of Normandy 41
Robertson, Rev. James 169
Roman army
helmet *26*
javelins *32*, 32
legions 26–7, *27*
IXth Hispana 18–19, 22, 37
scorpios (long-range catapults) 31
shield *26*, 27
sword (*gladius*) *26*, 26
wedge formation 32–4, *33*, *34–5*, 36
Roman occupation of Britain 7, 13–15, 37
Roundheads 119
see also Parliamentarian army
Royalist army 116, 117
areas controlled by 119
baggage train 116, 137
and the Battle of Newbury 120, *122–3*, 123
Bluecoats 129, 132, 135, 136
cavalry 129, *130*, 130–1, *131*, 135
defeat at Naseby 136–9
infantry 116, 129, 132–3, *134*, 135
and the New Model Army 124
pikemen 131, *132*, 135–6
and Prince Rupert 124–6
storming of Leicester 126
see also Rupert of the Rhine, Prince